Communicating Politics in the Twenty-First Century

Karen Sanders

palgrave
macmillan

First published 2009 by
PALGRAVE MACMILLAN

Palgrave Macmillan in the UK is an imprint of Macmillan Publishers Limited,
registered in England, company number 785998, of Houndmills, Basingstoke,
Hampshire RG21 6XS.

Palgrave Macmillan in the US is a division of St Martin's Press LLC,
175 Fifth Avenue, New York, NY 10010.

Palgrave Macmillan is the global academic imprint of the above companies
and has companies and representatives throughout the world.

Palgrave® and Macmillan® are registered trademarks in the United States,
the United Kingdom, Europe and other countries.

ISBN-13: 978-0-230-00028-5   hardback
ISBN-10: 0-230-00028-2   hardback
SBN-13: 978-0-230-00029-2   Paperback
ISBN-10: 0-230-00029-0   Paperback

This book is printed on paper suitable for recycling and made from fully
managed and sustained forest sources. Logging, pulping and manufacturing
processes are expected to conform to the environmental regulations of the
country of origin.

A catalogue record for this book is available from the British Library.

A catalog record for this book is available from the Library of Congress.

10   9   8   7   6   5   4   3   2   1
18   17   16   15   14   13   12   11   10   09

Printed in China

For Anna, Andrew and Elena Cruzado Sanders

Communicating Politics in the Twenty-First Century

Also by Karen Sanders

NACIÓN Y TRADICIÓN: Cinco discursos en torno a la nación peruana, 1885–1930 (1997)
ETHICS AND JOURNALISM (2003)
MORALITY TALES: Political Scandals and Journalism in Britain and Spain in the 1990s
(co-author with María José Canel, 2006)

Contents

Tables and Figures

Tables

Figures

1

Introduction

As I write, the US primaries for the 2008 presidential election are in full swing. The Democrats have an historic choice: they can nominate either the first female or the first Afro-American presidential candidate in US history.

I have followed the contest from my Madrid base: accessing Spanish, British and US newspapers and broadcast channels; tracking blogs such as the *Huffington Post* or the views and data of poll experts such as Mark Blumenthal; I have watched Hillary Clinton 'tear up' on a BBC-hosted video and the transformation of a Barack Obama speech into a song with a hip-hop beat on YouTube. Politics may still be about the achievement and exercise of power but communicating it has become a vastly more complicated exercise. As *Star Trek*'s Mr Spock might have said: 'It's life, Jim, but not as we know it'.

Political Communication: Research, Education and Practice

This book is about the contemporary world of political communication. It is a difficult enterprise. The field straddles a number of disciplines and draws on theoretical and methodological traditions developed by sociology, political science, psychology, political philosophy and literary studies. By 1990 it was considered that 'political communication has developed some identity as a more or less distinct domain of scholarly work' (Nimmo and Swanson, 1990: 8). By 2004 its range covered the examination of political messages, news coverage, public opinion and the role of the internet (see Kaid, 2004a). The scope of practice and research in political communication is now vast.

The United States dominates. The apparatus of US scholarship – associations, journals, university chairs and departments – has become well established since the founding of the International Communication Association's (ICA) Political Communication Division in 1973, quickly followed by a subject journal which became *Political Communication*. It has

1

generated many of the field's principal theoretical and methodological approaches, developed in the US political and media context.

There has also been extensive work carried out by British-based scholars inspired by the doyen of UK political communication scholarship, Jay Blumler. The mid-1990s saw a flurry of political communication publications: Franklin's *Packaging Politics* (1994), reissued in 2004, Scammell's *Designer Politics* (1995), Kavanagh's *Election Campaigning* (1995) and Negrine's *Communication of Politics* (1996). These books focused largely on the professionalization of British political communication and its impact on democracy. Preceding them, Seymour-Ure published significant studies of British media and politics in 1968 and 1974 and has continued to produce work on executive communication (2003). A more general overview of the field in Britain was McNair's very useful *Introduction to Political Communication*. First published in 1995, it was last re-issued in updated form in 2007.

Subsequently, more narrowly focused studies have included Wring's valuable studies of the history and impact of the UK Labour Party's communication and marketing transformation (1996 and 2005), Thompson's work on political scandal (2000), Street's (2001) and Davis's (2002) work on the impact of the development of media democracies and Lees-Marshment's chronicling of the development of political marketing (2001, 2004). Lilleker's publication of *Key Concepts for Political Communication* (2006) as well as Negrine and Stanyer's *Reader in Political Communication* (2006) and the latter's *Modern Political Communication* (2007) all demonstrate that the field of UK political communication study is also a well-consolidated one.

Further afield, political communication research has emerged as a key area of social scientific scholarship. Asian research is becoming well-established (see Willnat and Aw, 2004). In continental Europe, German researchers such as Donsbach, Holtz-Bacha and Noelle-Neumann have led the field in their specialist areas of media effects, political advertising and public opinion research respectively. Italy's Mancini has been a pioneer of comparative political communication research (see Hallin and Mancini, 2004) and Maarek (see 1995) has been a leading figure in French political communication studies as well as a promoter of international scholarship through his leadership of the Political Communication Section of the International Association of Mass Communication Research (IAMCR). In 2008 Spanish-based scholars and practitioners founded the Association of Political Communication, marking a key moment for the field's development in Spain.

The practice of, and burgeoning research in, political communication have prompted the creation of a number of university degree programmes. Since the 1990s, new graduate programmes have been developed in Britain, France, Spain and China, moving the subject beyond its traditional US heartland. Increasingly, undergraduate programmes in journalism, media, cultural studies and political science feature a political communication module.

International Perspective and Ethical Concern

My reasons for adding to the literature on political communication are three-fold. First, during 11 years at the Department of Journalism Studies of the University of Sheffield, I had the great fortune to teach and learn from an internationally diverse group of MA and doctoral students. I record my thanks to them all here. Several were political communicators of one type or another: journalists from Latvia, China and the Ukraine; communication specialists working for public institutions from Peru, Mexico and Indonesia; those who had worked for political parties from Zimbabwe and the Philippines. Their rich experience suggested to me the need for work that would indicate, in the first place, broader political communication horizons than national or Anglo-American ones and, secondly, explore a wider range of political communication themes than those typically covered in the texts available.

Both aims are, of course, impossibly ambitious. My work does have a British slant, partly because of my own research and experience and partly because political communication during the Blair years (1997–2007) was, I argue later, of particular interest to scholars of the subject. However, I hope that the book, in its examples and acknowledgement of the limitations of national prisms, provides a wider window on the world of political communication than is normally the case, although Oates's work (2008) is an important recent exception.

The second reason for writing the book derives from practical and theoretical concerns with what appears to me to be a growing disconnect in the public mind between politics and ethics and almost a reluctance to confront head on the subject of ethics in the literature on political communication (see Chapter 14). This 'disconnect' is nothing new. Both Machiavelli and Hobbes espouse a view of politics that attempts to divorce it from morality. They suggest that successful politicians must resist the moralization of politics and, certainly, the view that politics should be distinct from theocratic or pulpit politics is one I share. However, their critique – and one taken up by modern political theory – goes further: it claims that politics is an amoral enterprise geared to the successful exercise of power which should not be subject to ethical concerns. Lies and manipulation are entirely acceptable if they serve the ruler's purposes for the public realm. This view of the effective use of power being separate from ethics has seeped deep into the public consciousness: the popular sense that all politicians are liars does not date from the age of spin.

However, I argue that we must distinguish well between politics, on the one hand, and the exercise of power, on the other. Books such as Clausewitz's *On War* or the Japanese study of sword-fighting by Musashi are lessons in the exercise of power and can be used by business leaders, by military planners or by politicians; they all deal with the effective employment of power but not politics as such. Politics is about 'acts that are directed toward the determination and/or implementation of state goals in the context of power struggles' (Hösle, 2004: 68) or, in Bernard Crick's more poetic words:

> Politics is a bold prudence, a diverse unity, an armed conciliation, a natural arti-
> fice, a creative compromise, and a serious game on which free civilization
> depends; it is a reforming conserver, a sceptical believer, and a pluralistic moral-
> ist; it has a lively sobriety, a complex simplicity, an untidy elegance, a rough civil-
> ity, and an everlasting immediacy; it is conflict become discussion; and it sets us
> a humane task on a human scale. (1982: 161)

Politics implies a commitment to communicability and thus a notion of veracity. In this book I advance the view that the understanding and analysis of the communication of politics entails a fundamental, if not always acknowledged, position on ethics, for rhetoric is one of the key links between ethics and politics.

Finally, I have worked in, taught or researched issues related to political communication for virtually all my professional life and they continue to be an area of passionate interest. This book is an opportunity to draw together and reflect upon the themes that have been the subject of my work, research and teaching.

Structure of the Book

The book is structured in three parts. Part One – 'Political Communication: Themes and Context' – is divided into four chapters. I first set out an overview of the development of the field of political communication as a site of practice and scholarship. In Chapter 3, I examine perspectives on the relationship between the media and democracy, examining the contemporary context of mediated politics. The chapter explores the relationship between language, politics and persuasion, distinguishing between the latter and manipulation, propaganda and spin. The phenomenon of spin is set in the context of an analysis of the central place of the media in constitutional democracies. In Chapter 4, I explore the dramaturgical model of political communication. This model takes Edelman's insights into the central role of symbolism in politics and examines how politics, like money, has a real yet in part fictionalized existence – intensified in a mediated context – which owes much to the tropes of drama and the ritual and absolutes of religion. Finally, Chapter 5 examines the development of political marketing and debates about what it means for politics itself. Part One seeks to explore the fundamentals of the contemporary field of political communication and principally the debates raised by the development of what Silverstone describes as the 'mediapolis' (see Chapter 3).

Part Two – 'The Communicators' – examines key contemporary communicators, their roles, strategies and tactics. In Chapter 6, I explore the shift of government communication from its initial peripheral role to the central position it occupies in governance today, taking the Blair years as a case study. Chapter 7 examines the communication strategies of a variety of actors who are, legally or illegally, in opposition to the established governing powers. I explore how political parties in opposition, campaign groups and organizations such as Al-Qaeda or ETA operating outside the law use a variety of communication strategies to wrest power away from those in whom it is vested. Chapter 8 examines the development of the political persuasion industry including lobbyists, pressure groups and the more recent emergence of think tanks. It explores the reason for their development, their legitimacy and the ways they attempt to influence the policy process. Finally in this section, in Chapter 9 I explore the development of the global political communicators, examining the role of global news organizations such as Reuters, CNN and Al-Jazeera in setting the global news agenda and driving public diplomacy and the role of public diplomacy itself.

Part Three – 'Getting the Message' – consists of five chapters and explores some of the content of political communication, the forms used to communicate it and its impact. In Chapter 10, I look at the notion of public opinion, the ways employed to quantify it and the growing apparent disengagement of the people in post-industrial democracies. Chapter 11 examines the political campaign and in particular the election campaign, the principal historical site for political communication. and Chapter 12 assesses the questions as to whether and how people are persuaded by election communication and changing understandings of political news are examined in Chapter 13. Finally, the concluding chapter examines the ways in which political discourse can be corrupted or prostituted and how communication integrity, key for the future of political communication, can be fostered.

From running the British Chamber of Shipping's Press and Parliamentary office to developing and directing the University of Sheffield's MA in Political Communication, I have met many outstanding scholars, students and exponents of political communication from across the world. Many of those scholars are mentioned earlier in my cursory overview of scholarship. From Britain, Bob Franklin, Ralph Negrine, Margaret Scammell and Dominic Wring have been kind and encouraging colleagues. I owe a special debt to Philippe Maarek and Christina Holtz-Bacha, with whom I have spent many happy times and enjoyed fruitful discussions at research panels in political communication at IAMCR and ICA conferences. Several chapters draw on research presented at these meetings. María José Canel deserves special mention and thanks. Many chapters rely on research we have developed together in comparative political communication.

I wish to record my special gratitude to former colleagues at Sheffield's Department of Journalism Studies with whom I am privileged to have worked and, more particularly, to Mark Hanna from whom I have learnt a great deal. Jackie Harrison has always been a source of encouragement and support. The communication and journalism students I have taught in Sheffield, and now in Madrid, continue to be a source of inspiration.

The book's limitations are my responsibility. I am conscious, for example, that the medium of radio gets short shrift even though I know it is the means by which many people around the globe receive political news. I would also like to have dedicated more attention to parts of the world such as India and South-East Asia. I hope readers from those countries and regions will respond to the book with suggestions and examples. It is also true that I have largely avoided the summary textbook style. I understand its advantages, but I believe it can also encourage short cuts in understanding and knowledge that are not entirely beneficial. I have, however, attempted to give the reader a succinct view of each chapter's contents in the introduction while maintaining the discursive style of the main text. My awareness of the book's limitations, and my attempts to remedy them, are due to the helpful comments of the book's anonymous reviewers. I am grateful to them not only for pointing out areas for improvement but also for their very encouraging comments.

Many people were quick to respond to requests for help. My thanks to Carmen Isolina, José Carlos Lozano, Nyankiso Maqeda, Carla Montemayor, Joseph Shipley, Jeffrey Tatum, Jon Urkiola and the media offices of Amnesty International and Greenpeace. My thanks too to Linda Sanders who read and made many helpful criticisms of draft chapters and to María de la Viesca who helped me check the final manuscript.

Over the last ten years I have conducted a number of workshops and interviews, some specifically for this book, with journalists, lobbyists and campaigners. I use their insights throughout this study. They include Head of Politics at the BBC, Ric Bailey; former BBC journalist and specialist in spin, Nick Jones; CAFOD head of communication, Alison Fenney; head of news at Sky News, John Ryley; and former head of the East Midlands Government News Network, Peter Smith.

The writing of this book became the victim of a job, house and country move in 2007. I am grateful to my editors at Palgrave Macmillan, Emily Salz and Sheree Keep, who were understanding and encouraging in keeping me on course and to my dean, Francisco Serrano, for his support.

Finally, my thanks to family and friends who have been unfailingly supportive in getting me over the finishing line. You know who you are. I couldn't have done it without you.

Part One
Issues, Concepts, Debates

2

Introducing the Field of Political Communication

Introduction

Graffiti on the wall dividing Israel from the Palestinians, a joke or cartoon about French president Nicolas Sarkozy; Barack Obama's bestselling memoirs, Salam Pax blogging from Baghdad and CNN's Christiane Amanpour broadcasting from Pakistan; George Clooney visiting Darfur or José Luis Zapatero campaigning to be re-elected prime minister in the 2008 Spanish elections, all of these phenomena share one common feature: each can be considered an instance of political communication. Their diversity indicates, on the one hand, the richness and interest of the field but also the difficulties scholars experience in pinning down its limits for the purposes of study.

For the moment, I am going to leave aside the question of definition, returning to it at the end of the chapter. First, I will sketch in some of the historical background to the development of political communication and its emergence as a lively area of practice, debate and scholarship at the beginning of the twenty-first century.

Ancient Origins and a Continuous Tradition

As *practice*, political communication has existed as long as there have been human beings engaged in one of two activities:

- persuasive communication directed towards political goals
- informational communication about politics

Communication in both cases requires, firstly, the existence of actors: an 'I' who seeks to persuade or inform an 'other'(s). But for it also to be 'political', the appropriate communicational context and subject matter are required;

9

these provide the historical boundary posts for the practice of political communication.

Take context first. Ancient Egyptian civilization was founded on a belief in the pharaoh's divinity. Politics understood as an end in itself, a sphere of freedom constituted by citizens participating together in the public realm, did not exist. For fifth century BC Athenians, on the other hand, the *polis* – the city-state – was truly the realm of word and action. Speeches aimed at persuading fellow citizens to support war against Persia mattered. Despite its limited nature, the Athenian *polis* was the birthplace of both the theory and practice of political communication. The first great systematic study of political communication was Aristotle's *On Rhetoric: A Theory of Civic Discourse*, where he analysed the art and science of persuasion or rhetoric.

Aristotle (384–322 BC) considered rhetoric to be a necessary part of politics together with the knowledge of the arts of military leadership and economics. He was also the first to state that rhetoric was a worthy practice and to set out the essential ingredients for successful communication. Plato (427–347 BC) had earlier criticized the Sophists, professional public communicators, in *Gorgias*, arguing that rhetoric has no subject matter peculiar to itself and therefore, an ignorant man could mislead and manipulate other ignorant men in the pursuit of power rather than the achievement of good. The temptation to use rhetoric for ignoble ends has been constant down the ages and provides one of the enduring themes in the study of political communication.

Even in limited political contexts, the possibility of the loss, gain or consolidation of political power ensured the use of a number of communication strategies. Through the pageantry and ceremonial of courts, emperors and kings displayed and communicated the reality and appearance of royal power to friends and potential enemies. The choreographed victory processions of imperial Rome with their chants, flags and scent of incense symbolically enacted the City's dominance; Byzantium's coronation ritual was imitated by the parvenu Carolingian eighth-century court, emphasizing the continuities of royal power. The 'Forbidden Cities' of Chinese dynastic rulers across the centuries communicated their semi-divine status. The great Indian Mogal emperor, Akbar (1556–1605), used Catholic iconography for his own propaganda, emphasizing the symbolic coincidence of Jesus's virgin birth and that of his Mongol ancestors. Carefully controlled copies of the image of Akbar's exact contemporary, England's Queen Elizabeth I, and efficient dissemination of her speeches reinforced her standing and legitimacy as the country's 'Virgin Queen'. Leaders everywhere, despite the limited degree of consent they required for power, were conscious of communication's role in the maintenance of their position.

Spreading Democracy

It was only with the emergence of newspapers as a force in the formation of public opinion in the eighteenth century and the spread of democracy in the nineteenth century that the wider communication of politics became a pressing issue for the political classes. The Americas were the site of much of the political and media innovation which was key to the development of political communication. Alexis de Tocqueville's classic study, *Democracy in America* (1835/1840), examined the role of a free and thriving press in the democratic processes of the new nation of the United States. Newspapers had come to be seen as a power in the land in the build-up to North America's War of Independence in 1789, the first great age of newspaper power. As we shall see in Chapter 11, populist politicians like Ireland's Daniel O'Connell harnessed press power and his fine rhetorical gifts to build a mass campaign to win political rights for Irish Catholics. In the United States, Andrew Jackson's 1828 presidential campaign used rallies, parades, a campaign song, badges and insignia, professional speech-writers and producers of newspaper copy to win the election.

In Latin America, the end of the eighteenth and beginning of the nine-teenth centuries saw the sun beginning to set on Spain's extensive empire. From Mexico to Patagonia, it fragmented to create a number of independent states whose political identity had partially been forged by the early news-papers of the time (see Anderson, 1983). The great Latin American *Libertador*, Simón Bolívar (1783–1830), was a supreme manipulator of liberal public opinion during his years of exile in London and Washington. He was also adept at producing black propaganda to influence international public opinion, forging letters alleging planned Spanish atrocities. One of the first acts of Mexico's rebel leader, Miguel Hidalgo, was to take over the press.

It was also during this time that 'the prototype modern pressure group' (Johnson, 1991: 323) was born. The movement for the abolition of slavery galvanized the British public to boycott sugar, create correspondence com-mittees, produce publicity material and articles for the press, collect evi-dence for parliamentary committees and even to manufacture a Wedgewood pottery cameo of a slave in order to campaign for legislation to be passed by the British parliament banning slavery, an aim finally achieved by William Wilberforce and his supporters in 1833.

The Arrival of the Masses

The extension of the franchise, the growth of literacy and education, the increase in the number and circulation of newspapers, the march of business and the development of technology ushered in what the Spanish philosopher,

José Ortega y Gasset, described as the age of the masses. The first mass war – the First World War (1914–18) – provided the impetus for scientific investigation of the making of mass opinion. 'The present European war [...] deserves to be distinguished as the first press agents' war', claimed the *New York Times* (9 September 1914, cited in Kunczik, 1996: 175).

As part of the US government's effort to win over its reluctant public to the cause of the First World War, a Committee on Public Information, known as the Creel Committee, was appointed in 1917 by Woodrow Wilson. It was described by its chairman, George Creel, as: 'a plain publicity proposition, a vast enterprise in salesmanship, the world's greatest adventure in advertising' (cited in Kunczik, 1996: 187). Edward Bernays (1891–1995), nephew of Sigmund Freud, was a member of the Committee. Afterwards, he opened a public relations consultancy and advised virtually every US president between Coolidge and Eisenhower. His advice to the austere Coolidge to eat pancakes at breakfast with Al Jolson, the singer, was a media event. The *New York Times* headline was: 'Actors Eat Cakes With The Coolidges – President Nearly Laughs'.

As we shall see in Chapter 5, Bernays was the first to establish public relations on a pseudo-scientific basis. He termed its practitioners 'opinion managers', 'publicity agents' or 'public relations counsellors'. His last major book, *Engineering Consent* (1947), suggested that political leaders and governments could engineer public support in a rational, scientific manner through an understanding and manipulation of mass psychology. His theoretical outlook was greatly influenced by his uncle's pioneering work examining the subconscious irrational forces driving human desire and choice. The Freudian model suggested that human beings' motives often lay deeply hidden and unknown even to ourselves. He is considered as 'one of the most influential theorists and practitioners of public communication in the twentieth century and thus one of the key figures in laying the groundwork for the promotional culture in which we live' (Durham Peters and Simonson, 2004: 51).

Another member of the Creel Committee was the distinguished journalist and political commentator, Walter Lippmann (1889–1974), whose *Public Opinion* (1922) took a similarly bleak view of the public's capacity to arrive at an informed view on matters, and particularly political matters, beyond their immediate experience, reliant as they were on the partial, fragmentary information provided by the media (see Chapter 10).

The Modern Era of Political Communication

Economic, cultural and political conditions in the United States particularly favoured the development of 'designer politics' (Scammell, 1995) in which the burnishing of a party's and candidate's image became a core element of campaign strategies. Corporate public relations begat political public relations and the Democrats were the first US political party to set up a permanent public relations office in 1928, followed by the Republicans in 1932. The first political public relations consultancy, *Campaigns Incorporated*, was established in California by a husband and wife team, Clem Whittaker and Leone Baxter, in 1933 (see McNair, 2007: 119). It formed the model for what would become the contemporary billion-dollar political consultancy business. They advised on 75 campaigns, won 70 of them and considered that the frequent repetition of a single theme was the key to success. From 1936 onwards, candidates for office began to draw on the services of advertising agencies, and in 1946 opinion polling began to be used seriously.

The 1953 Eisenhower presidential campaign was the first time a television advertising campaign was used and polls extensively employed, highlighting the power of both for political campaigners. However, television's power in politics really came of age in the Kennedy-Nixon 1960 presidential debate (see Chapter 11). The putative impact of 'seeing' Kennedy rather than just hearing him became accepted as the starting point for the televisual age in politics.

Research published by McCombs and Shaw in 1974 based on an analysis of public opinion polls and newspaper content provided the first empirical evidence for the 'agenda setting' effect of the media. This confirmation of a 'fact' intuitively understood by political campaigners represented a significant moment in political communication research, pointing to the real contributions that researchers might make in understanding its practice. I will consider next the chief ways scholars have thought about the communication of politics.

Thinking about Political Communication

The study and practice of political communication is characterized by the application of a range of theoretical and methodological approaches. Such an embarrassment of scholarly riches is unsurprising. The field's multidisciplinary origins in psychology, sociology, rhetoric and political science and the complexity of the area of human activity designated as 'political communication' require the insights of diverse perspectives, each of which has its strengths and limitations.

Thinking about political communication necessarily implies theory building. The original Greek *theorein* means 'to look at' or 'contemplate'. In contemporary science a theory is a set of descriptions forming a model to explain the ways things are and offering predictions about what will happen in the future such as, for example, the theory of global warming. In ordinary use, 'theory' is often used in the opposite sense to its scientific one, as in 'that's fine in theory but how will it work in practice?' A good theory, however, should be practical and not only embrace concepts and definitions but also address processes to explore how, when and why effects occur. This understanding of theory is characteristic of one particular approach to the study of political communication but, as I shall now explain, there are others too that can provide useful insights into the field.

For heuristic purposes, I have divided them into three main perspectives:[1] the first can be described as positivistic in outlook, the second as critical and the third as hermeneutical. I will explain what each of these means, their organizing concepts, principal methods and concerns (see Table 2.1).

Positivistic Model: Emphasizing the Individual

Positivism is the view that all knowledge is derived from scientific methods. This derives from the commitment to a specific theory of knowledge, empiricism. Empiricism seeks to explain, predict and control observable phenomena by discovering necessary, general relationships among them.

This approach was first employed in political communication research by those examining media effects in propaganda and voting studies. Paul Lazarsfeld (1901–1976) established Columbia University's Bureau for Applied

Table 2.1 Approaches to the study of political communication

Theoretical perspective	Epistemological approach	Methods	Themes
Positivism	Empiricism	Content analysis Surveys Experiments	Media effects: Voting Agenda setting Priming Audience: uses and gratifications
Critical social theory	Materialism	Observation Document analysis Statistical analysis	Political economy of media Propaganda Manufacturing consent Moral panics
Hermeneutics	Phenomenalism	Discourse analysis Semiotics Observation Focus groups	Media events Reception analysis Moral panics

Social Research where, among other things, he initiated the first election studies (see Chapter 11), examining the effects of mass-mediated messages about politics. The Bureau's particular research emphasis was on effects and audience. This was not fortuitous. It arose out of the close connection between the academic establishment and the corporate world. Paul Lazarsfeld actively sought business funding for what he called 'administrative' research.

Lazarsfeld's contemporary, Harold Lasswell (1902–1978) taught at the University of Chicago and became the principal expert on the study of propaganda, publishing *Propaganda Technique in the World War* (1927). His statement that communication research was about 'who said what to whom in what channel and with what effect' became the guiding light of much future work. It expressed what has been described as the process approach to communication studies, examining the transmission of messages as a lineal process in which senders and receivers encode and decode messages.

Studies in the positivistic tradition draw chiefly on psychology, political science and sociology and favour the employment of quantitative methods such as:

- **Content analysis**. This seeks to produce an objective, measurable, verifiable account of content and functions through the identification and counting of chosen units in a communication system that are identifiable and occur with sufficient frequency for statistical methods of analysis to be valid.
- **Surveys**. Data are collected from the population to answer research questions and test hypotheses.
- **Experiments**. Social scientists set up experimental situations, for example, exposure to selected television images, to test hypotheses.

The empiricist approach has been criticized for being overly mechanistic. In its earliest form, researchers formulated a so-called 'hypodermic needle' model, where media cause and effect were conceptualized as being related in a simple stimulus–response way (see Chapter 12). However, the discovery that people responded differently to the same messages began to undermine this model fairly early on. Individuals do not simply receive messages and are acted upon by them uniformly and in a vacuum. Researchers adjusted their focus and began to examine how messages are filtered through various kinds of variables (see Chapter 11), developing a battery of statistical techniques and survey approaches to examine communication phenomena.

Critical Model: Emphasizing Structure

Critical theory owes much to Marxist thinking, especially in taking the view that theory should be directed towards achieving social change, analysing social and cultural structures (the superstructures of Marxist thought) in order to free those subject to their power. In other words, the exponents of critical theory seek emancipatory social change through critical reflection on social practices. They take Marxism itself not as a new kind of positivistic science but as a critique of prevailing ideologies. Ideology here refers to a system of beliefs characteristic of a particular group employed, according to Marxist theory, as a means by which the ruling group maintains subordination of the working classes.

Louis Althusser (1918–1990) developed the idea of ideology as a practice, and as being deeply inscribed in the ways of thinking and living of all classes and not simply imposed upon others by the dominant class. He described the process of 'interpellation' where, by responding to a communication, we participate in a particular ideological construction, forming social identities that are complicit with or even contrary to our own interests. Ideology constitutes me as female, male, black, white by the very fact that I am able to use and respond appropriately to signs, connotations and myths. In other words, the only means of making sense of our experience are always ideologically loaded.

Mass culture became a major concern of critical theorists such as Theodor Adorno (1903–1969) and Max Horkheimer (1895–1973). These post-1933 emigré scholars from the Frankfurt School, the Institute for Social Research at the University of Frankfurt, transferred the Institute and their intellectual concerns to Columbia University. There they developed their critique of the culture industries and what they considered to be their manipulation of the masses. In political communication, their approach inspired a rejection of positivistic, 'common-sense' understandings of the relationship between media and political structures in favour of a critical examination of the economic, cultural and social determinants that configure structure. Hermann and Chomsky's (1988) *Manufacturing Consent* is a classic example of this approach.

Hermeneutic Model: Emphasizing Culture

Critical theorists' concern with culture was taken up in the work of Stuart Hall (1973), one of the leading figures of cultural studies in Britain. His Marxist-influenced work emphasized the audience's active role encoding and decoding texts and in negotiating their meaning. Reception theory, as this approach is known, suggests that audiences can resist, oppose and negotiate meanings through their own interpretative strategies derived from their individual backgrounds and experiences.

The founding fathers of British cultural studies, the literary critics Richard Hoggart (b.1918) and Raymond Williams (1921–1988), had also emphasized the role of active audiences, of their ability to read and interpret texts so that communication is understood not just as the transmission of messages but as the construction of meaning. In this understanding of communication, determinants of meaning lie not only in the process itself but also in society and the individual. The interpretative arts, then, become central to understanding communication. The contributions of anthropologists such as Clifford Geertz (1926–2006) and philosophers such as Paul Ricoeur (1913–2005) and George Herbert Mead (1863–1931) emphasize our use of symbols to comprehend and interpret the world and make sense of our own place in it. In this view of communication, the term is linked to such notions as sharing, participation, association and fellowship. Communication occurs in our attempts to make sense of others' behaviour through our own interpretative activity.

The hermeneutic approach to understanding communication developed more under the influence of the humanities: literature, linguistics and philosophy and its insights are, I will suggest below, particularly valuable for understanding the communication of politics in a symbol-saturated world. Its characteristic, if not exclusive, epistemological inspiration is phenomenology. Phenomenology emphasizes a 'first person' approach to gaining knowledge rather than the 'third person' perspective of the scientific method, exploring the phenomena of conscious experience.[2]

Before concluding this necessarily cursory overview of approaches to thinking about political communication, two important qualifications should be made. First, while researchers may adopt fundamental theoretical commitments, tending perhaps more to an empiricist than to a hermeneutical outlook, these outlooks may in fact share certain features that permit a certain eclecticism. Second, this is also true in relation to the selection of methods. Much of the most valuable research undertaken in political communication uses a mixed methods design. Researchers employ two or three methods to examine their object of study, ensuring that they 'triangulate' – corroborate with diverse streams of evidence – their findings.

Defining Political Communication

It may seem perverse to deal with the definition of the object of this book towards the end of the chapter. However, having examined the kind of practice and area of scholarship involved, I hope it will now be easier to describe what I mean by political communication.

The cross-disciplinary field of inquiry known as 'political communication' emerged from the world of propaganda studies after the end of the First World War. It has been a field populated by psychologists, political scientists, rhetoricians and communication scholars. The discourse of US campaigns, and primarily presidential campaigns, provided one of the main sites of political communication research, and American scholarship still dominates the field, well exemplified by the front cover of the *Handbook of Political Communication Research* published in 2004, where stars from the American flag burst out of an Uncle Sam hat in a colour scheme of red, white and blue.

However, political communication is about much more than American presidential election campaigns. It has been broadly defined as the 'role of communication in the political process' (Chaffee, 1975: 15). An earlier attempt at definition was that offered by Eulau, Eldersveld and Janovitz (1956), who suggested that political communication could be understood as one of the processes, together with political leadership and groups, through which influence is transmitted.

Researchers have also approached the definition of political communication from a system-based analysis. Blumler and Gurevitch, for example, defined the components of a political communication system as consisting in (1995: 5):

- Political institutions in their communication aspects
- Media institutions in their political aspects
- Audience orientations to political communication
- Communication-relevant aspects of political culture. (1995: 5)

A more meaning focused definition describes political communication as 'any exchange of symbols or messages that to a significant extent have been shaped by, or have consequences for, the functioning of the political system' (Meadows, 1980: 4). This approach is adopted by Brian McNair, drawing upon that outlined by Denton and Woodward (1998) who define political communication not by its source, but by its content and purpose. Political communication, says McNair, is 'purposeful communication about politics' (2007: 4). This includes all communication by political actors for the achievement of specific purposes, all communication directed to them, and all communication about them and their activities. McNair specifically excludes interpersonal communication, as I largely will too. This is a useful starting point, although one might ask whether all communication is not in some way purposeful.

Another way of looking at what constitutes political communication is to examine research in the field. Johnston's survey (1990) of 1980s political communication research divided it into four categories:

1. Election communication
2. Political communication and news
3. Political rhetoric
4. Political attitudes, behaviour and information

A more recent compendium of political communication research (Kaid, 2004a) divided it into six sections covering theory and methods; political messages (including, for example, political advertising, rhetoric and campaign debates); news coverage of politics; public opinion (citizen's engagement and political knowledge, for instance); international perspectives and, finally, the role of the internet. It provides a useful snapshot of mainly American-based work in the field. It does not capture – nor does it intend to – the rich panoply of political communication practice.

The field of political communication is concerned with communication and its role in political processes, systems and institutions. However, for simplicity's sake, and to place political communication in the realm of not only the social but also the human sciences, this book will treat political communication as an area of practice and study related to the human activity of communicating about politics. Politics here is understood too as a human activity engaged in by groups where there are diverse interests conciliated by a settled order. The activity involves deeds and words with both instrumental and symbolic meanings (see Chapter 4) related to decision-making and the allocation of scarce, valued resources.

Guiding Principles and Organizing Themes

A number of commentators have suggested that traditional accounts of political communication are too restricted. Corner and Pels, for example, have argued that: 'Political communication is both too limiting in its suggested scope (centred, sometimes exclusively, upon political publicity and political journalism and with a bias towards electoral campaigns) and too functionalist in its implications of a defined role self-consciously performed' (2003: 5). They suggest a move towards the exploration of the aestheticization of politics, focusing on politics as performance, style and personality.

This is helpful. It opens up the range of political communication study, as we shall see. It suggests too the usefulness of briefly setting out the theoretical choices I have made and the methodological tools I have used to tell the story of political communication at the beginning of the twenty-first century.

Theoretical and Thematic Choices for Political Communication

In his helpful review of approaches to political communication, the British political scientist John Street suggests that broadly speaking there are three perspectives founded either on a pluralist, constructivist or structuralist understanding of the relationship between the media and politics where '[t]heir differences are revealed in their competing accounts of how they understand 'communication', the way they define the 'political' and the balance they strike between structure and agency' (2005: 18).

In simple terms, in first place for the pluralists the media are political players among others in the domain of politics (reflecting the positivist approach); for the constructivists, in second place, the media have colonized the political space, 'mediatizing' politics (this echoes the hermeneutical perspective). In Street's words 'the media are the playwrights' (2005: 23). Finally, structuralists challenge both these understandings, arguing that media and politics are structured by the political economy in which they are situated (this echoes the critical social approach). Writing about media systems, for example, Garnham suggests that they are 'just like supermarkets. They are systems for packaging symbolic products and distributing them as rapidly and cheaply as possible' (2000: 59–60). His approach eschews methodological individualism in favour of a focus on institutional, economic and regulatory structures.

Each of these paradigms provides insights for the study of political communication. However, the theoretical paradigm underlying the following account of political communication is based on an approach essayed by the sociologist Margaret Archer in a trilogy of books: *Culture and Agency* (1988), *Realist Social Theory* (1995) and *On Being Human: The Problem of Agency* (2000). In this work Archer sets out a view which conserves human agency and yet recognizes the grip of structural power. She rescues the self that has been dissolved by constructionists in discourse, turned into a rational essence by the champions of rational choice and entirely enmeshed by material forces by the structuralists. Acknowledging that we do not make ourselves on terms of our own choosing, Archer nevertheless argues that our relations with natural, practical and social reality allow for specific and personal human properties and powers to emerge.

Her social realist approach permits a view of human agency that allows us to discuss the importance of events for human beings without neglecting the role of structure and culture. Archer argues that culture is indeed structured: cultural capital is not equally distributed nor are we equal partners in any conversation, a metaphor she considers misleading (see 2000: 259).[3] Human beings are, first, *actors*, with their own personal, specific powers and properties; they are also *primary agents*, situated by structural and cultural constraints; finally, they may also be *corporate agents*, distinguished from the former by their strategic actions which contribute to the shaping of the structural and cultural domains.

My approach is to examine political communication in order to uncover the actions of human beings both as actors and as corporate agents. Strategic action implies engagement with power, understood as the domain of material and symbolic resources that shape the environment in which we act and by which we are acted upon. The development of the media and their contribution to the simultaneous dispersal and concentration of symbolic resources have galvanized a range of corporate agents and generated new cultural themes. They make media central to any account of political communication, the reason why I have not dedicated a separate chapter to the media as communicators or political players (although see Chapters 3 and 13). It suggests too the choice of a wider palette of topics than might be suggested by traditional political communication studies: certainly election campaigns are important, but so are scandal, terrorism, spin and political campaigns of various types (see Chapters 4, 7, 8 and 11). For similar reasons, the internet is not treated separately. Discussion of its role and impact in political communication is interwoven into each of the chapters' themes and topics since I think we can no longer doubt that the internet has become an integral part of the political communication environment.

Guiding Principles

The theoretical choices outlined imply the adoption of certain guiding principles for this study. I adopt them because I believe they make good some of the shortcomings or, to put it in more positive terms, enrich our approach to the understanding and study of political communication. I will give two examples to illustrate how the prevailing paradigms fall short in understanding political communication. Take the structuralists' view. Political economists have fruitfully examined the market imperatives driving the dynamic of media–political relations in industrial and post-industrial democracies. Critics in this tradition argue that the structural characteristics of capitalist economies, far from creating 'media democracies', have brought about propaganda states of disenfranchised citizens in which state power definitely has the upper hand. However, while this approach highlights some of the challenges to democracy generated by market-driven societies, it can fail to acknowledge the complexities and contradictions that also arise. Commercialism can indeed work against certain normative models of political communication; it may also be the means by which the media are stimulated to more critical scrutiny of politics (the endless stream of political scandals is a good example), framed in a more dramatic, personalized style. It is possible that increasing commercialism is driving the media to be more autonomous in post-industrial democracies and – to use the language of functionalism – 'differentiated' from the political system. The processes at work (the decline of strong ideological frameworks, the development of mass media, for instance) may give grounds for hypothesizing the emergence of a global media culture and environment for the practice and study of political communication.

To take a second example, theoretical perspectives taken from a positivistic model of the social sciences can and have provided useful insights into the development and practice of political communication, allowing us to define the field as a discrete area of scholarship susceptible of analysis in a global context. Here too, however, I would enter significant caveats. Empirical work grounded in the positivist social sciences can produce helpful evidence for questions regarding, for example, political communication processes, actions and effects. Nevertheless, its theoretical starting point has significant shortcomings for the study of human phenomena. Positivistic models often overstate reductionist and mechanistic explanations of human behaviour and underestimate the place of history, culture and agency. Indeed, much work has been dominated by a view which places instrumental rationality at the centre of thinking.

For this reason, while necessarily drawing on the contribution of critical and positivist traditions, this study argues that values and beliefs about the human being, rooted in religion and the contingencies of history, play a key role in understanding the development and practice of political communication in the context of distinct media and political cultures across the world. 'Our cultural arrangements do not just grow naturally, like a tree; they are founded, practiced and enacted by people' (Pitkin, 1998: 2).

My theoretical framework contains, then, two key components. First, it emphasizes the crucial contribution of comparative analysis for an understanding of political communication. Comparative work can help understand the ways in which a particular context has characteristics peculiar to itself and in what ways it is similar to others. It allows researchers to build models and develop theory in a more robust manner than is possible in its absence. This study will draw on both primary and secondary comparative research, as well as the work conducted over the last ten years with postgraduate students from all parts of the globe, to illuminate questions about political communication which too often have been examined only in an Anglo-American context.

The second key theoretical component is the notion that discussion of political communication always implies the formulation of a normative framework. This can be expressed along two axes: the first interrogates the 'architecture' of political communication, attending to the structural characteristics of the politics–media–public nexus and examining their implications for ideal-types of political communication; the second axis concerns the examination of the grounds and principles for right and wrong practice in political communication. An analysis of ethics in political communication will be one of the central theoretical concerns of this study.

3

Media Democracies

Introduction

The linkage of the existence of free media to the possibility of democracy is a long-established tenet of thinking about politics. In the Western tradition the development of democratic politics from the late seventeenth to the twentieth century was accompanied by that of a free press. In his *Democracy in America*, the French political writer, Alexis de Tocqueville (1805–1859) declared: 'The more I consider the independence of the press in its principal consequences, the more am I convinced that in the modern world it is the chief and, so to speak, the constitutive element of liberty' (1848/1994:193).

'Liberty', 'democracy', a 'free press' became the sacred watchwords of liberal societies. However, as governments became increasingly adept at 'spin' and the media were incorporated into powerful corporate conglomerates pursuing their own economic and political agendas, old liberal certainties were challenged. On the one hand, thinkers such as Edward Herman, Noam Chomsky and James Curran questioned whether media organizations, working to the logic of capitalist societies, could ever serve any interests other than the essentially mercantilist ones they were established to pursue. Far from establishing the grounds for political freedom, media organizations, it was argued, contributed towards the manufacturing of popular consent to the economic, social and political status quo (see Herman and Chomsky, 1988).

Another equally critical view of the media considers that democratic politics itself has been colonized by the imperatives of media spectacle. Politics are packaged and spun (see Franklin, 2004), the public manipulated, effectively disempowered and the press woefully inadequate to its civic task (Lloyd, 2004). These themes form the bedrock of the issues and debates to be found in political communication and, while this chapter will explore them in more detail, the questions raised will be found in every chapter of the book.

I will consider, first, the relationship of politics to communication and in particular persuasive communication in its various guises of rhetoric, spin and propaganda. This will be the prelude to a discussion of the tense relationship between the media and politicians in an era where the media increasingly appear to shape the rules of the political game.

Politics and Communication

Aristotle's famous dictum in *The Politics* that 'man is by nature a political animal' (*zδon politikon*) as well as his less well known definition of the human being as 'a living being capable of speech' (*zδon logon ekhon*) capture the ancient Greek understanding of the centrality of communication in constituting a truly human way of life. As the German political philosopher, Hannah Arendt, put it: 'To be political, to live in a polis, meant that everything was decided through words and persuasion and not through force and violence' (1958: 26). In the Aristotelian view, political activity was characterized by speech; speech (*logos*) and action (*praxis*) were the hallmarks of the *polis* – the city-state – and freedom was the fundamental ground of both. Politics was the realm of freedom not coercion; it was the sphere where words not brute force mattered. The science and art of argument – *dialectic* – and persuasion – *rhetoric* – were the weapons of those who dwelt in the polis and were its citizens. The need for argument and persuasion arises where different groups with diverse interests live together and where the fact of freedom is recognized. For, as Aristotle pointed out, an alternative to political rule is the rule of the dictator to whom argument and persuasion mean nothing.

Politics is irredeemably public, constituting by words and deeds a sphere where human beings and groups must make known to fellow citizens their views, their opinions, their policies. It is this quality of political life – 'its publicity' – which the political theorist, Bernard Crick, deemed to be the one which uniquely characterized political activity (1982: 20). Tyrants, oligarchs and kings do not need to enlist the public to their cause; they may simply impose their views through fear and force. However, whenever politics exists, so too must a constituency, be it of the narrowest kind, to whom words and actions will be addressed in persuasive appeal.

The Ancient Art and Science of Rhetoric

The ancient Greek polis was constituted by what we would consider today an unacceptably restricted constituency. Women, alien residents and slaves could not be citizens. This was the prerogative of a small number of free Greek men who were expected to be active in civic life and for this they were required to attain a certain mastery of oratory. To be an orator – *rhetor* – was to understand and be skilled in the art and science of civic discourse known as rhetoric. From the fifth century BC, the art of rhetoric was taught by groups of professional educators in communication known as Sophists, of whom Gorgias was one of their most famous representatives. In some ways they can be considered communication trainers, similar to contemporary political consultants and campaign strategists, and they too, like our modern communication specialists, were charged with being mercenaries and opportunists. The Sophists were not scholars or philosophers concerned with intellectual culture or transmission of ethical values. They wanted to teach people how to persuade others in order to achieve political or legal goals. The disassociation of rhetoric from dialectic (seeking of the truth) and rhetoric from ethics (seeking of the good) made Plato a fierce critic of rhetoric and of the Sophists, who he accused of being demagogues and of spreading illusion instead of knowledge. In his dialogue *Gorgias*, he has Socrates say:

> Do the rhetoricians appear to you always to speak with a view to what is best, aiming at this, that the citizens may be made as good as possible by their discourses? Or do they, too, endeavour to gratify the citizens, and neglecting the public interest for the sake of their own private advantage, do they treat the people as children, trying only to gratify them, without being in the least concerned whether they shall become better or worse by these means? (502e)

This criticism of those who engage in the persuasive arts has echoed down the centuries.

Plato's near contemporary, Aristotle, adopted a more sympathetic view of the role of rhetoric and, as we saw in the previous chapter, produced the first comprehensive theory of persuasion in his *Rhetoric or the Art of Civil Discourse*, thought to have been written in 336 BC.[1] Aristotle argued that rhetoric is acceptable provided that the speaker does not try to persuade the audience of what is debased. His defence of rhetoric goes to the heart of what we understand by communication and, more particularly political communication. As the Latin term *communicare* suggests, 'communication' is about more than emitting a message, more than just 'saying' something. To communicate involves two further elements: first, it involves saying something to *someone* and, second, that something which is said must be communicated, that is, be held in common between the communicator and the person to whom one communicates. Communication is more than information and for it to take place successfully the communicator must take into account three dimensions of communication, namely:

1. That language is an articulated system of signs – *syntaxis* – which must be used correctly.

2. That language is a vehicle of meaning – *semantics* – which implies a commitment to the notion that it can tell us about truth or, if preferred, reality.
3. That language has a practical dimension – *rhetoric* – which is about knowing how to communicate in such a way that we achieve the desired effect
   in our audience.

This last dimension is not trivial; it reflects both the character and style of
each human being and also the fact that human beings' experience of reality
is not straightforward. Each of us has our own communication style – man-
nered, elegant, ironic, understated or overstated – with which we seek to
communicate with others. For all of us reality is experienced in a partial,
fragmentary way, involving us in doubt, hesitation and reflection. For these
reasons, it has been said that human beings are 'naturally rhetorical because
they need to find the way of saying things' (Yepes Stork, 1996: 388). Think of
a teacher. It is not enough for a teacher to give a list of facts; a teacher must
know how to present these facts, clearly, succinctly, perhaps with some
humour. Thinking about what a good teacher does, highlights another
aspect of the rhetorical dimension of language which is of prime importance
for politicians and ethicists. A good English teacher can inculcate an abiding
passion for literature which never leaves us. We are in effect changed by the
ability of the teacher who has known how to communicate their love of the
English language. In other words, rhetoric can change us – our attitudes,
opinions, beliefs – and for that reason it is powerful and susceptible to abuse.

Persuasion

Aristotle's *On Rhetoric* explores within an explicit moral framework how to
be an effective persuader. He advocates knowledge of psychology and audience types and outlines three essential elements of persuasive discourse,
namely:

1. The trustworthy character of the speaker (*ethos*)
2. The logical argument set out in the discourse (*logos*)
3. The emotional effect created by the discourse on the audience (*pathos*)

Successful persuasion is very much anchored in the credibility of the persuader. This Aristotelian insight was understood by political scientists, who
in the American context, for example, accepted that perceptions of personal
attributes form a central component of American voting behaviour.
However, it was not until the 1970s and 1980s that research clearly showed
that election outcomes could be significantly affected by voters' evaluations
of the candidates (see Chapter 10). Indeed, candidate image has been shown

to be one of the best predictors of voting decisions (see Chapter 10). Knowing how to create the right emotional environment – appeals to patriotism, to altruism or fear – and the use of evidence and sound arguments all play their role in the persuasive arts.

The practice of persuasion is not of course the monopoly of politicians. We are constantly being exposed to persuasive messages from sources as varied as journalists, advertisers, friends, mothers and lecturers. According to one estimate, we receive as many as 1500 persuasive messages a day (Schultz, 1982). Great literature often explores the moral complexity generated by attempts at persuasion: Faust is persuaded to sell his soul, Macbeth to murder his king. In Jane Austen's novel *Persuasion*, Ann Elliot is persuaded by the over-worldly Lady Russell, against the reasons that her own heart gives her, not to marry the man she loves. Austen explores the central ethical dilemma of how we learn to weigh up persuasive messages and apply our own judgement to assess their cogency, a story going back to the Biblical accounts of that first seducer of humankind, the serpent in the Garden of Eden.

We can define persuasion as being communication intended to influence beliefs, attitudes and behaviour. Persuasion is at the heart of the democratic enterprise. But, of course, there is a problem here. The communication strategies and the strategists employed by politicians are often held to be manipulative. And, as Aristotle and Plato both noted, the risk of all rhetoric – and especially when employed by those who are powerful or unethical – is that it can be corrupted by an insufficient regard for the truth (the semantic dimension) or for the dignity of the listener. In other words, in the hands of the powerful or corrupt communication becomes solely rhetoric, the interests and goals of the 'communicator' paramount and those of the audience disregarded.

The Darker Arts of Propaganda and Spin

Propaganda

The slippage of rhetoric into manipulation is what gives political communication a bad name. The terms which have come to be synonymous with manipulative communication are 'propaganda' and the more contemporary word 'spin'. 'Propaganda' derives from the Latin term *propagandus* meaning 'what should be propagated'. It was first used in this neutral sense to describe the propagation or spreading of information, ideas and opinions by the Catholic Church. Founded by Pope Gregory XV in 1622, the 'Congregation for the propagation of the faith' or *Congregatio de Propaganda Fide*, was established to direct and coordinate the Church's missionary activities among non-Christian populations. In certain parts of the world – China, for example – 'propaganda' has maintained this more neutral sense. The Chinese

word 'xuanchuan' (宣传) for propaganda means to 'broadcast' or 'spread'.
The Chinese Communist Party's Central Propaganda Department actively
pursues the propagation of communist doctrine in the country's media, distributing directives to China's journalists – who normally have to be members of the Communist Party – about what can or cannot be published.
However, the benignity of the 'propaganda' function is being increasingly
challenged from within China itself.[2]

The negative connotations of 'propaganda' in the English-speaking
world are particularly related to its use in wartime and to the dawning of
the age of the masses and of mass media. During the First World War 'black'
propaganda techniques were used to spread false atrocity stories as a delib-
erate and systematic policy. Harold Lasswell pioneered the study of propaganda, focusing on Nazi techniques. In 1937 he founded, with others, the
Institute of Propaganda Analysis in the United States, specifically to combat
fascism and commercialism.

A different view of propaganda was taken by Edward Bernays: 'The only
difference between "propaganda" and "education", really, is the point of
view. The advocacy of what we believe in is education. The advocacy of
what we don't believe in is propaganda' (1923: 212). More recent communication analysts have located the differentiating characteristic of propaganda
in terms of the message structure. According to Johnson-Cartee and Copeland
(2004: 3), propaganda 'utilizes messages that tell individuals the attitudes,
beliefs, and behaviors found desirable by their social groups' so that propaganda, unlike persuasion, seeks to influence people as members of a group,
activating or reinforcing shared frames of reference in relation to, for example, nation, religion or race.

Propaganda as a practice is universal and from time immemorial. The
Romans were expert propagandists, employing a panoply of techniques to
impress on their own people and their enemies the might of Rome: the tri-
umphal procession of the conquering Caesar in the victor's chariot accompanied by trumpeters, dignitaries, booty, sacrifices to the gods, the captives
in chains, the singers and players, were all directed to reinforcing a message
of Roman invincibility and superiority.

Propaganda is also entirely contemporary. In February 2004, President
Bush announced the launch of a new Middle East television network called
Alhurra – Arabic for 'the Free One' – as part of his administration's programme for advancing democracy in the Middle East. Its target Arab audience might be forgiven for being sceptical about its claim to being unbiased
given its declared aim to counter what it considers anti-American sentiment
in Arab media. In the words of its critics:

> The propaganda techniques of the Cold War made sense once. But such state
> propaganda is not the real American way. Rather, our approach should be based

on Oliver Wendell Holmes' belief that 'the best test of truth is the power of the thought to get itself accepted in the competition of the market.' [...] Al Hurra should be closed down at once. (Lieven and Chambers: 13 February 2006)

The Politics of 'Spin'

The practice of 'spin', while not equivalent to propaganda, could be said to be one of the arms employed in its service. The term 'spin' was first used in 1978 by the *Guardian Weekly*. It is defined by the Oxford English Dictionary as:

> A bias or slant on information, intended to create a favourable impression when it is presented to the public; an interpretation or viewpoint.

In this sense, spin too has been around for as long as there have been humans interested in exercising social influence. Its contemporary rise to prominence is closely connected to the increasing emphasis by both politicians and journalists on message construction and management. This in turn reflects the reality of a ubiquitous 24-hour media world enveloping and, in some respects, constituting the world of politics.

By the end of the 1990s, 'spin' had become synonymous with a focus on message management rather than policy substance. This was said to be epitomized by Bill Clinton's 1992 presidential campaign and subsequent style of government. Clinton campaigned as a 'New Democrat' using daily polls conducted by pollster Stanley Greenberg, to craft carefully targeted messages coordinated by his campaign chief, James Carville, and future press chief, George Stephanopoulos. Carville ran the most technologically sophisticated campaign yet seen, establishing rapid response teams and tracking coverage by satellite from a central base in Little Rock nicknamed 'the war room' by Hilary Clinton (see Clinton, 2005: 425 and Gould, 1998: 162–71). He understood the absolute imperative of speed in the accelerated new media environment, printing the slogan 'Speed Kills....Bush' on T-shirts. He emphasized the importance of clear simple messages repeated constantly and consistently. These were summarized in three lines put up in a sign on the war room wall:

Change vs. More of the Same
The Economy, stupid
Don't forget health care

Helping out on the campaign was Philip Gould, a British Labour campaigner who, partly in response to what he had seen in Little Rock, was to become one of the architects of New Labour, which itself became synonymous with spin in the 1990s.

Spin doctoring is the antithesis of letting the facts speak for themselves. It aims to manage and shape impressions and perceptions in a way most favourable to the communicator's cause. The professionalism and perceived effectiveness of communication experts such as Peter Mandelson and Alastair Campbell, members of Tony Blair's team, and Dick Morris, Bill Clinton's campaign guru, raised questions about the integrity of political communication and the consequences for public discourse and democracy. In Britain, journalists (Jones, 2001; Pitcher, 2002) and scholars (Franklin, 2004) decried what they saw as its pernicious impact on politics. The spinners, it seems, were not so effective at spinning their own image.

Spinning into Trouble

Events in the UK Ministry of Transport just after the 11 September attacks in 2001 marked a particularly low point for British spin doctors. Within half an hour of the second plane's hitting the Twin Towers, the minister's political advisor, Jo Moore, sent a one-line email to her civil servant press colleagues: 'It's now a very good day to get out anything we want to bury. Councillors' expenses?' The leaked email sparked a debate about the nefarious effects of Labour's alleged spin culture and eventually led to Moore's resignation. The practice, however, of 'burying' bad news was nothing new in media management, as an anonymous letter writer to *The Guardian* who had worked for the Conservatives pointed out: 'on the day of the appalling Dunblane shootings [the murder of 16 young schoolchildren and their teacher], my colleagues and I were instructed by our chief press officer to release any "bad" news stories for the very reason that they would be overlooked or "buried" in the next day's coverage of events' (10 October 2001).

What made the Jo Moore case different was the increasingly held view that New Labour cared more about its image than anything else. This was not helped by the particularly crass language used by Moore in the email. The Moore incident simply fuelled the impression given by much of the British media and opposition that perception management was Labour's leading political strategy. Writing about the Blair government's crime and immigration policy, the Conservative analyst, Daniel Finkelstein made this the heart of his criticism (31 May 2006: 20): 'the aim has been to manage headlines rather than to manage crime and immigration. The important thing has not been to be tough on crime but to be seen to be tough on it, not to control immigration but to control media coverage of immigration.'

Others, however, took a more equanimous view of the spin phenomenon. McNair suggested that:

> The rise of spin [...] is not the cause of a deterioration in the quality of the public sphere, but a response to its technologically driven expansion, on the one hand,

and its democratization on the other. Both processes have combined to create a need for political actors to influence public opinion, and a profession geared to delivering that service. (2000: 138)

This is certainly the case. The question nevertheless remains whether the combination of rapacious media, hungry for news and entertainment, and the politicians' adoption of the techniques necessary to get the right kind of attention is having a deleterious impact on democratic politics.

Democracy and the Media

'Democracy' is a sacred term in contemporary political discourse even though many would agree with Winston Churchill's comment to the House of Commons that 'Democracy is the worst form of government, except for all those other forms that have been tried from time to time.' Free media have long been considered a vital bulwark of democratic politics, acting as a check on power – afflicting the comfortable and comforting the afflicted in the journalist's cliché,[3] by performing the role of watchdog (see Schultz, 1998 and Waisbord, 2000). This classic Fourth Estate function of the press was first expressed by the Anglo-Irish politician and commentator, Edmund Burke (1729–1797): 'Three Estates in Parliament; but in the Reporters' Gallery yonder, there sat a Fourth estate more important far than they all.'

The Fourth Estate view of the media extends beyond that of regarding them as a civic policeman. It is also about providing the means for citizens to be informed so that they can play their part in what the German philosopher, Jürgen Habermas, described as the 'public sphere', which he located in the emergence in eighteenth-century London of the periodical press and coffee shop society. In this world, the personal opinions of private individuals could evolve into public opinion through a process of rational-critical debate open to all, free from domination, with the press contributing to the formation and articulation of an orientative public sphere.

I will discuss next some of the difficulties associated with this view.

Perspectives on Media and Democracy

The possibility that the media really can serve democratic goals has been challenged by a number of thinkers from three basic perspectives. As we saw in Chapter 2, the first – the structural critique – argues that political and media systems in market economies are established in ways that necessarily militate against the existence of an effective democracy. In Table 3.1, I set out three structural axes which articulate part of the relationship between the media and politics. These can be summarized as: (a) the types of

Table 3.1 The relationship between the media and politics: three structural axes

	Media	Politics
Power	Reputation	Setting legal framework
	Image	Economic policy
	Agenda-setting	Provide information
	Framing	Sources
Rationale	Money	Obtain/maintain power
	Influence	Pursue/implement policies
Institutional practices	News values	Deliberation
	Official sources	Persuasive discourse

power, (b) exercised for overarching rationales, that (c) are embedded in specific institutional practices.

The media's power lies in its ability to shape reputation and image, set the agenda and frame narratives about politics. Politics sets legal frameworks, economic policy and provides the information and sources which are the life-blood of the media's coverage of politics. The media's rationale consists in money-making and the wielding of influence, that of politics the gaining and maintenance of power in order to pursue specific policies. The media's institutional practices and routines rely on sources and a 'canon' of news values, while politics must operate within a deliberative and persuasive framework. These different 'logics' often appear not only to clash but also to subvert each other. Take institutional practices, for example. The fact that the media tend to rely heavily on official sources for their information locks them into a necessary embrace with politicians who wield the source power required by journalists. At the same time, this acts to skew media access even more sharply in favour of those who are already powerful. On the other hand, media news values which stress the local, the peculiar and so on work against the grain of the reporting of the deliberative practice of politics which is one of its chief features.

The structural critique is helpful in underlining some of the real tensions in media democracies. A nuanced version of this critique is advanced by a number of scholars and journalists (see, for example, Blumler and Gurevitch, 1995; Fallows, 1997; Lloyd, 2004; Patterson, 1994; Rosenblum, 1993) who focus to a lesser or greater degree on the role of the media. The critical consensus is that 'the political communication process now tends to strain against, rather than with the grain of citizenship' (Blumler and Gurevitch, 1995: 203) and that much of the reason for this is a shift of power to the media, which filter not only politics but a great deal of contemporary human experience. This view holds that the media's arrogation of power is not accompanied by an understanding of their responsibility in a constitutional democracy:

> Journalists confuse being subservient to politicians (which no free media can allow themselves to be) with being subservient to democratic politics. The media have not come up with a better idea than democratic politics, and they do not officially claim to have done so; but in ways, explicitly and implicitly, they act as if they have. The media have claimed the right to judge and to condemn; more, they have decided – without being clear about the decision – that politics is a dirty game, played by devious people who tell an essentially false narrative about the world. (Lloyd, 2004: 20)

The losers are the public.

A second view, what might be called a post-modern perspective, takes the view that society is organized around play, image and simulated reality, more real to us than reality itself. Computer games, televised sport, the tellingly named reality shows make up our world where we experience the 'ecstasy of communication' and become, in Baudrillard's words, 'a pure screen, a pure absorption and re-absorption surface of the influent networks' (1988: 27). Politics is part of the game, there to amuse and entertain the masses who exercise the power of non-participation. This ultimately nihilistic view removes value, belief and meaning from human existence and, in that sense, while succeeding in giving a sense of the texture of twenty-first century life, represents a dead-end.

Finally, what might be called the elitist perspective, considers not only that the media are incapable of providing citizens with the wherewithal to make rational and informed judgements but also that it is unnecessary for them to do so. Walter Lippmann, journalist and political analyst, did not believe that the press could do much to improve American democracy and that, in any case, elites rule. In these circumstances the best the press can do is to provide simple, clear signs to serve as 'guides to reasonable action for the use of uninformed people'. The central task for democracy is to find ways for people to act intelligently but in ignorance. Lippmann's diagnosis may be unappealing but in some respects it may not be inaccurate. In a seven-question political knowledge quiz of 2000 British adults only 45 per cent got four or more answers correct and only three per cent got all answers correct – only 27 per cent knew that a general election does not have to be held every four years and 'only 49 per cent knew that the House of Commons has more power than the Lords' (Power Report, 2006: 75).

Each of these perspectives provides insights into the troubled relationship of the media and political systems in liberal post-industrial democracies. We should, however, be conscious of the specificity of the socio-economic, cultural and political characteristics of any given media-political system and beware of extrapolating generalizations made from Anglo-American experiences to the rest of the world. Comparative political communication research seeks to address this tendency (see Canel and Sanders, 2006; Hallin and Mancini, 2004). Having said this, it is not unreasonable to point to structural features and their operational logics and, with all the proper caveats, suggest that tension – understood as uncertainty and strain – will be a characteristic quality of media democracies. In particular, the media act as power brokers in three arenas which make them uncomfortable bedfellows for politicians: first, they act as cultural power brokers, mediating versions of values and truth in ways many politicians would never dare to contemplate; second, they are economic power brokers, acting as players in the global economy; third, they are political power brokers, mediating and colonizing democratic politics, guarding, distributing and destroying the symbolic capital of reputation which is the foundation of the universal currency of politics, trust. Confucius advised his disciple Tsze-kung that three things are needed for government: weapons, food and trust. If a ruler cannot hold on to all three, he should give up the weapons first and the food next. Trust should be guarded to the end for 'without trust we cannot stand'.

The Unbearable Tensions of Media Democracies: The Case of the Blair Government's Communication about Iraq

On 24 September 2002, the Blair government published a dossier entitled *Iraq's Weapons of Mass Destruction. The Assessment of the British Government* (see Figure 3.1 for a chronology of events). In the run up to the invasion of Iraq, the dossier was used to make the case for war to the British people. In the executive summary, Blair stated:

> I am in no doubt that the threat is serious and current, that he has made progress on WMD [Weapons of Mass Destruction], and that he has to be stopped.
>
> Saddam has used chemical weapons, not only against an enemy state, but against his own people. Intelligence reports make clear that he sees the building up of his WMD capability, and the belief overseas that he would use these weapons, as vital to his strategic interests, and in particular his goal of regional domination. And the document discloses that his military planning allows for some of the WMD to be ready within 45 minutes of an order to use them.

Sept. 24 2002 WMD dossier	**June 26** Campbell demands BBC
Feb. 3 2003 Second dossier published	apology. They refuse
Feb. 6 2003 Channel 4 reveals second	**July 10** Newspapers name Dr Kelly as
dossier is plagiarized	the source of Gilligan's allegations
March –May 1 Iraq War	**July 15** Kelly gives evidence to
May 29 Gilligan's BBC broadcast alleg-	Foreign Affairs Committee
ing Downing St 'sexed up' dossier	**July 18** Kelly commits suicide
June 1 Gilligan publishes article alleg-	**July 20** BBC reveals that Kelly was
ing that Campbell forced 45-minute	source
claim to be included	**July 21** Hutton Inquiry into circum-
June 19–25 Gilligan and Campbell	stances surrounding Kelly's death
give evidence to Foreign Affairs	announced by Blair
Committee	**August 11** Hutton Inquiry begins∂

Figure 3.1 Chronology of a communication controversy

The 45-minute claim received particular attention from the British press. That day the London *Evening Standard* ran the headline '45 MINUTES FROM ATTACK', followed the next day by *The Sun*'s 'BRITS 45 MINS FROM DOOM'. Some months later, on 3 February 2003, a second dossier, entitled *Iraq – Its Infrastructure of Concealment, Deception and Intimidation*, was posted on the government website. The US secretary of state, Colin Powell, used it in his presentation to the United Nations. It quickly became known, however, as the 'dodgy' dossier when UK Channel 4 news revealed on 6 February that most of it was copied without acknowledgement from three different articles.

The failure to find WMD after the invasion of Iraq in March 2003 intensified media questioning of the Blair case for war, culminating in the following allegations made by a BBC reporter, Andrew Gilligan, on the country's most influential radio news programme:

> What I have been told is that the government knew that claim [the 45-minute claim] was questionable even before the war, even before they wrote it in their dossier.
>
> I've spoken to a British official who was involved in the preparation of the dossier and he told me that in the week before it was published, the draft dossier produced by the intelligence services added little to what was already publicly known. He said: 'It was transformed in the week before it was published to make it sexier. The classic example was the claim that weapons of mass destruction were ready for use within 45 minutes. That information was not in the original draft. It was included in the dossier against our wishes, because it wasn't reliable. Most of the things in the dossier were double-sourced, but that was single sourced, and we believe that the source was wrong.' (BBC *Today* programme, 29 May 2003)

The ensuing fallout from the broadcast, including the suicide of the source, government scientist Dr David Kelly, led to the most far-reaching examination of the workings of government and media yet undertaken. The Hutton Inquiry laid bare the conversations of journalists with sources, the notes they took, emails sent from members of Blair's 10 Downing St team to the head of intelligence and all of it was posted on the internet.

The material revealed some of the tensions that characterize media democracies and, in particular, the promotional dynamic that can corrupt political discourse. In an off-the-record conversation with the BBC reporter, Susan Watts, Dr Kelly expressed the problem when describing the putting together of the dossier:

> you know the word-smithing is actually quite important and the intelligence community are a pretty cautious lot on the whole but once you get people putting it/presenting it for public consumption then of course they use different words. I don't think they're being wilfully dishonest I think they just think that that's the way the public will appreciate it best. I'm sure you have the same problem as a journalist don't you. (Kelly cited in Coates, 2004: 31)

The hardening up of the opaque language and uncertain truths of human intelligence for the purposes of persuasion and the right kind of headline revealed how far what might be called the journalistic logic of communication had permeated politics. Intelligence material had never been publicized in this way before and yet the British government felt constrained to do so.

If we examine the communication logics of politicians and journalists (see Table 3.2), we can immediately see the difficulties. While politicians deal in complexity, the press deal in simplicity; politicians seek to control information, the media to release it. Most crucially, as we saw in Table 3.1, politicians seek to maintain and obtain power. For this they must be trusted and yet the means for them to achieve this is not entirely in their hands. The media shape perceptions of reputation and image and, if we look at the evidence of polls, politicians are not faring well nor are, in Britain at least, some groups of journalists (see Table 3.2). Leading politicians score only around 20 per cent in the trust stakes, although this looks quite high when compared to 12 per cent for journalists on populist ('red-top') newspapers.

Decline in trust in politicians and public disengagement from politics are often blamed on the media. However, research shows that each link in this causal argument is unproven. The 'media malaise' case – that negative media reduce trust and public engagement – is not supported by the evidence (see, for example, Norris, 2000), which shows that higher levels of media consumption are correlated with higher degrees of political participation. The

Table 3.2 Trust in occupational groups in the UK

Who do we trust? % saying they trust each of these group's great deal' or 'a fair amount'		
	Now	**Change since early 2003**
Judges	77	+9
Journalists on mid-market newspaper	36	–
Leading Conservative politicians	19	−1
Journalists on red-top newspapers	12	−2
Journalists on up-market newspapers such as *The Daily Telegraph*	62	−3
Family doctors	89	−4
Ministers in the Labour Government	20	−5
Estate agents	11	−5
School teachers	81	−7
My local MP	44	−8
Plumbers, electricians	46	−9
BBC News journalists	71	−10
Leading Lib Dem politicians	25	−11
Managers of NHS hospitals	24	−12
ITV News journalists	67	−15
Senior EU officials	16	−19
Senior police officers	52	−20

Source: The *Daily Telegraph* and YouGov, 22 May 2006.

'Don't blame the messenger' thesis was also the conclusion of the review of evidence by a major investigation into the state of British democracy:

> Our view is that, as with the popular hostility towards politicians, more pro-found structural problems have promoted disengagement and alienation, and that negative media coverage is a symptom rather than a significant cause. It seems to us that while there clearly is a problem with the media the answer is where to start and, in light of the evidence, we believe that if we get the political system right this will change the atmosphere and culture and the press will follow. (Power Report, 2006: 69)

This may be a little over-optimistic. Structural change to the voting system, control of the executive, better education about politics would all surely help improve the participatory political culture but, given the structural imperatives outlined earlier, it may be difficult to change media culture.

Table 3.3   The tense tango

Politicians	Media organizations
News provider	News purveyor
Deliberation	Speed
Control	Revelation
Steadiness	Novelty
Complexity	Simplicity

In liberal democracies much of politics is about getting attention and, in doing so, it must compete in a crowded and difficult field. How can most national politicians compete with Ronaldo, Madonna or George Clooney? Being a highly talented footballer, entertainer or actor wins attention on its own terms: we know that their business is performance, entertainment. They are not automatically under suspicion (unless they stray out of their fields). The tense tango of contrasting yet related political and media logics set out in Table 3.3 can lead to excessive mutual suspicion and blame-mongering: heavy-handed politicians who berate the media for their low ethics and cynical journalists who write off the whole political class. Neither attitude is good for democracy.

It Takes Two to Tango

Like partners in a dance, each requires the other: for politicians, their visibility within the *mediapolis* (see Silverstone, 2007) is an index of power; for media organizations and journalists, while not their exclusive concern, scrutiny of power entitles them to claim the privileges of being the people's tribune.

Of course, within mainstream media organizations, journalists are not lone rangers, able to pit themselves against political and corporate power. In their study of influences on media content, Shoemaker and Reese (1996) identified 5 levels of influence (see Figure 3.2): the individual level refers to the evidence for the impact of personal characteristics such as gender, education, religious or political affiliations on the work of a journalist; the second – media routines – describes sets of practices and values such as the notion of objectivity, of exclusivity, of news hierarchies and so on that systematically structure news content; the organizational level refers to the particular features of the media organization itself, whether it is a state, public or commercial enterprise, whether it targets an elite or popular audience; the extra-media level encapsulates the regulatory, commercial and

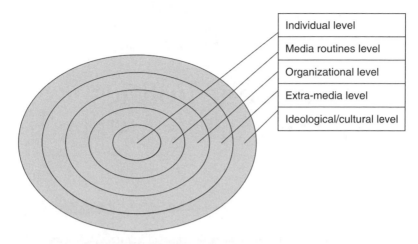

Figure 3.2 Influences on media content
Source: Shoemaker and Reese, 1996

political environment in which content is produced; finally, the ideological – to which I have added the cultural – level refers to the tacit assumptions which undergird news production such as, for example, the historical tropes which inform and frame coverage of issues.

These influences – of which Shoemaker and Reese find the first the least powerful – structure the environment in which journalists work. It is not difficult to see how often journalists themselves can experience a great sense of powerlessness in this complex universe of power. However, where there is a basic disagreement on fundamentals between politicians and journalists, notably on such issues as the need for scrutiny (the journalists' role), the legitimacy of persuasion (the politicians' role) and the general need for information flow, democratic politics cannot even get off the ground.

Mainstream media *are* political actors in the contemporary political environment. Their legitimacy flows from, 'The public's right to know – the ethic that has sustained journalism's claim to be a central part of the democratic process for the four centuries of its existence, and which sustains it still' (Lloyd, 2004: 6). If this 'right to know' is, however, not robustly upheld by the media, increasingly there are available alternative avenues for public knowledge as I shall explore in more detail in Chapter 13.

4

Symbolic Politics:
'All the world's a stage'[1]

Masks are arrested expressions and admirable echoes of feeling. At once faithful, discreet, and superlative. Living things in contact with the air must acquire a cuticle, and it is not urged against cuticles that they are not hearts; yet some philosophers seem to be angry with images for not being things, and with words for not being feelings.

George Santayana, *Soliloquies in England and later Soliloquies*. New York: Scribner's, 131–2

Introduction

Spanish-American man of letters, George Santayana (1863–1952), points to the existence of a deep-seated unease about our relationship to words and images. We must use and have them and are yet somehow suspicious of them as not being the 'real' thing, which of course they sometimes are not. Nevertheless, display and spectacle, image, ritual and symbol are intrinsic to, and constants of, human culture. Humans truly are symbol-using animals as the philosopher Ernst Cassirer described. I will examine in this chapter what this means in relation to the contemporary communication of politics where its mediatization pushes image, display and spectacle into the front-row of political activity. In particular I will discuss the rise of what has been called '*symbolic politics*', with the accompanying emphasis on *the personal* and on *scandal*, and what light theories about the *dramaturgical nature of communication* can throw on the symbolic strategies pursued in political communication. First, I will discuss the basic concepts of *person and image, symbol, ritual and religion, spectacle and performance* and their *relationship to the practice and understanding of politics*.

The Drama of Politics

In media democracies much of politics is cast in dramatic form. Media stories of politics are populated with villains and heroes, tales telling the cost of hubris, the rewards of courage or the risk of action. Paradoxically, the fact of significant and real human agency can be lost. The reality of politics as the art and science of government, as human action and the exercise of power in groups can disappear over the horizon of our understanding, not least because politicians themselves seem at times to connive in the creation of a politics of pure drama. Of course, politics is also about drama – sometimes tragic, others comic. It is about performance, spectacle, the use of symbol and ritual, the creation and management of images. As American sociologist, Michael Schudson, put it: 'Politics is a set of symbols, meanings and enacted rituals' (2001: 423). But it would be a mistake to claim that these elements are the essence of politics. However, as we shall see in this chapter, there are those who, faced with the logic of media democracies, consider the 'packaging' of politics to have usurped its content. In order to assess this claim, it will first be helpful to clarify some of the central concepts underlying discussions of symbolic politics, namely the notions of person and image, of symbol and ritual.

Person and Image

Distinguishing between the notions of 'person' and 'image' is a key starting point in any discussion of symbolic politics. *Prosopon* is the Greek term from which we derive our word 'person'. In Ancient Greece it referred to an actor's mask translated into the Latin *per-sonare*, underlining how the actor made his voice sound out through the mask. This appears to be very remote from our current understanding of 'person' as concrete individuality in the tradition of Boethius (480–525), who defined person as 'an individual substance of rational nature'. However, the original sense of the word points to something which is entirely contemporary, namely that human beings in some sense frequently perform roles. This view of the human person was explored by Erving Goffman (1922–1982) in his *The Presentation of the Self in Everyday Life* (1959), in which he defined the self in terms of behaviour selected from a repertoire as appropriate for differing sets of contingencies. In this account the person really is a set of masks and here the 'presentation' of the self, the image and display in which we engage in social life is effectively what we are. 'Image' – usually understood as the figurative representation of something or someone – becomes here the public showing forth of the person in accordance with the role being played. Human action is considered as essentially dramaturgical, played out in staged settings with an audience complicit in upholding the agreed definition of the situation. This can lead to circumstances where 'one finds the performer can be fully taken in by his own act; he can be sincerely convinced that the impression of reality which he stages is the real reality' (Goffman, 1959: 17). Goffman presents us with an account of human beings as enigmatic selves, of whom we know nothing, and who themselves can become knowing dupes of their own performance. But the question remains as to who is this self who mysteriously knows how to don the correct mask for each role. The relationship between the real and presented self is left unclear.

Nevertheless, Goffman undoubtedly points to features of human action common to all of us which have been made particularly salient by contemporary conditions. We all engage to some degree or other in image-making but, as we saw in the previous chapter, this has now become a central activity of politics. A frequent criticism levelled at twenty-first-century politicians is that image-making appears to trump the making and execution of policy: how stories *play* and how politicians *appear* to the public matters above all else. Image apparently swallows up the human person and with it any sense of authenticity. The attacks on Tony Blair's premiership, for example, were partly founded on claims that he was insincere and false, more interested in spin than substance. On learning of Princess Diana's death in 1997, Blair's description of her as the 'People's Princess' was considered by some commentators as more directed towards clever populist phrase-making than expressing genuine sadness. One of Blair's harshest critics describes him in the following Goffmanesque terms: 'this man is a pathological confidence-trickster. To the extent that he ever believes what he says, he is delusional. To the extent that he does not, he is an actor whose first invention – himself – has been his only interesting role' (Parris, 18 March 2006: 21).

However, as we shall see, although contemporary conditions may have reinforced presentational politics, this is not the same as saying that the possibilities of authenticity have entirely disappeared. On the one hand, the presentation of authenticity is a necessary strategic goal for politicians and on the other, simply because it is presented does not make it necessarily false. To put it another way, the *role* of politician is probably more difficult to play than it has ever been but, despite the growth of presentational politics, politics itself continues to be a field in which authentic human action is possible because, after all, politicians continue to be human beings.

Understanding Symbols

In presenting ourselves, we make use of a repertoire of words, actions and gestures, much of which can be described as symbolic. The Greek word *symballein*, from which our word 'symbol' comes, referred to one-half of an object broken in two – a seal, for example – and presented as a way of authenticating someone's identity: the seamless join of the two broken parts brought together attested to the person's identity. Symbols came to mean signs which make things present: the wearing of a black armband in memory of someone who has recently died *symbolizes* mourning and to wear one is to partake in a ritual of mourning. In Western culture black is the colour symbolizing death; in some parts of the East it is white.

Signs can be understood as proxies for something, as standing in for and pointing to something else. When we see a sign – Welcome to Dublin! – we look elsewhere for the real thing. 'Here is Dublin', we think, as we cross the River Liffey. Signs can share characteristics with what they represent, but they may not. Mathematical symbols are an example of the latter. Signs can also be understood as showing us what things are for. For example, understanding the meaning of a word, a kind of sign, is knowing how to use it. This Wittgensteinian idea suggests that signs establish communication. Signs which also *symbolize*, however, often seem to embody a connection to that which they symbolize. The Eiffel Tower is in fact an iconic building in central Paris and at the same time immediately conjures up all the charm and romance of that city. It is the vehicle for people's beliefs, feelings and attitudes and its symbolic power rests on them. The latter characteristic of symbols is well shown in the example of a country's flag. The colours and design may have some representative role (the Peruvian flag's red-white-red design, for example, is said to represent the impressive sight of a flock of flamingos taking flight). However, the emotional power of national flags has far more to do with the symbolic richness with which they are invested. So, for example, Spain's General Franco was careful to ban the Basque flag, the *Ikuriña*, knowing that it symbolized Basque distinctiveness and claims for independence.

Symbols, then, are a kind of sign which, through a variety of material means (marks, sounds, colours, words and so on), represent something (take 'x' to be the number of books John has on his shelf) and/or act as a vehicle for emotions, attitudes and beliefs on the basis of shared conventions. One further feature of some symbols is their quasi-sacramental character. A soldier who raises a white flag surrenders. The correct use of the symbol realizes what it symbolizes. Symbols are conventional but can also have natural properties through which they aspire to the condition of bodily experience. Think of a word with onomatopoeic qualities like 'hush' or 'mumble'; we can 'feel' the meaning of this word in a way similar to how we experience and understand poetry or music.

Ritual, Religion and Politics

Ritual is highly symbolic. It consists of pre-established, formalized symbolic actions usually directed towards upholding definitions of events, expressing shared cultural and social understandings and values. According to the English philosopher, Roger Scruton, rituals are 'moments that stand outside time, in which the loneliness and anxiety of the human individual is confronted and overcome, through immersion in the group'. He adds that 'by calling these moments "sacred", we recognise both their complex social meaning and also the respite that they offer from alienation' (August 2007).

Ritual and various kinds of symbolism are historically strongly connected and rooted in religion and the sense of the sacred, those places, times, objects that are set apart from the ordinary. Once one crosses the threshold into sacred space or time – a Mosque, the Sabbath, a memorial service – a different standard of behaviour comes into force. Rollicking laughter, immodest dress are inappropriate; one finds oneself present or participant in sacred action which, in its most solemn form, takes on the attributes of great drama. The dramatic spectacles of religious ritual and symbolism claim a fully sacramental character: in other words they state that certain symbols not only mean something – the water of Christian baptism symbolizes spiritual rebirth – but that they do in fact realize what is represented. This startling claim makes clear that in religion the sacred really is a different place where the transcendent is thought to be made present.

If we think about this in relation to politics we can see how the great pre-arranged State occasions – the funeral of a president (think of John F. Kennedy), the State opening of the Westminster parliament, a coronation – are carefully choreographed rituals replete with symbolism; this kind of politics becomes special, set apart from the ordinary rough and tumble of political life. These grand occasions become types of *media event*, a 'narrative genre that employs the unique potential of the electronic media to command attention universally and simultaneously in order to tell a primordial story about current affairs. These are events that hang a halo over the television set and transform the viewing experience' (Dayan and Katz, 1994: 1). Not only confined to political occasions, media events are only possible in an era of mass media. But the transformation of politics into liturgy (a term taken from the Greek originally meaning 'public work' or 'duty') pre-dates the television age and points to the linkages between politics and religion.

Religion and Politics

Politics' occupation of religion's psychological and sociological space was the subject of study of the philosopher, Eric Voegelin (1901–1985). His work examined the notion of 'political religion', charting its development from the ancient Egypt of Akhenaton (1380–1362 BC), to Fascism, Nazism and Communism, noting these ideologies' structural and sociological similarities to mainstream religion.

The term 'civil (or civic) religion' is probably more useful and appropriate for the analysis of constitutional, representative democracies. Sociologists of religion and political scientists use the term to refer to it in its various manifestations. At its most intense, elements of civil religion can be found in explicit invocations of a specific religious tradition in political discourse, the use of religious symbols in the public context and the establishment of foundation stories or myths. The US sociologist Robert Bellah has used the notion to explore his country's political culture which, despite the constitutional separation of state and religion, is imbued with Christian symbolism. From the country's coinage – stamped with the words 'In God We Trust' – to the president's oath of office sworn on the Bible, US politicians 'do God' in ways that other political traditions do not. The US civic religion combines strong references to the Christian tradition with the sacralization of its republican and democratic heritage: the celebration of Thanksgiving Day and the fourth of July are good examples of this. At the lower end of the scale of civil religion, countries such as France that specifically exclude religion from the public realm, nevertheless exhibit characteristics in their political discourse that suggest the persistence of practices typically associated with religion such as veneration of the flag and other national symbols; the quasi-canonical status of the constitution; patriotic holidays; national hymns and sacred places.

Presidents, prime ministers and governments, parliaments and oppositions, campaigning groups and politicians can draw upon the symbolic repertoire that their historical and cultural traditions make available to them and make them anew for their generation: Barack Obama, for example, announced his intention to become the next US president from the Old State Capitol in Springfield, Illinois, where Abraham Lincoln had given a famous speech against slavery. The use of symbolism in politics is, of course, as old as politics itself but, as I shall discuss next, the mediatization of politics has led some commentators to argue that 'symbolic politics' has become especially significant in the contemporary era with substantial consequences for politics itself (see, for example, Stanyer, 2007).

Symbolic Politics

Political scientist, Murray Edelman (1919–2001), was the first to develop the notion of 'symbolic politics'. Drawing on the work of the influential American philosopher and social psychologist, George Herbert Mead, he emphasized how much of politics used symbolic forms (rite, ritual and myth) or had a symbolic function.

Edelman characterized political actions and events as being both instrumental, where they have actual effects, and expressive, that is, as having a dramaturgical and symbolic value according to which actions are presented to the public. As he put it:

> The patterned nature of so much of the publicized political process provides a
> revealing clue to the function of political spectacle [...] it is dramaturgy rather

than policymaking. Like drama, it is constructed to be presented to a public. (Edelman, 1967/1985: 210)

In Edelman's view, the instrumental dimension of politics was being increasingly overlaid by the dramaturgical, symbolic one where political players employed symbols and rituals for the media for subsequent public consumption. Everything could be converted into drama. 'In politics the names of goals are potent symbols', he said (1967/1985: 206) or 'Polls and surveys generate numbers that have the dramaturgical look of hard data' (p. 208). Edelman's work (see also 1988) anticipated and paralleled work taking place in the fields of rhetoric, political science, sociology and literary theory that explored underlying, persistent patterns of human communication that mark the kind of communicational strategies commonly employed by politicians.

Dramaturgical Communication

The work of American literary theorist and philosopher, Kenneth Burke (1897–1993) also emphasized the political and social power of symbols.[2] He described communication in terms of what he called a *dramatistic pentad* including the dimensions of act, scene, agent, agency and purpose. According to Burke's notion of *dramatism*, life is not like a play, it *is* a play. Rhetoric, the essential human communication mode, is what drives the drama because language is a form of action. Burke's *pentad* (see 1969) describes the dramatic structure of this action which can be analysed according to the following questions:

- **Act**: What purposeful act has taken place?
- **Agent**: Who carried out this action?
- **Agency**: How or with what did they do it?
- **Scene**: Where, when and in what context did the act take place? This includes not only the physical place but also the cultural and social context.
- **Purpose**: Why did they do it? What was their intent?

Burke considered that the *pentad* could be used to analyse the motive(s) of a speaker, how they attempt to persuade us that their view of reality is the correct one, partly by examining the weight of importance given to a related pair of elements or what Burke called the *ratio* between, for example, agent and scene, agency and act, or act and scene. So, for instance, George Bush's speech declaring the end of 'major combat operations in Iraq' in May 2003 was given on an aircraft carrier after he became the first US president to land on a moving ship. Bush's rhetoric was transmitted as much by the *mise-en-scène* as by anything he actually said. The scene transmitted the message of US military might and its commander-in-chief's martial prowess, a message that became difficult to sustain as the US army failed to win the 'war on terror' in Iraq. In other words, the choices made about the elements of the *pentad* indicate communicational motives. This point was made by Hilary Clinton, reflecting on some advice given to her by one of her aides: 'merely by travelling to South Asia as First Lady with Chelsea would send a message about the importance of daughters. Visiting poor rural women would underscore their significance. I understood her point, and I soon became a convert to the view that I could advance the Clinton agenda through symbolic action' (2004: 265).

The Rhetoric of Identification, Division and Scapegoating

Burke's arguments are not always entirely clear. He was not a systematic thinker and his discursive method was directed to provoking discussion and thought rather than closing it down. His discussion draws on literary, anthropological and philosophical sources to explore the 'grammar' of language. He also uses theological concepts to identify the deep motives of rhetoric and, in this respect, his ideas are reminiscent of those advanced by the French philosopher and literary theorist, René Girard. Burke suggests that we seek through rhetoric or public discourse to purge ourselves of guilt (understood as all kinds of negative feelings), to identify the external enemy, the victim, and find the perfect scapegoat, who is the source of all our woes. Much of political news, of communication about politics is indeed suffused with conflict and division. However, the existence of division does not negate, according to Burke, the possibility of identification, the possibility of identifying that which is held in common or at least of persuading someone else that such grounds of identification exist. In Burke's words:

> We need never deny the presence of strife, enmity, factions, as a characteristic motive of rhetorical expression. We need not close our eyes to their almost tyranneous ubiquity in human relations; we can be on the alert always to see how such temptations to strife are implicit in the institutions that condition human relationships; yet we can at the same time always look beyond this order, to the principle of identification in general. (1969: 20)

Indeed, the fact of human separateness is a spur to identification in Burke's view. Where strategies to achieve identification fail, purgation re-establishes social order through the language of symbols and the form of rituals including the identification of the scapegoat. Scapegoating language is typical of election campaigns. In the Spanish 2008 'pre-campaign', the governing Socialist Party expended some energy in setting up the Catholic

Church and, by association, the opposition People's Party, as the enemy of progress and democracy.[3] During the US presidential nomination campaign, Obama's opponents spread the rumour that he was in fact Muslim;[4] the fact that this was considered potentially damaging was a sad indictment of the divisions that had opened up in the world post-9/11.

Girard's analysis of literature and history is the basis for a wide-ranging and controversial theory of human behaviour with important implications for communication (see, for example, Girard, 1989). He considers that much of human behaviour is based on the urge for 'mimesis', imitative conduct focused on acquisition and appropriation, and that it is this rather than scarcity or aggression which is at the heart of human violence.[5] Violence, he suggests, is a constant in human history as is the identification of the 'other' who acts as a lightning rod for strife and conflict, discharging the burden of tension that builds up in human communities. For Girard, this role is played by the scapegoat, the community or figure configured as 'different', but often all too similar to those by whom she is condemned. Both Girard and Burke point to the key role of the scapegoat in the configuration of community and communication. Girard, for example, considers that the attacks of 9/11 and subsequent events owe much to this account. In an interview with *Le Monde* he declared:

> No doubt terrorism is bound to a world 'different' from ours, but what gives rise to terrorism does not lie in that 'difference' that removes it further from us and makes it inconceivable to us. To the contrary, it lies in an exacerbated desire for convergence and resemblance. Human relations are essentially relations of imitation, of rivalry. (Girard, 6 November 2001)

This mimetic impulse leads eventually to an explosion of violence. In the case of Al Qaeda's attack against New York's Twin Towers, this analysis may seem counterintuitive given the 'othering' of the West and of radical Islam in each other's eyes. But Girard's claim is that the organization's leaders are in fact very close to the Westerners they so hate. They want to regain the dominance once held by the Islamic world before the West rose to prominence. The rhetorical creation of a godless America together with that of an 'infested and defiled Arabian landscape' and 'the subjugated and abused Muslim peoples', according to Katchadourian (15 May 2006), 'the two most important images in bin Laden's rhetorical arsenal', is part of their strategy to re-establish the caliphate. Godless America is the scapegoat and communication strategy, as we shall see in Chapter 9, is intrinsic to the creation of the reality they say they wish to transform.

Scapegoating, however, becomes a double-edged sword in the post-Christian world where, in Girard's account, the scapegoat, the victim at the heart of Christianity, Jesus Christ, reveals his essential innocence in an act of forgiveness at the moment of his death ('Forgive them Father for they know not what they do'). These words ironically transform victimhood into the strategy of the victor. Being the underdog, the victim, can work to undermine rhetorical strategies of division but in politics this communicational approach is all too rarely used.

The Rhetoric of Ritual and Symbolic Action

Affirmation of leadership, anniversaries, parliamentary debates, inaugurations, press conferences and deaths use the patterned symbolic communication of ritual. Verbal symbols and non-verbal symbols generate attention. They reduce the complexity of political problems, communicate a certain way of looking at the world and stimulate emotions. Great political leadership is often about having a sensitivity to symbols and mastery of their use. Ritual functions well where there is consensus. These occur, for example, in relation to the high feastdays and the everyday rubric of political life. Symbolic action, of which they are both examples, can also be used in a structured, purposeful but non-ritualized way to communicate specific messages. I will look at an example of each next and the concern that symbolic action has become a surrogate for 'real' action.

High feastdays. These include events such as in Britain, the State opening of parliament and the monarch's annual Christmas address to the nation. Delivered traditionally by radio, Queen Elizabeth II became the first English monarch to use television and, in 2007, her broadcast was made available on YouTube, continuing even in this modern 'scene' simultaneously to symbolise and enact national unity and identity. High feastdays include elections, resignations and presidential debates.

Everyday rubric. Ordinary political life is shot through with symbolic action. From the symbol-festooned presidential podium, to the tradition of bowing to the Speaker on entering the chamber of the House of Commons, the ministerial red boxes used to present Britain's annual budget and the conventions of parliamentary debates and the dress styles adopted by leaders.

Purposeful symbolic action. This is often employed as a way of communicating salient aspects of political policy, style or character. The wearing of indigenous-style dress by South American leaders such as Bolivia's Evo Morales and Venezuela's Hugo Chavez, for example, had huge symbolic significance as a way of communicating both men's identification with their indigenous communities. In the case of Morales it also had economic importance: a Bolivian businessman undertook the production of a cheap version of the leader's alpaca jumper describing it as a 'symbol of the President' (BBC, 20 January 2006). Gandhi, his dress and his spinning wheel, symbolized the new independent India and its simple agrarian values; Harold Wilson, British Labour leader, was often pictured with his pipe, associated with the working class, rather than the cigar he was alleged to smoke in private; Fidel Castro's beard was considered so iconic that the CIA plotted to make it fall out.

Political leaders are symbols and symbol makers, an activity they engage in to foster belief, loyalty, and to build an iconography of themselves, their political groupings and their policies. As Hilary Clinton put it on becoming First Lady: 'Now I was a symbol-and that was a new experience' (2004: 140).

Political symbols can be used, for example, to signal significant policy change. As Blair's press secretary, Alastair Campbell, writing about Blair's decision as leader in opposition of the Labour Party to push for the renunciation of Clause 4 (the Party's commitment to 'common ownership of the means of production, distribution and exchange'), commented: 'He knew that in terms of the political substance, it didn't actually mean that much. But as a symbol, as a vehicle to communicate change, and his determination to modernise the party, it was brilliant' (Campbell and Stott, 2007: 11).

However, symbolic representation is one dimension of the notion of representation. It does not capture the matter of agency, the notion of acting for, and this is at the heart of criticism that considers that symbolic, dramaturgical communication transforms politics into performance and spectacle, symbolized by chat show politics and the importance of the personal.

The Rhetoric of Performance and Spectacle

For some commentators (see Alexander, Giesen and Mast 2006), the breakdown of social consensus makes ritual and myth more difficult to sustain. Ironically, the consequence in media-saturated societies, where politics must desperately compete for attention, leads to the politics of spectacle and performance and, it is suggested, to the possible growth of 'symbolic government'. This has been described as government-related activities where:

> the creation of symbolic images, symbolic actions and celebratory rhetoric have become a principal concern. Symbolic government is about the appearance of action or communication rather than the fact of action or the factual content of information. Appearances therefore do not just matter. They are a main part of its business. (Henneberg and O'Shaughnessy, 2004)

According to this analysis, symbolic politics has moved from the 'micro' level (Churchill's cigar) to the 'meso' level, where actions acquire a more systematic, strategic orientation, and to the 'macro' or systemic one.

Communication, particularly considered as a symbolic enterprise, comes to shape the very conduct of politics. Symbolic acts and imagery are vital; policies and announcements are couched in ways that build images of competency, relying particularly on data symbolism: 'Hospital waiting lists have been halved'; '5 economic tests for joining the Euro'. In fact, there is nothing new in data symbolism. Mao Tse-Tung was a past master. However, the argument is that partly because of a defensive response by political actors to pressures from the media and partly as a result of taking a political marketing path (see Chapter 5), the politics is being sucked out of politics to be replaced by spectacle and performance. In the words of one critic:

> In an age of spectacle politics, presidencies in the United States are staged and presented to the public in cinematic terms, using media spectacle to sell the policies, person, and image of the president to a vast and diverse public. The media are complicit in the generation of spectacle politics, reducing politics to image, display, and story in the forms of entertainment and drama [...] the public comes to see presidencies and politics of the day as narrative and spectacle in an era in which entertainment and information inexorably merge. In the media entertainment society, politics and everyday life are modelled on media forms, with entertainment becoming a dominant mode of media culture and a potent and seductive factor in shaping politics and everyday life. (Kellner, 2003: 160)

In Kellner's view, the transformation of politics into spectacle also has an alienating effect: 'The concept of the spectacle is integrally connected to the concept of separation and passivity, for in submissively consuming spectacles one is estranged from actively producing one's life' (2003: 3).

In contemporary society, where celebrities are the icons of media culture, there are countries where being a politician and being a celebrity seem to be converging phenomena. France's Nicolas Sarkozy, elected as the country's president in 2007, seems to be an example of this development. His personal life – the separation from Cecilia Sarkozy, his relationship and marriage to a former model, become part of the spectacle of his presidency, transforming him into a celebrity figure who dominates the pages of *Hello!* magazine and the gossip segments of television magazine programmes. 'Sarko, c'est un spectacle permanent' [Sarko, he is a permanent spectacle] in the words of a Belgian newspaper. In countries such as the Philippines, politicians literally *are* celebrities, famous for being singers or actors before taking up politics but continuing to use their celebrity status to buttress their political ambitions. Politics as spectacle can have a disorientating impact on journalists. It seems to mix up genres transforming politics into the subject of the entertainment pages.

On the other hand, politics has always had the dimension of 'performance'. In his classic article 'Politics and the English language' (1946), George Orwell stated: 'Political language [...] is designed to make lies sound truthful and murder respectable, and to give an appearance of solidity to pure wind'. Politicians seek resounding language: 'The Founding Fathers', 'The American Dream', the 'War on Terror', 'Sleaze', 'Free enterprise'. They have always been actors but there is a sense in many long-established constitutional democracies that politics is indeed a play and the performance arts more important than the arts of government.

There are two comments that should be made here. First, politics does not cease to be real simply because it uses symbols. Second, while the players may primarily be the politicians, journalists and the public are, as I shall explore in later chapters, increasingly able to influence some of the terms of the performance. However, I would argue too that the prevalence of symbolic politics also has a number of unfavourable consequences for the conduct of substantial politics. First, there is the tendency for journalists to convert all politics into some kind of game of Chinese whispers. As former UK newspaper editor Peter Wilby explains in reference to the parliamentary lobby (the UK corps of parliamentary reporters):

> it allows no political event [...] to have meaning in itself, like a piece of poetry in a postmodern university literature department [...] What does an NHS reorganisation or an 'initiative' on behaviour in schools mean for doctors, patients, teachers or children? The political journalists cannot tell you. They can tell you that this is a Blairite or Brownite idea, that it shows the minister is 'getting a grip' or losing it, that it will pacify backbenchers or enrage them. (13 June 2005: 23)

A further, and paradoxical, consequence of performance politics is the attempt by journalists to pierce the carapace, to tell us what politics is really about and who politicians really are. Here we can find some of the explanation for the rise in scandal coverage and the politics of authenticity, of the personal.

Symbolic Capital, Scandal and the Personal

Two noted developments of late twentieth- and early twenty-first-century politics are the prevalence of scandal and the coverage of the personal in political communication (see, for example, Canel and Sanders, 2006; and Stanyer and Wring, 2004). These phenomena can be partly attributed, as I shall discuss next, to the significance to the symbolic in contemporary politics.

Symbolic Capital and Scandal

Politicians need visibility because they need our attention. Political leaders seek to establish relationships with their followers in order to gain support from them. This support is based mainly on credibility: if a leader wants to be followed, she needs to be trusted. Being a leader requires one to look after one's own reputation, for which it is important to be known, heard and viewed by those from whom one seeks support. Reputation becomes a kind of resource or, as one of the foremost scholars of political scandal explained it, 'a sort of "symbolic capital" [...] a valuable resource, because it enables individuals to exercise a certain kind of power' (Thompson, 1997: 47). The notion of 'symbolic capital' was developed by Pierre Bourdieu (1930–2002) and refers to the power bestowed by systemically defined goods such as reputation, being listened to and honour, those non-economic goods deemed socially valuable and given concrete expression in such things as academic degrees, positions and titles.

In media-saturated democracies, symbolic capital can become very much the plaything of the media and thus a source of danger for politicians. In this atmosphere the reputation of the leader becomes vulnerable and herein lies the scope for scandal (see Canel and Sanders, 2006). Scandals cause politicians to lose their reputation and relationships between political leaders and the people become pervaded with distrust.

It is this potential for damage to the reputation of the leader which makes the media so powerful in scandals. It is also why management of visibility has become one of the main aims of communication strategies of political institutions. Strategies move from disclosure of information to secret-keeping, but all for the sake of controlling the story-line in the candidate's or politician's favour.

This is why we seem to like scandal and the concentration on process – who is up, who is down. On the one hand, it treats us as insiders. On the other, it ruptures the controlled narrative. The Dean scream – the moment the possible 2004 Democratic presidential nomination, Howard Dean, let out a Neanderthal shout – was a highpoint of campaign coverage. The UK deputy prime minister, John Prescott's right-hook to an egg-throwing protester during the 2001 campaign seemed the most exciting moment of the election race. Politicians 'package themselves for protection – and end up looking phony as well as flawed' (de Zengotita, 2005: 138), protecting themselves from us and the media. It is only at times of crisis – the look that flashed across Bush's face in a Florida schoolroom when he is given the news of the 11 September 2001 attacks – and scandal that they seem really real.

The Shift to the Personal

Campaigning in the 2008 US primaries in New Hampshire after the demoralizing loss to Barack Obama in Iowa, a voter asked Hilary Clinton: 'How do you do it? How do you keep up?' Her emotionally charged response, revealed in the images of the encounter, was: 'You know, this is very personal for me. It's not just political, it's not just public. I see what's happening, and we have to reverse it.' Hilary became real for an instant and her tearful moment was credited in part with her totally unexpected victory in the New Hampshire polls.[6]

The personalization of politics is not only the result of the pursuit of scandal by journalists. Long before the Clinton-Lewinksy scandal at the end of the twentieth century, politicians themselves had pushed the personal to communicate aspects of their lives they thought might find favour with the public. Twenty-first-century media made this far more difficult to control and the outcome appears to be the acknowledgement by politicians that the intimate presentation of the self must be a part of contemporary political communication.

It is a difficult balance to strike: an over-choreographed presentation undermines its symbolic value as a pledge of authenticity; if it is too spontaneous the person can be accused of lack of control. In Hilary Clinton's case, she was accused by some critics of contrivance and by others of a worrying over-emotionalism; among those who mattered, the voters, she was believed. France, a country utterly unused to the employment of the personal in public life, was in 2007 treated to the spectacle of the personal in epic terms, to the conversion of their president into the romantic hero of a sentimental novel, moving from the liberation of the Bulgarian nurses in Libya, to the break-up of his marriage and then to the sojourn in Egypt with his new girlfriend, all presented to the press in a kind of presidential performance never before witnessed by the French. The magazines loved it, but it was greeted by very mixed reviews in the wider press.

Sarkozy's performance, in itself symbolic of the rise of the personal in politics, should not, however, obscure the abiding significance of the power of character and of words themselves – the traditional tropes of Aristotelian rhetoric – in political communication. Reporting on the Obama campaign in South Carolina, a veteran British sketch-writer for a conservative newspaper, could not fail to be moved by his words. In an article entitled: 'Obama's soaring rhetoric captures the mood of nation hungry for change', he relates how he came upon the memorial inscription to an eighteenth-century South Carolina politician, Hon. Henry Deas (1770–1846). It read: 'With earnest patriotism and enlightened devotion to constitutional liberty, he zealously engaged in eventful political measures [and] by his graceful, earnest and persuasive eloquence and by the moral force of a pure and elevated character exerted a prominent influence on public affairs' (Gimson, 12 January 2008: 20–1). It will be interesting to see whether in an age of symbolic politics contemporary leaders can continue this authentic rhetorical tradition.

5

Political Marketing: The Death of Conviction?

'This is the beginning of a whole new concept. This is it. This is the way they'll be elected forevermore. The next guys up will have to be performers.' Roger Ailes, Nixon's campaign manager in 1968.

Joe McGinnis (1968) *The Selling of the President*. London: Penguin

Introduction

American journalist, Joe McGinnis's account of Richard Nixon's successful campaign to win the US presidency, for the first time opened the public's eyes to the arrival of the marketing concept in US politics. This chapter explores the background to and the *development of political marketing* in an international context. Political communication is not only an area of scholarly investigation but also of professional practice. The area of political marketing seeks to combine the science and art of persuasion with marketing concepts and techniques in order to achieve political goals. I will discuss the *marketing concept in politics*, its *application in campaigns and government communication* and whether political marketing's emergence is a sign of the *triumph of market over conviction politics* and marks *the death of ideology*.

The Development of Political Marketing

The history of political marketing has yet to be told in systematic fashion. Its story is scattered in the history of propaganda and political communication studies, the development of public relations and the art and science of marketing as part of management studies. It is also, of course, ineluctably tied to the story of democratic politics itself.

Like all human practices, the set of understandings, actions and instruments which comprise political marketing are situated, culturally established activities that have developed in particular historical circumstances, shaping our current understanding and application of them. Thus, before embarking on definitions of political marketing, it will be helpful to examine some of the historical background to its emergence in twentieth-century politics.

Mass Society

Fear of the 'mob', the inchoate human collective that functions as one irrational actor to overturn the established order, runs through history. The fourth-century BC Greek philosopher Diogenes described the mob 'as the mother of tyrants' and Edmund Burke's *Reflections on the Revolution in France* (1790) made clear his condemnation of the revolutionaries who he believed had mobilized the masses to pursue abstract political ideals through violence and turmoil. Burke was writing at a time when industrialization was just beginning in Europe. It would eventually contribute to the creation of a mass, urban-based society which, through the extension of education, voting rights and of ideologies challenging the status quo, would become a transforming force in modern democracies.

The rise of mass society fed fears that democracy would become a tyranny under another name. The warning, commonly if mistakenly attributed to Thomas Jefferson, that 'A democracy is nothing more than mob rule, where fifty-one percent of the people may take away the rights of the other forty-nine.' This warning was echoed in the work of nineteenth-century intellectuals who examined the psychology of crowds. *The Crowd: A Study of the Popular Mind* (1896) by the French intellectual Gustave Le Bon was one of the first to identify the potential power of the unconscious and the risks of its manipulation.

Plato's rejection of democracy had rested on his view that the masses were unfitted for the tasks of government which should be undertaken by a specialized elite. A number of commentators at the beginning of the twentieth century expressed their fears at the rise of the masses in similar terms. In his *The Revolt of the Masses* (1930), Jose Ortega y Gasset painted a dystopian picture of contemporary society composed of the masses living without moral code, increasingly unwilling to defer to the dominant minorities. For Ortega, Bolshevism and fascism were symptoms of the usurpation of power by 'mass man'. In the United States Walter Lippmann wrote of the 'bewildered herd' and in his influential work *Public Opinion* (1922) argued that ordinary human beings were unable to formulate well-founded views on public affairs and thus needed to be wisely led by expert elites.

The Power of the Ego and the Growth of Consumer Society

Le Bon had identified the possible power of the human unconscious. This insight was fully developed by Sigmund Freud (1856–1939). His work suggested that there are subconscious mental processes and forces beyond human consciousness which play a key role in life and behaviour. He explored the power of irrationality in human beings and came to a very bleak view of their susceptibility to manipulation, given tragic credence by the events of the First and Second World Wars. War had been one of the great drivers of the development of propaganda aimed at mobilizing the masses in common cause (Knightley, 2004).

Freudian ideas about the power of the repressed and the irrational began to filter into the intellectual milieu after publication of Freud's works in English in the 1920s. One of his principal American evangelists was his nephew, Edward Bernays. On Bernays's return from a First World War peace conference, he decided: 'If you could use propaganda for war, you could certainly use it for peace.' And, pragmatically, as 'propaganda got to be a bad word because of the Germans using it so what I did was to try to find some other word so we found the words "councillor on public relations".'[1] Understanding public opinion was of increasing interest in a context where the United States had become a mass industrialized country and businesses were looking to promote consumption of their goods. The development of mass production shifted the philosophy of sales of goods from a need-based, functional basis to a desire-driven culture. Citizens were becoming consumers and the trick was to persuade people to purchase objects they did not need, but somehow could be prompted to desire.

Using Freud's writings and particularly his *General Introduction to Psychoanalysis* (1920), Bernays explored how there is much more at work in human and especially group decision-making than the rational processing of information. Asked by a major tobacco company how the female market could be activated (it was considered unfeminine for women to smoke, especially in public), Bernays turned to a psychoanalyst. He advised that cigarettes are a symbol of male sexual power which women should be shown how to challenge. Bernays decided to recruit a number of rich debutantes who, at a New York parade, would at a declared signal all light up a cigarette hidden in their garter. Bernays alerted the press, told them they were suffragettes and described the cigarettes as 'torches of freedom', resonating with symbols such as New York's Statue of Liberty. Journalists wrote the next day of 'Group of girls puff at cigarettes as a gesture of freedom' and thus, cigarettes became socially acceptable with a single symbolic act. Bernays originated the idea that consumption was not just about buying something you needed, but that it was also something which made you feel better, that bestowed identity, creating an emotional connect. He showed US companies that by associating merchandise with unconscious desires, human beings could come to desire things they did not need. The self became a central focus in consumer society; in an ironic turn of events, techniques honed in the era of the masses became in part the means for the exaltation of the individual.

Political Marketing and Public Relations

Bernays was one of the architects of modern persuasive techniques. He used celebrity endorsements and product placements to promote Randolph Hearst's women magazines and associated erotic desire with the purchase of cars. Submerged irrational emotions were harnessed to encourage consumption. These promotional techniques, commonly employed by marketing and public relations (PR) departments, were developed by corporate United States but were soon taken up by politicians. As we saw in Chapter 1, President Coolidge drew on Bernays's help to improve his dull, humourless image. Bernays persuaded celebrities to visit the president and the next day newsreels ran with the headline 'Famous friends visit President Coolidge' and every newspaper had as their front-page story, 'President Coolidge entertains actors at White House.'

In 1928 the Democrats became the first political party to set up a permanent public relations office and the Republicans followed suit in 1932. The first political public relations consultancy, Campaigns Incorporated, was established in Los Angeles in 1933 (McNair, 2007: 119). Journalists began to chronicle the impact of PR and advertising men (and they were mostly men) on presidential campaigns. Theodore White's classic account of Kennedy's campaign in *The Making of the President* foregrounded the role of image-making. Joe McGinnis's *The Selling of the President* told the story of 'the packaging of Richard Nixon'. He cited Republican chairman, Leonard Hall, commentating on Dwight Eisenhower's hiring of an advertising agency for his 1956 re-election (1968/1988: 27): 'You sell your candidates and your programs the way a business sells its products.'

The Bernays consumer model and its bleak characterization of the manipulation of the relationship between human beings, the market and power found its counterpoint in those who argued that, in fact, marketing and public relations placed reciprocity at their heart and the customer as their focus. Opinion polling and focus groups, techniques that came to be used in the 1930s and 1940s, were about finding out what people wanted, allowing the views of the public to be known on matters of importance. The election of Franklin D. Roosevelt in 1933 ushered in this dispensation as the new president employed Dr George Gallup to chart public opinion about the issues of the day. This attempt to find out what the citizens thought reflects more accurately what political marketeers would themselves believe they are doing namely, identifying the goods and/or services wanted or needed by the public in exchange for their vote and support. Nevertheless, those who observed the work of the marketing, advertising, PR men at close hand considered that in politics they had ensured that 'style becomes substance' (McGinnis, 1968/1988: 30) and a number of academics have also been trenchant critics of the impact of marketing in politics (see, for example, Franklin, 2004). Before considering their arguments, we will first examine what marketing means for politics.

The Marketing Concept

Marketing was traditionally understood as the set of activities in profit-seeking enterprises aimed at understanding and supplying customers' needs and wants. It is predicated on the notion of the existence of a market in which goods and services are exchanged in competition with others. Kotler and Levy (1969) were the first to consider the application of marketing to non-profit or service organizations and in the last 20 years, a number of scholars have used the insights of marketing to examine their implications for the conduct and understanding of contemporary politics (see, for example, O'Shaughnessy, 1990, Newman, 1994, Scammell, 1999, Wring, 2005; Henneberg, 2006). As a result political marketing has become a dynamic subfield of marketing research (Kotler and Kotler, 1999).[2] Here I will examine a number of issues raised by their discussions related to the specific contributions of marketing to our understanding of politics.

The Political Marketplace

Politics has been variously conceived of as theatre, a (horse) race, as warfare and as a marketplace. The notion of politics, and particularly electoral campaigns, as a marketplace where voters make economically driven rational decisions was formulated in Anthony Downs's *An Economic Theory of Democracy* (1957). His adoption of rational choice theory to explain voting decisions sought to show how political parties are pushed to take up centrist positions in response to voters' moderate opinions (see Chapter 11).

Changes in voting behaviour from the 1970s onwards, in particular the decline of the stability of voter preferences associated with class and party and evidence of more voter volatility, suggested that examining political choice from a market perspective might provide valuable insights into voting decisions and the conduct of campaigns. Election campaigns had been typically examined from the perspective of political scientists and communication scholars. For Scammell, however, the distinctiveness of the marketing perspective is that it 'offers a rational economic theoretical basis for explaining party and voter behaviour that is more broad and inclusive than either the conventional political science campaign studies or political communications approaches' (1999: 739).

Political scientists typically examine campaigns and the introduction of political marketing as the application of techniques, the influx of marketing and communication experts and the application of positioning and audience segmentation strategies. Communication scholars, on the other hand, have understood the marketization of campaigns as a consequence of modernization, taking this as the theoretical framework for changes in campaigning practice. This perspective identifies modernization as being at the root of such phenomena as the development of non-ideological parties ('catch-all', big tent parties) and the transformation of the media into a major political actor. From both points of view, marketing is the by-product of wider forces. In Scammell's view, this is to misunderstand the direction of influence. In her words, political marketing 'effectively reverses the perspective offered by campaign studies/political communications approaches. Political marketing is no longer a subset of broader processes: political communications becomes a subset of marketing [...] The prime drivers of change in campaigning practice and communications are not the media, nor American influence [...] but campaigners' strategic understanding of the political market' (1999: 723). So that, for example, the importance of candidate or party image comes to be seen not as a product of Americanization, modernization or the power of the media, but as a strategic calculation responding to market demands. Echoing a claim made in one of the first examinations of marketing's contribution to political science (see Harrop, 1990: 277–91), strategy applied to specific market conditions is understood to be the key driver of campaign practice. This has a number of important consequences for understanding what political marketing is but also provides a rather restricted model for understanding the conduct of politics, as we shall see below.

What is Political Marketing?

The American Marketing Association defines marketing as 'the process of planning and executing the conception, pricing, promotion and distribution of ideas, goods and services to create exchanges that satisfy individual and organizational objectives' (the term 'ideas' was added to the definition in 1985). Lock and Harris described research in political marketing as 'the study of the processes of exchanges between political entities and their environment and among themselves, with particular reference to the positioning of those entities and their communications' (1996: 21). Political marketing is decidedly not simply equivalent to the use of promotional tools in politics, something with which it is often confused, nor is it just a collection of techniques often equated with the processes associated with the 'marketing mix' of the 4Ps, the traditional framework used for commercial marketing. In the political context these can be understand as:

- **The product**, the actual good or service and its satisfaction of customer needs and wants. This is a complex construct in politics and refers to a series of characteristics conditioned by the particular political, media and economic environment in which the product is offered. At election time, for example, this might include a party, its leaders and its policies. Voters' images and knowledge of each will weigh differentially according to the kind of political system (presidential or party-driven), voting system (first past the post or proportional representation), media landscape (heavily partisan, mixed, public service oriented) and so on.
- **Pricing** refers to what is exchanged for the product or service which can be a monetary or other value. In politics this is the least easily definable marketing variable but can usually be identified by the values proffered by the campaign slogans of parties and candidates. For example, Herbert Hoover, in a naked appeal to their materialist instincts, offered Americans 'A Chicken in Every Pot. A Car in Every Garage' in his 1928 Republican presidential campaign. Nazi Germany offered its people 'Ein Volk, ein Reich, ein Führer' ('one people, one country, one leader') and Thatcher's Conservative Party told the British people in the election campaign of 1978 with reference to the incumbent Labour Party and the high unemployment rate, 'Labour is not working.' This last example demonstrates the two-pronged tactics parties often adopt in defining the values offered to the electorate: they imply what they can do or what they represent by pointing out where the others fail (Labour isn't working but the Conservatives will work and thus improve the economic state of the country).
- **Promotion** refers to all the ways the product is promoted. These can be broadly divided into free and paid for media (see Maarek, 1995). Paid for or controlled media include all the ways in which political campaigners market their goods through means they control and pay for, such as advertising (paid or statutorily provided for as in many European countries), rallies, tours, direct marketing, telephone and door-to-door canvassing and websites. Free media is coverage generated by campaigns, but not controlled or paid for by them. Politicians have invested significant resources in attempting to control free coverage, organizing press conferences, employing media advisers and so on. However, the evidence from recent US presidential campaigns is that this is becoming increasingly difficult to control for two reasons. First, the abundance of

media outlets, vastly expanded by the internet, means that comprehensive media control is simply unfeasible. Second, the ease with which new
technology allows access and distribution of non-mainstream media
material or user-generated content.

- **Placement** or place refers to the channels through which a product or
  service is distributed, in which geographic region or industry, and to
  which segment (young adults, families, business people). In political
  campaigns these activities refer to the rationale for the geography of campaigning, shaping which areas of a country are targeted, how audiences
  are segmented and how different campaign vehicles are employed.
  Barack Obama, for example, intensively targeted resources towards the
  internet during his 2007 campaign for the Democrat presidential nomination, garnering substantial economic resources in the process.

In election campaigns pricing, promotion and placement tactics are shaped
by previously conducted market research and collection of relevant intelligence related to key voters, campaign issues, opposition research (finding
out opponents' weaknesses and strengths). However, where the marketing
concept truly prevails (see Scammell, 1999; and Lees Marshment, 2001) the
product itself is submitted to the market. In other words, politicians seek to
discover the needs and wants of the voter at the beginning rather than at the
end of the process of defining policies. Here citizen-customers become the
arbiters of political content and, in an analogy taken from service industry
relationship marketing, voting is understand as an exchange between the
politician providing what the citizen-customer wants, with the latter invest-
ing their trust and, all importantly, giving their vote to the candidate.
Campaign strategies seek to build trust, emphasizing honesty as well as
expertise and reputation in relevant policy areas. External accreditation and
endorsement are used to construct the kind of images that pollsters and
market researchers have discovered voters desire for their leaders.

A marketing perspective will also affect politicians' long-term strategic
behaviour in relationship to competitive positioning (see Collins and Butler,
1996). Politicians may seek to steal ground from competitors, adopting in
some aspects a 'following' strategy and others a 'leading' or challenging one
(see Butler and Collins, 1996; Henneberg, 2006). British Labour's promise not
to increase taxes in 1997, and its subsequent emphasis on financial prudence,
reinforced the perception that the Conservatives were no longer the party of
economic competence. Parties may also adopt niche strategies, positioning
themselves as the champion of green issues, for example. However, the discussion of competitive positioning throws up a serious objection to the political marketing perspective, namely that it does not work in certain kinds of
political environments where coalition and consensus building are the norm
(see Ormrod, 2006). I shall return to these criticisms at the end of the chapter.

Political Marketing and Campaigns

Work has been developed on the theoretical underpinnings of political marketing (see Henneberg and O'Shaughnessy, 2007), its adoption by political actors besides politicians and the understanding of political marketing in government (see Nimmo, 1999), at a local level (Franklin and Richardson, 2002) and in a comparative context (see Lilleker and Lees-Marshment, 2005). The main focus of political marketing scholarship, however, has been on its impact on campaigns with a heavy focus on the analysis of the application of marketing instruments (see, for example, Kavanagh, 1995; Lees-Marshment, 2001; Maarek, 1995; Newman, 1994; Scammell, 1995).

Wring's analysis of the British Labour's party adoption of marketing tools and concepts (2005) provides a useful historical grounding for the understanding of the development of political campaigning. He uses a model of the relationship between parties as electoral organizations and voters, showing how it has shifted from being one of mass propaganda to that of promotional media campaigning and, finally, to that of political marketing. Wring's work is a helpful counterpoint to overstated descriptions of the adoption of political marketing as a 'revolution' (see, for example, Gould, 1998). Lees-Marshment's pioneering work in political marketing provides a structurally similar model to Wring's. Her analysis of British politics pinpoints three types of political party namely, the product, sales and market oriented party. These can be seen to be roughly equivalent to Wring's tripartite classification, where the first is focused on telling the public about its product, the second in selling it to them using modern communication techniques, and the third in adapting its products to the needs and wants of its market. To do this, Lees-Marshment suggests it must implement the following stages (2001: 25):

Stage 1 Obtain market intelligence
Stage 2 Product Design
Stage 3 Product adjustment
Stage 4 Implementation
Stages 5 and 6 Communication and campaign
Stage 7 Election

The usefulness of her approach has been shown to be limited outside the British context for two reasons (see Ormrod, 2006; Lilleker and Lees-Marshment, 2005). First, political markets are not always zero sum competitive arenas as they are in countries with first past the post electoral systems. Multi-party systems throughout Europe are characterized by coalition governments which seek win-win alliances. Second, her approach also raises questions, which I will return to later, about the usefulness of political marketing as an analytical tool shorn of a richer understanding of politics and public decision-making. One way of exploring some of the questions raised is to examine, as I shall now, some notable examples of the application of political marketing to contemporary politics.

Political Marketing in Practice

Campaigns have been the main focus of political marketing research for the simple reason that they have been the most conspicuous and common example of its practice. However, political marketing is not restricted to campaigns and in this section I will examine how it came to be associated with Bill Clinton's governing style during his second term in office. Before that, it is worth exploring one of Clinton's sincerest imitators, the British Labour Party.

Clinton and New Labour

The gestation of New Labour can be traced to the traumatic period following its calamitous campaign for the 1981 general elections. Among those who pushed for the introduction of a marketing perspective for the next campaign was poll expert Philip Gould. In his *The Unfinished Revolution*, he set out his creed for a successful campaign):

> An agreed, early strategy
>
> Selectivity of target audience
>
> Simple message often repeated
>
> Orchestrated, cohesive presentation of the message
>
> Clear allocation of responsibility for tasks. Clear lines of authority and accountability Adequate structures of co-ordination
>
> Positive, proactive press relations
>
> A shift in campaigning emphasis from 'grass roots'/opinion forming to influencing electoral opinion through the mass media
>
> Proper use of outside expertise
>
> Less publicity material, used more often
>
> Highest-level political authority and support for the early and continuing implementation of these principles. (Gould, 1998: 55–6)

The initial phases of shifting from using marketing tools to applying a marketing perspective in the Labour Party was marked by the establishment of the Shadow Communications Agency, which met for the first time in March 1986. Working with communications expert Peter Mandelson, Gould and his team began the process of redesigning the Labour image, ditching old symbols and style for an unthreatening red rose and slickly organized campaigning events. However, while the presentation had improved, the policies were fundamentally unchanged and Labour's leader, Neil Kinnock, failed to convince the electorate in 1992 that the party should be given power.

Gould's experiences in the Democrat election camp the following year convinced him that a new approach was required. He asked his creative team 'to undertake a political communication revolution' for future electoral campaigns. He wanted 'a consumer not a political campaign, using normal consumer language and not "political" terms.' (1998: 59). He spoke about developing 'symbolic policies' which would indicate to the public that there had been a radical shift in Labour's perspective, no longer statist or averse to a law and order agenda embodied in slogans such as 'Freedom and Fairness', 'Tough on Crime and Tough on the Causes of Crime'.

With the Democrats, Gould had learned that the consumer was king. Politicians had begun to heed the lessons of business, which had started to use focus groups to discover customers' deepest desires. Until the 1960s and 1970s, asking customers what they wanted and then giving it to them was not a commonly accepted notion. Focus groups were used to explore feelings about products and consumers were no longer classified by social class, but by how they identified themselves as aspirers, succeeders or reformers. Ordinary people were no longer so easily ascribed to social groups. Economic reforms in Reagan's America and Thatcher's Britain were loosening social bonds and identities, making way for a new individualism in which marketing and advertising could play their part in constructing new categories of social identity. Politicians could map these and respond in formulating appropriate policies. Gould would offer the raw material from focus groups for politicians to formulate policy. Phrases were copied from the United States. For Gould, it meant that the time for elitist politics in Britain was finished and it was now time for the transference of power to the individual. This was the lesson Gould learnt at Clinton's base in Little Rock, Arkansas, and one which was executed with successful effect in 1997 by Tony Blair's New Labour.

Political Marketing in Government

Politicians saw the potential for marketing their own products in election campaigns. Thatcher's Conservative Party, for example, was a noted customer of advertising and marketing services (see Rosenbaum, 1997). However, the apogee of the marketing concept came with its arrival in government in the person of Dick Morris, brought in by Clinton as campaign manager for his 1996 re-election campaign 'to save his butt', as Morris later put it. Clinton's popularity was at a low ebb. He needed to win back the key swing voters who would decide the next election and, in Morris's view, this could best be done by treating them as consumers. Therefore, all ideology should be laid aside and politics turned into a form of consumer business. Politics had to be transformed and be as responsive to the whims and the desires of the marketplace as business was, radically changing its view of the voters, treating them not as targets to be manipulated but as customers to be learnt from.

Morris's approach brought lifestyle marketing into politics, employing neuro-personality polls to elicit responses from thousands of voters about their intimate selves. They were asked questions such as: 'do you consider yourself to be the life and soul of the party?'; 'are you a planner or are you spontaneous?'[3] These polls were used to segment the American population and produce profiles with names such as caps and gowns or pools and patios. Tiny details of people's lives and their anxieties were used to develop small-scale policies, what Morris called 'small-bore politics', such as school uniforms and V-chips for televisions. The strategy of 'triangulation' emphasized issues that crossed the ideological divide, co-opted Republican policies and reflected back to voters their concerns and lifestyles. Morris and pollster Mark Penn called swing voters every night to check every detail of policy. Polling became a virtual religion and suburban voters a prime influence in 1990s' US domestic policy.

To conclude, political marketing is not simply a set of concepts and techniques to be used in election campaigns. It can also be applied in government so that marketing becomes a governing tool and public office 'a full-time campaign platform' (Nimmo, 1999: 75). Again, however, strategic political marketing is more than the application of certain methods and techniques. It occurs when there 'is some level of recognition, even if not fully articulated, that elections and democracy itself are a competitive "marketplace", voters and citizens are "consumers", and that this development is underpinned by the rise of an advanced consumerist material culture' (Henneberg and O'Shaughnessy, 2007: 21). The concern must be that by adopting the political marketing concept we create Bernays's vision of consumerist democracy where people's desires are in charge, but not the people themselves. Democracy becomes the means to try to satiate what may be contradictory desires such as wanting both lower taxes and better schools. I will next examine some of the issues raised by critics of the application of marketing to politics.

The Limitations of Marketing for Politics

Critics of political marketing fall into three camps. The first fears that political marketing subverts politics and democracy, allowing style to triumph over substance, negating conviction and principle. The second argues that marketing and politics are ill-suited bed-fellows as politics cannot simply be reduced to transactions in a marketplace. The third is more sympathetic to political marketing, but considers that it lacks the theoretical and methodological ballast to make a significant contribution to the understanding of contemporary politics. I will examine each of these areas of criticism in turn.

'Candy Floss' Politics

As the UK Conservative Party prepared for the country's 1992 general election, they sent observers across the Atlantic to learn from American campaigners. Members of their team concluded:

> The cross-party consensus was clear: the coming general election campaign would be the most carefully orchestrated ever. In the probing light of the television camera, in the shadow of the instant headline, one slip of the tongue could lose the election. Therefore the aim should be to reduce risk, to eliminate spontaneity, to curtail the cut and thrust of political debate. Words should be written down on autocue, photographs plotted in advance, sound-bites pre-cooked and wrapped in clingfilm: for Britain was bound to follow the Americans further and further down the path of candy floss politics. (Hogg and Hill, 1995: 164)

The idea of 'candy floss' politics, of politics converted into a nice, fluffy, saccharine, superficially attractive but ultimately unfulfilling experience, has been a frequently expressed concern by politicians and academics (see Henneberg, 2004). Political marketing is seen as contributing to a more manipulative, populist, unprincipled kind of politics where it becomes 'counter-productive to have a fixed principled stance' (Wring, 2005: 179). The criticism does not simply apply to the use of communication methods but also to the marketing strategies and techniques used to focus campaign energies on certain kinds of voters –swing voters in first past the post systems, for example – leaving huge swathes of citizens virtually ignored. We can identify four specific allegations about the impact of political marketing on politics:

- It disenfranchises citizens in certain kinds of electoral systems
- It is manipulative
- It encourages populism
- It encourages unprincipled politics

Does political marketing necessarily have these outcomes? I would argue that it depends. Certainly the use of political marketing to employ limited resources effectively can contribute to a sense of public disenfranchisement and falls in voter turnout. However, as the Power Commission concluded on this issue (see 2006), this problem has more to do with the nature of the electoral system itself than with the practice of politics.

Does it produce more manipulative politics? Here, I would suggest, far more empirical and conceptual work needs to be done to provide the instruments and body of evidence with which to answer this question. We need to understand what manipulation is (see Chapter 3), how it is produced, variables which intensify its impact and so on. Is, for example, negative advertising manipulative? And what about the technique of triangulation? There does appear to be prima facie evidence for arguing that the panoply of potentially manipulative techniques has expanded but whether this is a function of political marketing or of technological developments is a moot point.

Finally, is it true that political marketing contributes to more populist and less leader-led politics? Depending what is meant by 'populist', there are certain senses in which this might be said to be true. If one understands this as a greater attentiveness to, and impact of, citizens' views on policies, then this is probably a consequence of political marketing and one which could be said to be positive. This may be linked, however, to what could be considered as a further negative consequence, namely the death of conviction and principle in politics. If politicians adopt simply a 'following' mentality, what place is there for ideas and leadership? In fact, there are two further issues here. On the one hand, leadership is a political category which is highly valued by the public so that the adoption of a follower strategy could be ultimately counter-productive even from a marketing point of view. Second, Butler and Collins have pointed out that service and non-profit marketing perspectives show that in this kind of marketing, the emphasis should be placed on a 'long-term interactive relationship rather than on simple exchange' (1999: 55). The very notion of relationship implies a value or ethical category going beyond the mutual benefit obtained in a market exchange. Applied to the political realm, this might suggest that qualities which sustain relationships are considered valuable in their own right. Consistency and integrity, for example, and the maintenance of views grounded in deeply held values would, then, be considered an asset for politicians.

An Uneasy Fit

Marketing developed in a business environment and it is clear, as Lock and Harris have pointed out (1996), that there are crucial differences between political and service or product marketing including:

- The same day choice of voters in election campaigns
- The utility maximizing framework applying to purchases and services fits electoral choice poorly
- Voters must live with collective choices in a way they don't have to with other kinds of choices
- Winner takes all in certain kinds of elections

- The complexity of the 'political bundle'
- The difficulty of introducing new brands
- Brand leaders tend to fall behind once in power

More fundamentally, one might object that the notion of a political market by itself is conceptually too threadbare to do justice to the complexity of political reality. In my view, this criticism is justified. Attempts to apply marketing analyses to election campaigns have not always provided significant theoretical insights (see, for example, Lilleker and Lees-Marshment, 2005). A sensible approach is taken by Henneberg and O'Shaughnessy who conclude from their study of the 2000 US presidential campaign that: 'A political marketing analysis is only one tool in getting to grips with political persuasion and not a paradigm through which to explain all political persuasion' (2007: 5).

Expanding the Research Agenda

The political marketing perspective is a useful part of the mix in understanding the relationship between politics, communication and the public. As a relatively new area of research, there are a number of issues that are ripe for further exploration. A number of scholars have indicated what these might be. My personal list would include the following:

- A deepening understanding of what political marketing means for governance and politicians in government.
- Attention to cultural, historical and religious contexts in the development of political marketing concepts and models.
- More emphasis on the regional and the local.
- Attention to the dimensions of ethics and responsibility, a notably under-researched area in political marketing (see Henneberg, 2004: 9).

The area of ethics is a particularly important one for political marketing. Conceptualizations of relationship and value ineluctably throw up an ethical dimension. Ethics is after all about human behaviour and here, perhaps, is one of the central challenges for political marketing theorists and practitioners. How can the political marketing perspective – derived from a rational choice paradigm where the human being is understood as *homo economicus* – work out a theory of value which is not purely economistic and instrumental? Political marketeers may often act ethically, but political marketing itself often appears to be a normative-free zone as far as research and also, at times, practice is concerned. One clear task is to work out the grounds of ethical and non-ethical behaviour in political marketing, providing an account of overarching regulative ideals and its defining substantive goods. It is a subject to which I will return in the final chapter of this book.

Part Two

The Communicators

6

Communicating Government

Introduction

President Eisenhower, good soldier as he was, thought that the facts should speak for themselves. His wiser press secretary, Richard Neustadt, knew better. He understood that presidential power lay partly in the ability to persuade: political leadership requires effective communication.

At the heart of governing in a democracy is finding the ways and means to communicate effectively government messages and policies, not only to the elite groups – congress, party members – envisaged by Neustadt but also to the mass publics brought into being by the mass media age. Whether it is persuading the public about the case for war, promoting a healthy eating campaign or trumpeting the latest welfare initiative, governments must constantly engage in communication with the multiple publics they rely on for support.

In the mediated twenty-first century world, command of rhetoric in the restricted arenas of traditional politics is no longer enough. Broader communication issues such as politicians' relationships with journalists, image construction, the question of trust and the salience of scandal all become key to examining how governments communicate. In an environment where those who govern must 'go public', in Kernell's (1986) well-known phrase, governing itself becomes a 'permanent campaign'. The permanent campaign combines 'image-making with strategic calculation', refashioning 'government into an instrument designed to sustain an elected official's public popularity' (Blumenthal, 1980: 7). And so political consultants and pollsters are brought into the very core of the political system and image-making becomes a central concern of government. Of course, they are not the only or primary concerns; delivering on policy and responding well to crises make up the core business of government. How well governments do, however, will in part be a function of how effectively they have communicated what they do.

This chapter will examine *the development of government communication* in relation to that of *the mediapolis*. It examines its shift from its initial peripheral role to the *central position it occupies in governance* today. It will examine *leadership communication* focused on *character and image* and *government communication during times of crisis*, focusing particularly on *the Blair years (1997–2007) as paradigmatic of many of the controversies surrounding government communication.* Finally, it will consider what is necessary for *effective government communication.*

Moving Communication Centre Stage

In 1983, Britain's Labour Party produced a manifesto described as the 'longest suicide note in history'.[1] Communication was not the party's strongest suit in the late 1970s and early 1980s. Managing the media consisted of leaving piles of badly photocopied press releases for collection outside the parliamentary press gallery (interview, PA chief political correspondent, 1997). Previous Labour governments had not been so cavalier about the need to manage communication. Harold Wilson's governments in the 1960s had taken seriously communication's key role in achieving policy goals (see Wring, 2005: 1–2).

Across the world, since the early 1950s, television had begun to occupy its dominant position in public culture, opening up a window on the political world and underscoring the importance of image-making in political communication. Over the past 50 years communication moved to the centre stage of government and democratic politics, contributing to change in the business of politics itself. The technological, social and economic drivers of these developments have contributed to the ever-accelerating expansion of media space/time which exists like a kind of fourth dimension, mediating, representing (some would say 'distorting') much of what we experience. It is conjured into existence through five features of the contemporary media environment: *ubiquity* – the media are (almost) everywhere; *speed* – news 'breaks' as events happen; *quantity* – in the digital era blogs, multi-media devices, radio and TV channels abound in contrast to the analogue world of spectrum scarcity; *accessibility* – computers, once huge hulking machines stored in basements, give an entrance ticket to a worldwide stage, as the Baghdad blogger found when he told his eye-witness story of the invasion of Iraq (McCarthy, 30 May 2003); *fragmentation* – special interests, hobbies, campaigns, religion and ethnicity form the rallying point for the creation of a multiplicity of groups no longer so easily addressed by one blunderbuss mass medium. I will examine these features next.

The Expansion of Political Space and the
Compression of Political Time

Until relatively recently, the places, times and circumstances in which political leaders could communicate were very restricted (see Seymour-Ure, 2003).

Previously, institutional settings such as parliamentary chambers, official residences or foreign visits were largely outside the public's field of vision. They might read about parliamentary debates, but in Britain, for example, they couldn't hear their political leaders until the 1920s and they couldn't see them until 1988 when MPs approved the televising of parliament. The opening up of the places of public communication offers opportunities to leaders but also poses threats. It means that the communication dimensions and consequences of every action have to be considered as the distinction between private and public actions becomes increasingly blurred.

Take two examples. In July 2006, Israel commenced a punitive bombing campaign against the Shiite militia, Hezbollah, based in the Lebanon. At this time, the Spanish government leader, José Luis Zapatero, was photographed wearing the *kuffiyeh* (Palestinian scarf), bringing condemnation from the Spanish Jewish community. The photograph had been taken at a gathering of young Socialists and captured the moment – Zapatero quickly removed the scarf – when a young Palestinian had placed the scarf around the president's neck. Did Zapatero act deliberately knowing that the image would indicate his support of the Arabs and disapproval of Israel's action? His party denied that that was his purpose. However, the incident illustrated the ability of the media to fix a fleeting moment and convert it into an event of symbolic force. A second example is the reporting of former French President, Jacques Chirac's disparaging comments made to fellow world leaders at the 2005 G8 conference in which he said, 'The only thing they (the English) have ever done for European agriculture is mad cow disease' and 'One cannot trust people whose cuisine is so bad. After Finland, it is the country with the worst food.' The comments were overheard by French reporters and duly published in the French newspaper *Libération*. Political leaders find their every word, expression and gesture open to scrutiny.

These features of the media environment have a number of consequences for the conduct of politics and journalism which interact often to the detriment of both. I will consider these next.

The Importance of Image

One aspect of the changing relationship between the media and politicians is the increasing need to focus on leaders' images. As we saw earlier, image has always been central to leadership communication. But, in an age of ubiquitous technology, no leader can neglect the language of image in almost all places and at all times. Allegedly, the choice of Tony Blair as leader of the UK Labour Party in 1994 was made in part because he was more telegenic, had 'more media and public acceptability' than his main rival, Gordon Brown (Gould, 1998: 198).

The focus on image also requires government leaders to be sensitive to the personal areas of their lives, previously considered out of bounds. The gravitas and power of office do not protect office holders from the contumely of the masses. In the past, social conventions of deference and differing assessments of the relationship between the private, the social and the public placed certain aspects of leaders' private lives off limits. Excessive drinking was never an issue for Winston Churchill, but it became so for Charles Kennedy who, because of it, was forced to step down as leader of the British Liberal Democrat Party in 2005. It was unthinkable, for example, that the full extent of Franklin D. Roosevelt's disability would have been shown to the public in the 1930s or 1940s. Contrast this with the detailed medical bulletins and images of an ailing Pope John Paul II shown to the world in the years leading up to his death in 2005. However, even where there is a genuine wish for privacy – and a broad consensus about its legitimacy – politicians may still not be safe. Witness, for instance, the long-lens photos taken of the Clintons waltzing together in their bathing-suits on a secluded beach. Ironically, because of the increasing stage-management of even the most seemingly private of events, they were accused of having deliberately choreographed the photo opportunity (Clinton, 2004: 438).

This example highlights the risks of image making. Those politicians who appear to overplay the role of image, risk entering a hall of mirrors in which no one knows any more – perhaps not even them – what is real and what is contrived. On the other hand, an apparent contempt for image-making – the position taken by former Spanish prime minister, José María Aznar (1996–2004) – can be construed as equally contrived (Sanders, 2004) and, if it goes wrong, quite disastrous for communication purposes. In other words, as far as image-making is concerned, politicians are damned if they do and damned if they don't.

The Permanent Campaign

A second development is the arrival of the 'permanent campaign'. The techniques of election campaigns – gathering intelligence, targeting audiences, promoting messages, rapid rebuttal – have become part of the machinery of government. The ubiquity, speed and quantity of contemporary media have resulted in governments making substantial institutional and personal investments in communication, employing communication specialists to advise on strategy and carry out communication functions. In his speech to the Reuters Foundation just before stepping down as prime minister, Blair admitted as much:

> I am going to say something that few people in public life will say, but most know is absolutely true: a vast aspect of our jobs today – outside of the really major

decisions, as big as anything else – is coping with the media, its sheer scale, weight and constant hyperactivity. At points, it literally overwhelms. (12 June 2007)

As if to prove the point, 11 days later the Spanish government announced it would open a press centre at the prime minister's residence and workplace, La Moncloa, as part of the drive towards greater 'transparency' (Aizpeolea, 23 June 2007); Russia announced the opening of a press and information centre in January 2008. In reality, governments have little choice in a media-saturated environment other than to engage with the media. As Blair put it, for a politician 'not to have a proper press operation nowadays is like asking a batsman to face bodyline bowling without pads or headgear' (12 June 2007).

The permanent campaign is a fixture of governmental politics. Leaders and their advisors give considerable time to planning and implementing communication strategies. If they don't, they can find their policy agenda being knocked askew by opponents and the media. It was something that Bill Clinton felt he had got wrong when he became President in 1992: 'I gave almost no thought to how to keep the public's focus on my most important priorities, rather than on competing stories that, at the least would divert public attention from the big issues and, at worst, could make it appear I was neglecting those priorities' (2005: 467). As a result of the inattention to 'messaging', Clinton found the public agenda was being set by his political enemies and, in consequence, he was perceived through the prism of controversies related to an expensive haircut, an investigation into fraud at the White House Travel Office and his plan to allow gays to serve openly in the military. Inadequate time and thought given to communication means that government policy priorities fall off the radar screen, something no government can afford to happen.

Organizing Communication: The New Labour Experience

The expanding importance of multifaceted communication operations is a well-attested finding of political communication scholarship (see, for example, Seymour-Ure, 2003). From a preoccupation with effective parliamentary performances to the creation of the contemporary government communication machine, British politicians have responded – in a way similar to those in comparable liberal democracies – to the demands of the complex communication environment they inhabit. There are certain features of developments in Britain which make it worth closer study.

Blair's years of office (1997–2007) marked a particular intensity in the debates and controversy surrounding the issue of spin (see Chapter 3). These debates occurred in other countries (see Kurtz, 1998), but the amount of media, political and critical attention paid to them in Britain is perhaps unrivalled in other liberal democracies.[2] There are several reasons for this. First, Britain has an extraordinarily competitive media scene so that any subject elevated to the status of controversy or scandal is endlessly chewed over and analysed. Second, Blair and his team – as he himself acknowledged – were particularly preoccupied with effective communication when he won office. In Blair's words: 'We paid inordinate attention in the early days of New Labour to courting, assuaging, and persuading the media' (12 June 2007). His justification was that 'after 18 years of Opposition and the, at times, ferocious hostility of parts of the media, it was 'hard to see any alternative'. Third, the government of Blair's predecessor, John Major, had followed (probably more out of necessity than conviction) what might be called the apparently more traditional, information-focused Whitehall model of government communication (see Bale and Sanders, 2001) in contrast to New Labour's more modern and communication-focused 'Millbank' model. I will next examine the features of each model and the issues they pose for communicating government.

The Whitehall Model

Situated in the heart of London's administrative district, 'Whitehall' is a street that stands as a metonym for the cadre of civil servants who comprise Britain's administrative class and, by extension, the ethos of probity and political impartiality they are charged to uphold. As an ideal type, the Whitehall model of communication has a number of structural, environmental and cultural characteristics rooted in the development of twentieth-century UK government and politics which I shall examine next:

- **Structure**. As communication became a concern for government, civil servants were entrusted with its execution. War was a great spur to the development of communication or, perhaps more accurately, propaganda campaigns to rally support for war aims: the first Ministry of Information was established in 1918 and refounded in 1939. It was superseded by the creation of a non-ministerial department, the Central Office of Information (COI), responsible for communication and marketing services, and the creation of a cadre of information officers in 1949. This Government Information Service (GIS) was renamed the Government Information and Communication Service (GICS) in 1997 in response to an internal review recommending changes to government communication (see below).

    The growing significance of media relations was recognized with the appointment of the first chief press secretary in 1932 and, after Churchill unsuccessfully attempted to do without a press secretary in 1951, they became a permanent fixture of UK administrations. Two types of press secretary predominated: the first consisted of those who were recruited directly from the civil service and often had a journalistic background; they were most often used by Conservative governments. The second consisted of those who had been journalists and often had a party connection. This model was favoured more by Labour governments (see Seymour-Ure, 2003).

Whitehall communication consisted, then, of three central structural features:

The Chief Press Secretary (1932–1998)/Prime Minister's Official Spokesperson (1998–2001)/Prime Minister's Spokesperson. As occupied by a civil servant, this job has retained common functions. It was summed up by one of Blair's two civil service spokesmen from 2001 to 2007, Godric Smith, in the course of questioning during the Hutton Inquiry. He described it as being: 'to provide media advice to the Prime Minister as appropriate; to liaise with other Government departments on the coordination and presentation of Government policy; and probably most importantly to brief the press during Parliament in formal briefings at 11 o'clock and 3.45.'[3]

The corps of civil servants engaged in explaining government policy to the media known as the Government Information Service and, from 1997 until 2004, the Government Information and Communication Service.

The Central Office of Information providing press and publicity service and expertise to government bodies.

- **Environment**. The environmental features refer to the peculiarities of the British political press corps and its relationship to power. Organized from the late nineteenth century as the lobby, this group of accredited political journalists (see Chapter 12) was permitted to assist at Prime Minister Spokesperson's (PMS) briefings on a non-attributable basis only until 1998. From 2000 transcript summaries of the briefings became available online, allowing a little more light into a clubby, secretive world. Opacity had long characterized the Whitehall world and this was reflected in the ethos of the journalists who reported it, creating an environment where political news was often more about rumour than knowledge.

- **Culture**. The Whitehall approach to communication had three leading cultural features. The first refers to the generalist tradition of the civil service which prized general intellectual abilities above specialist skills (see James, 2005) and the second to the lowly status which communication work held compared to those engaged in policy matters.[4] In keeping with this, communication activities were considered best left in the hands of superior minds and capable technicians. Famed for his insouciant attitude to communication, the post-Second World War prime minister, Clement Atlee, for example, was only persuaded to have news agency tape machines at No. 10 when he found out they reported the cricket score (see Rose, 2001: 92).[5] The Whitehall model is characterized, finally, by a firm commitment to the possibility of a non-political, impartial approach to government communication. A Cabinet note submitted in 1985 attempted to sum up what this meant in practical terms for government information campaign spending, stating that:

- Publicity should be relevant to government responsibilities
- Content, tone and presentation should not be party political
- Cost should be justifiable. (Ingham, 1991: 368)

The Millbank Model

When the Labour party achieved office in 1997, the 'Millbank model' of communication created by the party in opposition was transferred from their Millbank headquarters to Downing Street. They found a communication service which they considered not fit for purpose and the head of the civil service established an internal review of government communication in 1997 (the Mountfield Review) which replaced the Government Information Service with the Government Information and Communication Service (GICS) to emphasize the need for a proactive approach to the communication of policy rather than the reactive answering of questions.[6] In my view, the Millbank model had four principal features:

- **Strong central control and coordination**
  This had been a principal characteristic of the communication regime instituted by Peter Mandelson and recommended by polling expert Philip Gould (1998) for the Labour general election campaigns. In practical terms, it meant that Mandelson took on a coordination role of communication and policy in the Cabinet Office. He and the newly appointed Chief Press Secretary, Alastair Campbell, decreed that 'all major interviews and media appearances, both print and broadcast, should be agreed with the No. 10 Press Office before any commitments are entered into. The policy content of all major speeches, press releases and new policy initiatives should be cleared in good time with the No. 10 private office; the timing and form of announcements should be cleared with the No. 10 Press Office' (cited in Mountfield, 1997: 7). To achieve these aims they set up the Strategic Communications Unit to monitor the media and collect data and intelligence; devise and advise on government communication strategies and coordinate communication across government.
- **Setting the agenda and proactivity**
  The Labour government exerted considerable effort to set the media and public agenda. In his evidence to a Commons Select Committee,

Campbell gave an example of what this meant: 'Today it was in the inter-ests of government communications that the main focus of today's news was Education Action Zones. I am pleased to say that that issue has led every single bulletin throughout the day. What you would not want is that happening on the same day as there was a major announcement by Frank Dobson [Health Minister] in relation to the Health Service' (Minutes of the Select Committee on Public Administration, 1998).

To help control the agenda, the government introduced *Agenda*, a com-puter system which came into operation on 25 February 1998. *Agenda* monitored events likely to have an effect on the day's news agenda and helped ensure that significant messages were not announced on the same day. The aim was to keep everyone on message with the Press Secretary as the lynchpin of this effort and government communicators taking a proactive role to get the government's messages out. Setting the agenda involved techniques such as repetition and 'trailing' – pre-announcing policy initiatives – to the media, building coverage before, during and after the actual initiative (see Barnett and Gaber, 2001: 102–25). Campbell explained this approach in a letter to the GIS which was subsequently leaked to *The Times* and published on 2 October 1997: 'The Government must lay down big messages around every event [...] There are three parts to any story – the build-up, the event and the follow through. My sense is that the middle of these three gets all the attention. There is insuf-ficient attention to advance publicity – the briefing of editors, feature writers and others both before and after.' This practice, perfectly appro-priate for an opposition party, could at times supplant the accepted constitutional convention that policy statements should be first announced in the House of Commons and brought several rebukes from the Commons' Speaker.

■ **Rapid and robust response**
In the leaked letter, Campbell asked department heads of information to 'raise their game' and went on to say: 'We should always know how big stories will be playing in the next day's papers. If a story is going wrong, or if a policy should be defended, we must respond quickly, confidently and robustly.' Observing the 1992 US presidential campaign, Labour's campaign advisor, Gould, had learnt the importance of rapid rebuttal in a 24-hour news cycle: 'Any political assertion, however false, can spread through this media jungle with the speed of a panther. The world of pol-itics is littered with assertions that are untrue, but are believed to be true because they were not effectively answered' (1998: 295).

Rapid response had been one of the characteristics of the Labour 1997 campaign. It was one of the main changes noted by a GNN head of region since the arrival of Campbell (interview with author, Smith, 14 March 2002). In the past, rebuttals were just not done and 'no comment' was an acceptable response; that was no longer the case with Campbell (interview with author, Smith, 14 March 2002).

Mandelson and Campbell carried robust rebuttal into government in ways some journalists found unacceptably close to bullying (Jones, 1997; 2001) or duplicity (Oborne, 2005). New Labour's approach to criticism was swift counter-attack and rebuttal, at times focusing on one inaccuracy as a way of undermining an entire story. This technique was seen to particularly controversial effect in Campbell's response to the BBC's report on the alleged 'sexing up' of the first Iraq dossier (September 2002).

- **Import of political staffers into the government machine**
One of the most significant changes introduced when Labour assumed power was the substantial increase in political appointees in government. Political advisers like civil servants are funded by the public purse, but unlike them may take a party political line on matters of policy and communication. Blair's time in government saw them rise to over 100 compared to 40 political advisors during his predecessor's administration. Not all were or are communication advisors but there were enough to cause, as we shall see, some tension in their relationship with civil servant communicators. Alastair Campbell's position was particularly noteworthy in that his appointment as chief press secretary (from 2001 director of communications and strategy) was in a political capacity but with powers – granted by a special order in council – to direct civil servants.

The Possibility of Non-Partisan Government Communication

The 'Millbankization' (see Gaber, 1998: 14) of government communication was in some ways, as even critics acknowledged (see Barnett and Gaber, 2001: 117–23), a necessary effort to modernize an antiquated communication machine. However, it also resulted, according to its critics, in a number of damaging consequences for the perception of government's integrity and, therefore, for public trust. The most trenchant critics allege that it undermined government's commitment both to parliamentary accountability and, in giving unelected officials such power, to public accountability, contaminating a civil servant's political neutrality with partisan aims (Jones, 2001: 242); it produced great centralization of control in Downing Street, and took 'trailing' as a way of governance (Ingham, 2003: 89); it spread scepticism about politics so that communication rather than policy substance became the obsession (Ingham, 2003: 64). In sum, on this account, it converted legitimate government communication into spin doctoring, 'helping to sustain a media culture that places the greatest value on speculation, exclusives and others devices for manufacturing news, rather than on the reporting and analysis of what has happened' (Jones, 2001: 207). These are serious accusations. One of the gravest – for the British political culture – was that of politicization. I will examine this next and discuss whether a non-partisan government communication service is a realistic ambition in the twenty-first century.

The Politicization Debate

As Mountfield put it in a note he subsequently wrote about the Labour government's communication controversies: 'The dread word 'politicization' was not much heard before the 1997 Election' (25 April 2002). Blair's prime-ministership was beset by this criticism. It was linked with the accusation that 'spin' – presentation of policy – had become the principal preoccupation of Blair's government. Indeed, 'spin' became the media leitmotif of Blair's time in office just as 'sleaze' had been for Major.

The concerns about politicization and spin are not entirely new. The controversies and discussion in the 1980s raged around the role of the COI and Margaret Thatcher's chief press secretary, Bernard Ingham. As the advertising and publicity agency, the COI's budget for these items rose significantly as it became involved in the costly campaigns to sell privatization (see Franklin, 2004). Ironically, as the shadow spokesman for Trade, Tony Blair became the chief opposition critic of these developments. Ingham himself was criticized for bullying, cultivating favourites among journalists and undermining government ministers through selective leaks.

In Major's time, there were few if any controversies of this kind. His chief press secretaries were all uncontroversial civil servants, who were scrupulous about not stepping over the political/governmental divide (see Bale and Sanders, 2001). However, there was a general recognition that government communication was in need of reform.

As we have seen, three developments were considered particularly controversial and conducive to the politicization of government communication during Blair's time.

First, the role of the director of communications and strategy, Alastair Campbell, was considered particularly troublesome. He was a special advisor not a civil servant, but was allowed to have a management role over civil servants. He was head of the Government Information and Communication Service (GICS), three 10 Downing Street departments (the press office, the strategic communications unit and the research and information unit) and, from 2002, the COI, an unprecedented accumulation of power for an unelected, political appointee. He was also accused of overbearing behaviour with ministers, accused of bullying and exercising favouritism with journalists and an overweening ambition to dominate media headlines.

The second development considered prejudicial to political neutrality was the influx and role of special advisers together with the departure of senior career civil servants. From the top 44 information posts, 25 had resigned or been replaced as at July 1999. Third, the emphasis on promoting coordinated, positive government policy messages sometimes, it was alleged, crossed the line of acceptable civil service practice by straying into party promotion rather than legitimate government publicity.

Did these developments amount to 'politicization' and, if they did, does it matter? To answer these questions, we first need to answer what is meant by 'politicization'.

Duty to Explain and Mission to Persuade

As we have seen, the British civil service has, including in its upper echelons, an ethos of political neutrality. This is almost unique in liberal democracies. Apart from Canada, in every other country governments make political appointments to the top and often second- and third-tier jobs in their administrations (Mountfield, 25 April 2002). In Britain all civil servants are expected to serve governments of all political stripes, providing advice and analysis on how best to achieve their policy goals. With regard to communication of government policy, the Mountfield Report declared that:

> It is entirely proper to present and describe the policies of a Minister, and to put forward the Minister's justification in defence of them, and this may have the effect of advancing the aims of the political Party in Government. It is not, however, proper to justify or defend these policies in Party political terms, to use political slogans, expressly to advocate policies as those of a particular political Party or directly attack (though it may be necessary to respond to in specific terms) policies and opinions of Opposition Parties and groups. (November 1997)

This is clearly a fine line and one may ask why trying to maintain and police it matters. The simple answer is trust. One approach to building trust, clearly not the only one, is political neutrality. The point of the British civil service's political neutrality is that it can provide some kind of counterweight to a political party's tendency, even in government, to see itself as having principally a mission to persuade rather than a duty to explain. Politicians are in the business of persuasion and this does not change when they assume power. Governments also have the duty to explain to citizens and this may sometimes be complex, uncomfortable and full of risks. It can be argued, as I will do at the close of the chapter, that an emphasis on explanation is the most persuasive form of communication in an information-rich environment. However, where persuasion becomes the principal communication value, it can come into conflict with that of explanation. Certainly, there is no doubt that New Labour placed a notable emphasis on persuasive communication. As the head of the civil service put it in his evidence to Parliament: 'There is a more systematic determined effort to coordinate, in a strategic way, presentation of the Government's policies and messages in a positive light across the whole of government, than I can remember since I have been in the Senior Civil Service' (Wilson, 1998, para 18). This process was facilitated by the three developments outlined above and, to the extent that as a result the duty to explain consistently played second fiddle, then I think it is reasonable to suggest there was a politicization of government communication during Campbell's time in office until his resignation in 2003.

Trust and Government Communication

'Propaganda of all shades' is how Bush's communication management of the 'war on terrorism' came to be categorized, reflecting the view that what lay behind his government's communication strategies was mere manipulation of public opinion (Hiebert, 2003: 243).

A similar panorama occurred in Britain. The aftermath of Blair's attempts to persuade the British public of the case for the Iraq war from the publication of the September 2002 dossier on Iraq's weapons of mass destruction to the suicide of Dr Kelly in July 2003 'reinforced an already growing public distrust of government communication' (Stanyer, 2004: 433). In the aftermath of Kelly's suicide, Campbell resigned (29 August 2003) and an independent review, the Phillis Commission, was established with a remit to 'conduct a radical review of government communications'.[7]

Published in 2004, the Phillis Report recommended that communication be based on the following seven principles:

1. Openness, not secrecy.
2. More direct, unmediated communications to the public.
3. Genuine engagement with the public as part of policy formation and delivery, not communication as an afterthought.
4. Positive presentation of government policies and achievements, not misleading spin.
5. Use of all relevant channels of communication, not excessive emphasis on national press and broadcasters.
6. Coordinated communication of issues that cut across departments, not conflicting or duplicated departmental messages.
7. Reinforcement of the Civil Service's political neutrality, rather than a blurring of government and party communications.

The recommendations, accepted by government, included the creation of the Government Communication Network (GCN), headed by a permanent civil servant responsible for establishing standards of excellence and training for the civil service corps. Campbell's powers to instruct civil servants were abolished.

The re-establishment of something more like the Whitehall model was consolidated by Gordon Brown's appointment of a civil servant as his director of communications and official spokesman on becoming prime minister in June 2007. A political press adviser was also appointed and, in 2008, a non-civil servant director of strategy and principal adviser, responsible for advising on communication (see Figure 6.1).

Ethical codes and principles of good practice were buttressed. The Civil Service Code, introduced in 1996 to govern the work of civil servants was revised in 2006. It was supplemented by *Propriety Guidance* which sets out the expected standards of behaviour for those working in government communication based on the following general conventions regarding communication which:

- should be relevant to government responsibilities;
- should be objective and explanatory, not biased or polemical;
- should not be – or liable to be – misrepresented as being party political; and
- should be conducted in an economic and appropriate way, and should be able to justify the costs as expenditure of public funds.

An example of unacceptable practice would be: 'if a speech by a minister included an attack on their political opponents, it would be improper for the department to issue it as an official text. The political attack would have to be omitted from the official release. If the minister wished the full speech to be issued, it would have to come from the press office of the political party' (*Propriety Guidance*).

The ethical turn showed that the spin label had done its damage. What seemed to have occurred was expressed by Mountfield (25 April 2002): '"spinning" has so far over-reached itself that it has become almost counter-productive, and [...] a self-correcting mechanism is therefore at work.' In other words, a law of diminishing returns operates when politicians at least allow the perception to spread that they greatly care about presentation: journalists seek ever harder to penetrate what they deem to be the 'reality' behind the appearance; the public becomes ever more distrustful of what they are being told – and are prone to believe – is a game of smoke and mirrors.

However, is it naive to imagine that government communication can ever be truly politically neutral? As the distinguished political columnist, Hugo Young, put it (29 July 2003): 'Few official facts and figures are politically

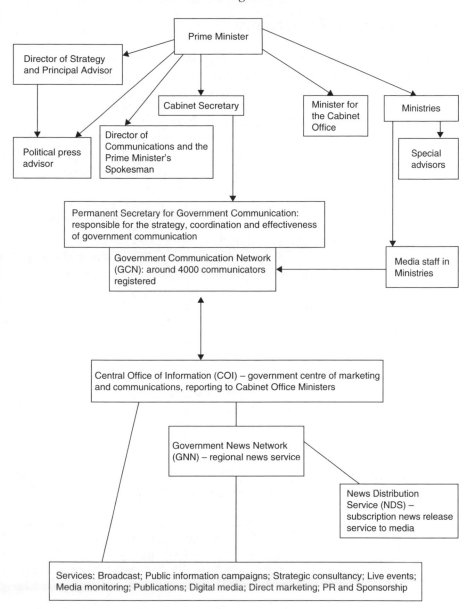

Figure 6.1   British government communication 2008

neutral, and none is incapable of manipulation one way or the other. In the struggle to capture the public mind, spinning is the most elementary weapon.'

How can governments get it right? How can they communicate effectively, a legitimate aim, and not yet be accused of sophistry?

Communicating Effectively

Communicating effectively in the contemporary media environment is no easy matter. Before considering what effective communication is, I will outline three basic elements governments need to have in place.

- **Experienced media operators and specialists**
  No government can do without experienced, tough staff able to deal with the media on their own terms. In this sense, much of the criticism of Campbell's robust style seems overdone. The world of political journalism is not for the faint-hearted. It thrives on failure, crisis and scandal. It is no wonder, then, that those who observe this world do not doubt that a Campbell-like figure is necessary. In the view of *The Guardian*'s Hugo Young (29 July 2003):
  `Sitting in government, watching quite a lot of political journalism chasing itself in a downward spiral of propaganda, innuendo and competitive truth-stretching, in a context that assumes the worst motive for every political act or speech or alliance, could anyone disagree that every prime minister will need an Alastair, fighting back on their behalf?'

  Managing communication involves knowledge of what works and what doesn't. On a trip to Russia it took just one glance from Campbell for Blair, who was hanging from a strap on a Moscow underground train, to adjust his position (interview with Jones, 26 November 2002).
  Managing an organization's presentation sensibly include the kind of rules devised by John Major's former press secretary (see Figure 6.2) for media relations.

  The employment of those with specialist communication knowledge is also now a necessary part of sensible organizational practice. Indeed, it is perhaps ironic that after heralding Gordon Brown's changes to the communication structure *The Guardian* had asked, 'WILL GORDON STOP

1. Be accessible	8. Try to make news; speak in
2. Be helpful	memorable, useable phrases
3. Be friendly but know the relationship is adversarial	9. Don't waste time remonstrating with the press
4. Don't waffle	10. Make sure the terms of briefing are
5. Don't lie	clear and usually have everything
6. Don't have favourites	on the record
7. Take journalists seriously	

Always try to ensure that communication is at the heart of policy making.

Figure 6.2   Ten Commandments of media relations
Source: Sir Christopher Meyer, Press Secretary to Prime Minister John Major, Ambassador to Washington (1997–2003) and head of the UK Press Complaints Commission, 12 October 2004, University of Sheffield.

THE SPIN? (16 June 2007). When he became Prime Minister a year later, it was being reported by the Daily Mail that 'GORDON BROWN HIRES SPIN DOCTOR TO STOP VISUAL GAFFES' (7 April 2008).

Communicating effectively is not only about media relations It also requires media monitoring, audience research and the understanding of new media as well as understanding the importance of strategy, tactics, coordination, speed, data and intelligence.

■ **Strategy and tactics**

The word derives from the Greek *stratēgos*, which referred to a 'military commander', and is about designing long-term actions to achieve a specific goal. Clinton described the difficulty of getting messages heard in the contemporary media environment: 'We [...] didn't give messaging anything close to the amount of the attention that we had in the election, though it's harder in government, even for the President, to get out the message you want every day [...] everything happens at once, and any controversy is more likely to dominate the news than a policy decision, no matter how important the decision might be' (Clinton, 2005: 468).

Communicating – even to the extent of just being heard – requires the design of strategy and appropriate tactics: the timing of announcements, creating grids to ensure stories do not overlap, maintaining contacts, providing photo opportunities. More questionably, there are also tactics for avoiding what one might not wish to be the focus of media attention. 'There is nothing new in government spin doctors releasing bad news when the attention of the press is focused elsewhere', claimed one former spin doctor in a commentary on the Jo Moore case. 'Every press officer in Whitehall has done it – and so have most ministers' (Wegg Prosser, 9 October 2001, *The Guardian*). This kind of tactic has to be weighed against the loss of credibility it can produce.

Timeliness – announcing policies and reacting to crises, responding as and when appropriate – is at the heart of all effective communication and requires careful tactical thought. Repeat announcements dressed up as new policy can undermine trust in government communication; slow responses can allow a problem to become a crisis. It will be difficult to get the strategies and tactics right without coordinated communication based on good intelligence and accurate data.

■ **Coordination, intelligence and data**

Tight coordination 'is really common-sense, if inconvenient for journalists trying to make a story from inconsistent reports from different sources' (Mountfield, 2002). Joined-up government is difficult without joined-up communication and, although it can smack of authoritarianism or 'control freakery' (see Jones, 2001), it is difficult to see what the alternative to coordination might be especially in the high-speed world of modern media where rumour hardens into fact in a matter of minutes. As Blair put it (12 June 2007): 'You have to respond to stories also in real time. Frequently the problem is as much assembling the facts as giving them'.

Mechanisms for gathering data rapidly and accurately, for using intelligence prudently (the mistake with the September 2002, Iraq dossier) and for providing some independent validation for the data provided are all key to effective communication.

Finally, what do I mean by effective communication? For government communication to be effective, speciously persuasive communication is not enough. This is the great lesson of Blair's time in office. For all the initial success in controlling the agenda, in ensuring a more organized communication operation, the mismatch between rhetoric and reality undermined the government's trustworthiness. The use of a language of targets, statistics, czars who were going to fix social problems, increased investment in health and education conflated real government action with achieved reality. Effective communication, then, should inspire trust and to do this it must know and listen more to its audience. Without an aspiration to trustworthiness, communication specialists might successively put a positive gloss on the news but they won't be believed.

Democratizing Communication

The perceived breakdown of trust between government, the media and the public was the background to the work of the Phillis Review. As mentioned earlier, one of its main recommendations was the creation of the Government Communication Network (GCN), tasked:

- To provide overall strategic direction and leadership on cross–government issues
- To integrate communication into policy
- To set standards and advise on propriety
- To deliver a regional media handling service to departments and agencies through the Government News Network (GNN)
- To deliver media monitoring services across government through the Media Monitoring Unit (MMU)

It also re-affirmed the importance of maintaining the political neutrality of civil servants.

Four main themes emerged from their report, later explored in a speech by the first head of the GCN, Howell James (20 January 2005), about the place and character of communication in government:

- **Communication as integral to good government**
  The basic premise is that good governance requires serious attention to communication, integrated into the heart of policy-making and not thought of as optional add on.

- **Communication as an area of expertise and knowledge**
  For this to be so, government must be able to draw on well-trained professionals, expert in the various tasks of communication – marketing, e-communication, press relations – who are attuned to their audience's needs.
- **Communication as dialogue and debate**
  Both Phillis and James emphasized the importance of government communication paying more attention to listening to the public and other stakeholders, developing regional and local networks, building a more interactive approach through new media and using web-based strategies to communicate with citizens. These are the kinds of strategies already being rolled out through e-governance,[8] initiatives found extensively throughout South-East Asia and pioneering countries like Lithuania. However, the suggestion is that government communicators have to do more than just enable the public to fill out their tax form online but also genuinely engage them in the early stages of policy development.
- **Communication as trustworthy and credible**
  All governments are political and are engaged in persuasion. They are also, however, the guardian of a public trust, responsible for the provision of key data about the economy, law and order, education and health in which citizens need to be able to have confidence. In examining how to restore public confidence, the Phillis Review concluded that: 'The tradition of Civil Service impartiality is a key bulwark on which to rebuild trust, and steps need to be taken to preserve and reinforce it' (2004: 2). This is not the only way to ensure that government communication is trustworthy. Indeed, without additional mechanisms laying down appropriate principles, practice and procedures, it is unlikely that even civil service impartiality would succeed in restoring public trust.

  The issue of trust was highlighted by a survey by the Office of National Statistics which showed that 68 per cent of the public thinks official figures are changed to support politicians' arguments and 59 per cent that government uses them dishonestly (see Toynbee, 22 November 2005). All Labour's attempts to build trust through independent league tables and audited figures had come to naught. For, as the political analyst Polly Toynbee stated: 'Politics is an art, not a statistical science. Belief […] is a matter of engaging emotions that intersect only glancingly with fact. Everyone has a dangerous taste for facts that suit their beliefs – but everyone starts with belief' (22 November 2005). Her damning conclusion was that, as Blair's time as prime minister drew to a close, belief in Labour's political projects had also ebbed away so that 'Current absence of trust is also a symptom of lack of things to believe in.'

7

Communication in Opposition, Protest and Violence

Introduction

This chapter examines the *communication strategies* of a variety of actors who are, legally or illegally, *in opposition to the established governing powers*. It will explore the role and strategies *of political opposition groups* as well as *protest movements* seeking political change.

It may seem perverse to include groups using violence and terror to attain their political goals in a discussion about communication. However, the reality of *global terrorism* is that the organizations involved are *highly sophisticated political communicators*. Brute force may be their method, but they are also intent on telling very specific stories.

The Challenges of Opposition

In democratic politics, it is inevitable that there will be political parties without power who seek it. In some countries – Britain and Canada, for example – the main political party not in office holds a constitutionally defined position as the main 'Opposition' party (in Britain, it is known as 'Her Majesty's Official Opposition'). The possibility of gaining power offered at election time directs a great proportion of opposition effort into planning, funding and implementing election campaigns. However, if their effort is restricted to election time, they are likely to be left behind in the race for power, a race in which the incumbent usually has a head start (see Trent and Friedenberg, 2004: 81–99). The advantages for the incumbent lie in the economic, political and symbolic resources at his or her disposal. These can, of course, be offset by the reality check placed on performance by the incumbent's actual record in office.

Challengers for public office have to employ a two-pronged strategy requiring them, first, to convince the electorate that change is necessary, and second, that the electorate should trust him or her to bring it about. Creating both perceptions takes considerable time, especially when the opposition leader is a relative unknown or the party was kicked out of office for perceived policy failures. Oppositions must use a kind of 'soft power' to achieve their purposes (see Nye, 2004), persuading voters to support them not through coercion, threat or direct financial incentives but through 'an attraction to shared values, and the justness and duty of contributing to the achievement of those values' (Nye, 2004). Communication is key: communicating the values, style and goals of the opposition – the party and its leader – in well thought-out actions are a *sine qua non* for winning power. However, it is also true that communicating effectively is only half the story, as UK Labour leader, Neil Kinnock, found out in the 1987 election campaign. His party had begun to use effective communication strategies but, on the one hand, the policies were simply not popular with the electorate (see Gould, 1998) and, on the other, the leader still lacked credibility. In Aristotelian terms, the *ethos* (the source of the message) was not convincing.

Opposition parties commonly use a number of communication strategies (Trent and Friedenberg, 2005: 99–111) and, as with all political communication, timing and knowing the audience are essential in ensuring their success. Calls for change and repeated attacks on the incumbent throughout the election cycle without an accompanying positive story may not give voters the reasons they need to vote for a challenger. Telling a story that does not resonate will also end in failure and leaving it to an election campaign to articulate a compelling political narrative is almost certainly too late. Opposition parties need to perform a difficult trick: keep their own side on board while at the same time convincing swing voters – the approximately 10 per cent who decide elections – who didn't vote for them last time. I will next examine what I consider to be four key ingredients in a challenger's approach to the task of convincing the people that change is necessary and that he or she is the right one to carry it out.

Telling a Coherent Story

Opposition parties often have to throw off the shackles of past failures and loss of popularity as government parties – the case of the US Democrats when they fought to regain power in 1992 – or perceptions of unsuitability for office – the case of the British Labour party in its wilderness years of the 1980s and early 1990s. One of their first tasks is to convince the electorate that they have changed, that they have a convincing political project and that this somehow draws on their best traditions: in other words, they must have a coherent story to tell about themselves. The British Labour Party managed this with great success in the late 1990s, finally convincing the electorate that the party had indeed changed, that it offered an attractive project while at the same time remaining true to itself. Of course context and personalities matter too. New Labour's landslide victory in 1997 could not have been achieved without the unpopularity of the governing Conservative Party and the credibility engendered by Blair's leadership.

Imitating New Labour's strategy, the new British Conservative leader, David Cameron, declared in an article in the *Spectator* magazine in October 2005 that under his leadership, 'the Conservative Party will look, feel, think and behave like a completely new party.' Two years later, his deputy, George Osborne, declared that the party was the 'heir to Blair'. The risk of this approach is that the challenger's traditional supporters may wonder whether it is any longer *their* party. In other words, challengers who wish to suggest they have changed must be clear about how they have changed, why they have changed and how these changes relate to their defining identity. Simply executing political and communication strategies suggesting change that are not accompanied by clear policy messages can make opposition parties appear muddled. This was the view of a Thatcherite critic of the Cameron approach: 'In the Eighties, the Conservative Party under Margaret Thatcher was obsessive about changing Britain. Today, the Conservative Party is merely obsessive about changing itself' (Harris, 2 June 2007). A member of Cameron's team saw matters differently: 'We have learned something important during the long years in opposition. It is no good having lots of policy detail if people aren't listening. And they only listen if we get the tone right' (Giddens and Willett, May 2007). Nevertheless, heeding criticism of this approach and poll evidence suggesting that voters saw him as 'lightweight',[1] Cameron set out his vision for Britain in a speech (18 June 2007) full of triggers (or what have been patronizingly called 'dog whistles'[2]), evoking themes dear to the party faithful.

Spain's main conservative party, *Partido Popular* (PP), followed a rather different strategy after its loss of power in March 2004, following the Madrid train bombings in which 191 people were killed. Its leader, Mariano Rajoy, pursued policy themes which buttressed the established view of PP as the party that takes a robust, uncompromising line on terrorism, security and the unity of Spain. There was no suggestion that the party was seeking to renew itself as it retained in top party positions two former ministers from the government that lost power in 2004.

Attacking the Government's Record and Calling for Change

Oppositions are expected to examine and criticize the government's actions and policies. It is what they should do. Where they don't, it is usually the sign of a weak and divided party (the British Conservatives from 1997 to 2004) or an over-powerful executive (Russia from Putin's time in office in 2000). Attacking a governing party's record is a stock weapon in the opposition's armoury. However, it can be a strategy with diminishing returns if used indiscriminately. A common public complaint about politicians is the 'ya-boo' style of politics where politicians are seen as squabbling schoolchildren uninterested in the common good.

The main Spanish opposition party took the defence of Spain as the central plank of a policy designed to make the governing Socialist Party's relationship with the country's regional parties and, above all, its policy towards the Basque country appear to be betrayals of Spain. Accusing the government of selling out to ETA terrorism and compromising the country's territorial integrity, the PP supported or called a number of massive street protests in early 2007 'not in defence of a party nor an ideology but [...] in defence of Spain' (Rajoy, 21 March 2007). This tactic was clearly aimed at shoring up its core support as well as winning over those swing voters unconvinced by the Socialist Party's record on security.

Attacking the government's record necessarily implies a call for change. The change demanded usually involves a number of elements: it tends to be forward looking – John Kennedy wanted to get the country moving again; it often appeals to older traditions so that Margaret Thatcher, for example, while implementing a radical package of reforms when in office, spoke of wanting to make Britain great again; in some cases, the challenger is positioned as being from outside the political class, ready to shake up the political establishment. Silvio Berlusconi used this tactic to win the Italian elections in 1994 and again in 2008; Jimmy Carter emphasized his non-Beltway status to win the post-Watergate election of 1977.

Keeping it General, Central and Upbeat

Challengers can enjoy the luxury of not having to spell out the specifics of their policy positions on the range of issues candidates are expected to pronounce on. Being too precise offers too many hostages to fortune as the Labour Party learnt to its cost in the 1992 elections. They produced a detailed account of their tax proposals allowing the Conservatives to scare voters with attack ads headlined 'Labour's Tax Bombshell' and 'Double Whammy-more taxes, higher prices'. Astute opposition campaigners keep it general: Franklin D. Roosevelt never spelt out the details of his 'New Deal' and Germany's Angela Merkel was criticized for following a similar tactic in her 2005 campaign. As *Spiegel* (20 June 2005) reported it: 'So far, she hasn't said much about what she stands for. And it's intentional. The less she says, so goes the strategy, the fewer flanks she'll leave open for attack. But many think she's setting herself up for failure.' The critics were proved wrong.

In American politics positioning oneself in the ideological centre has been an effective challenger's strategy. Bill Clinton's 'Big Tent' politics,

emphasizing the inclusivity, flexibility and pragmatism of his political platform, has been imitated in a number of Western democracies, not least by
Tony Blair who himself has found imitators. The UK's Conservative leader,
David Cameron, made it one of his main strategic aims to situate himself as
the occupier of the political centre ground. In part, this is about parties identifying the central issues preoccupying voters and formulating policies and
communication actions that show they have understood. Early in his leadership, Cameron staged a photo opportunity above the Arctic Circle on a
dogsled to show his concern with ecological issues and issued his appeal to
show love and understanding to disaffected adolescents. His political rivals
labelled it his 'hug a hoodie' proposal (see BBC, 10 July 2006), but it effectively communicated to voters that the Conservatives were listening to public concerns about the environment and moving away from the 'flog' em
and hang 'em' image. This strategy has its risks and often needs to run as a
twin-track approach in which party traditionalists receive reassurance.
Cameron was forced to do this after causing consternation in his party
when he appeared to abandon the Conservatives' policy on selective education (see Hennessy, 17 June 2007).

Creating Credibility

Voters form impressions of politicians through a variety of means including
direct or vicarious experience and facts known about them. There is a far
greater cache of information to be drawn upon for incumbents allowing
them to play the credibility card: their experience makes them a safer bet.
For challengers, this is normally not so easily the case (except where a former incumbent is challenging again for power), but they have the advantage of having more of a blank slate to draw upon. Communication scholars
have found (see Chapter 12) that voters seek a number of attributes in their
leaders including competence flowing from trustworthiness and expertise
(bestowing credibility), integrity (related to perceptions of character, who
the person really is) and leadership capacity (related among other things to
charisma and dynamism).

Establishing the first of these attributes – credibility – is key for all politicians; a long tradition of research has shown that highly credible sources are
more persuasive than those that are not (Hovland, Kelly and Kelley 1953).
Here opposition politicians may be at a disadvantage. Incumbents can use
scare tactics playing on the 'Better the devil you know' mentality that seeks
the security of the tried and tested over the inexperienced. However, this tactic can be countered by opposition politicians in two ways; namely using
strategies to establish, first, trustworthiness based on character, and second,
leadership capacity based on charisma and dynamism. Barack Obama

employed these tactics in his campaign against Hilary Clinton for the Democrat presidential nomination in 2007. His positive vision and high integrity were skilfully expressed in his best-selling book *The Audacity of Hope* (2007). Providing an upbeat vision for the future is an effective way of suggesting dynamism, of creating the impression of an active, positive leader.

Of course, opposition style strategies can be co-opted by incumbents. In the 2000 US presidential campaign, the vice president, Al Gore, chose to distance himself from Clinton not wishing to be judged guilty by association with his President's scandals. Nicolas Sarkozy similarly distanced himself from his predecessor, Jacques Chirac, in the 2007 French presidential elections. Even though both men had held high office in their country's government and were running as the government party's candidate for pragmatic electoral reasons, they decided to use challenger strategies, positioning themselves as the candidates for change, with rather more success in Sarkozy's case than Gore's.

Protest Politics

In democratic societies knowledge and information sources, systems and networks disperse power in ways unthinkable before the developments of, for example, the internet (1983), the World Wide Web (1991), the mobile phone (1983) and Google (1996). Even non-democratic governments are challenged in their attempts to contain and control knowledge and information.[3] This allows far greater scope for the exercise of soft power by non-government groups. Groups seeking political power have a more restricted range of communicational strategies open to them compared to those holding power who generally control the lion's share of resources. However, all persuasive communication is about the use of what Joseph Nye has called 'soft power', a concept he borrowed from Antonio Gramsci (1891–1937), the Italian Marxist theorist. Gramsci considered that coercive or 'hard' power was the domain of the state and consensual or 'soft' power that of civil society, the latter achieved by cultural means such as the media, theatre, education and so on. Each establishes a kind of hegemony; soft power frequently buttresses that of the state but it can also be the means by which countervailing values are established. At the beginning of the twenty-first century, the US government's use of hard power in invading Iraq is a stark example of how coercive power is insufficient when the tide of soft power flows against it. The Iraq invasion showed not only the limitations of hard power but also undermined the United States' status as a hegemonic soft power. As Gardels put it: 'Much of America's winning story which accounted for it being a soft superpower – human rights, the rule of law, an historic liberator instead of occupier – was further undercut by the images of humiliation, torture and sexual abuse at Abu Ghraib prison' (2005).

Soft power strategies have become ever more attractive particularly to oppositional groups who need to be able to get their message out and use narrative power to obtain their objectives. Contemporary information technologies permit groups and individuals to form global coalitions and have their voices heard with greater ease. The Mexican Zapata movement represents one of the earliest examples of an opposition group effectively using information technology to build a worldwide alliance (see Castells, 1996).

As Nye puts it: 'the information revolution is creating virtual communities and networks that cut across national borders. Transnational corporations and nongovernmental actors will play larger roles. Many of those organizations will have soft power of their own as they attract citizens into coalitions that cut across national boundaries' (2004). He argues that the sharing of information and credibility become increasingly sources of power as the balance shifts towards those groups who can use 'multiple channels of communication [...] to frame issues', and have 'cultural customs and ideas that are close to prevailing global norms and credibility that is enhanced by values and policies' (Nye, 2004). This rather generalized diagnosis can be examined in examples demonstrating the communication processes and models at work in mass peaceful protest.

Mass Peaceful Protest

At the end of four days of peaceful action by millions of Filipinos the authoritarian regime of Ferdinand Marcos had been overthrown and Corazon Aquino had become the first woman president of the Republic. The 1986 Philippine People Power Revolution[4] was a mostly peaceful mass demonstration and showed that sheer might of numbers could, in certain circumstances, demonstrate the illegitimacy of certain kinds of power. The Philippine protests took place in a decade of oppositional action to entrenched powers in Eastern and Central Europe and in the People's Republic of China. The Gandhian principle of *Satyagraha* – from the Sanskrit 'holding on to truth' – conceives non-violent protest as a moral imperative, directed to bringing about a change of heart in those to whom the protests are directed. The protestors seek to communicate, to signify through their actions the need for change and this can be effectively achieved where two principles are at work. The first is what social psychologists call the principle of social proof which states that we establish what is correct in behaviour, attitudes or beliefs by finding out what other people think is correct. The more people who are thought to hold something as correct, the more effectively does the principle of social proof function (see Cialdini, 1993: 99–142). Organizers of mass protests and demonstrations always stress the highest figures in calculations of turnout. On the one hand, weight of numbers is thought to imply democratic legitimacy and on the other, it is an application of the social proof principle. However, for this principle to be effective, publicity must be achieved for the action and it must be communicated to third parties. The lack of images and control of information by the Chinese authorities about the repression of the 1989 Tiananmen Square protests greatly confined their national effect. However, their symbolic power is attested to by the Chinese government's continued attempts to prevent all public mention of them.[5] In the West, the iconic image of the lone student standing in the path of a tank as well as the reporting of foreign correspondents tarnished the Chinese government's image.

Communication is essential to non-violent action and works on a number of levels. Martin and Varney (2003) have outlined the following dimensions of non-violence as communication:

- Conversion, persuasion, symbolic action: dialogue with opponents
- Power equalization via non-cooperation and intervention: preparation for dialogue with opponents
- Mobilization of third parties: the chain of non-violence
- Collective empowerment: dialogue within activist groups
- Individual empowerment: inner dialogue

In late 2004, Ukrainians who disputed the results of their country's presidential vote overthrew them in what became known as the Orange Revolution after the colour adopted by the main opposition party, led by Viktor Yushchenko.

The Ukrainian protestors were adroit choreographers of their actions: their perseverance in the cold winter weather, the festive air of the crowds entertained by rock music and puppet shows and the appearance of Lech Walesa, the seasoned Polish Solidarity leader, gave credibility to the opposition's claim that theirs was a moral protest against the corruption and intimidation of the electoral process. The images of protest acted as the symbolic correlate of the rightness of the cause, as they were beamed across the world showing the appropriate visual and sound accoutrements of banners, flags, slogans, music and song as well as the presence of iconic and legitimizing personalities.

Web Warriors and Subversive Texters

Described as a 'cliché of online political activism' (Russell, 2005: 560), the Zapatista Army of National Liberation (*Ejército Zapatista de Liberación Nacional*, EZLN) began their armed revolt against the Mexican government in 1994, seeking social justice for the long neglected and impoverished people of Chiapas. Supported by the indigenous population, the group attempted to inform the Mexican people of their cause in eloquent communiqués and letters which the mainstream media refused to publish. Using the internet they began to get their message out, building support in urban areas as well as an international web of campaigners, partly established by the astute myth-making surrounding *Subcomandante* Marcos (see Russell, 2005).

EZLN provides early evidence for how digital communications can allow protest groups greater autonomy from the mainstream media, allowing them to subvert and bypass them using the internet. In Castells's analysis (1996) network power lies in users' ability to control their messages and to construct identities unshackled by pre-network constraints of time and space. Political protestors can create network identities – the anti-globalization protestors are a good example – that the professional mediators or the politicians find difficult to co-opt. The Zapatistas were very effective in doing this, garnering considerable overseas support and coming to be seen as part of the wider anti-globalization, anti-neoliberalism movement.

The internet creates opportunity structures. This was demonstrated by the events following the March 2004 Madrid bombings (see Canel and Sanders, 2004; Sampedro, 2005). Speculation about the government's attempts to promote the thesis that ETA was responsible for the attacks and to keep information from the public spread like wildfire on the internet, undermining efforts by government spokespeople to demonstrate that they were being as transparent as possible. The internet and mobile phone text messages were also the vehicle for the mass mobilization of opponents of the government party, who demonstrated outside their offices accusing ministers and the outgoing prime minister, José María Aznar, of lying. These were, to say the least, unhelpful images for the governing party's reputation just a few days before the election of a new government.

Meme Warfare and Culture Jams

Global protest or activism, largely targeted against companies perceived as exploitative or hegemonic, have made highly effective use of varied media, including the internet, for what have become known as meme warfare and culture jams (see Pickerel, Jorgensen and Bennett, 2002). One of the pioneers of this kind of media-geared action is Kalle Lasn, editor of *Adbusters* magazine. This group engages in 'culture jamming', the subversive reworking of messages, advertising on billboards or the internet, for example, to undermine what is being promoted. According to Pickerel, Jorgensen and Bennett: 'The basic unit of communication in culture jamming is the meme: the core unit of cultural transmission. Memes are condensed images that stimulate visual, verbal, musical, or behavioral associations that people can easily imitate and transmit to others' (2002). One much cited example is the Nike 'swoosh'.

Meme warriors transfigure it to awaken associations that undermine the dynamic, 'cool' message Nike is seeking to transmit. One activist took Nike at its word that it would provide customized running shoes. His request was for the word 'sweatshop' to be imprinted on his Nike shoes. When the company refused, the news spread in viral fashion around the internet.

Waking people up from their media consumer-induced trance is one of the objectives of those who use the methods of meme warfare and culture jams. They use the power of symbolic surprise, often laced with humour, to puncture our ordinary expectations and alert us to the often unsavoury reality that underlies some of our consumption choices.

The Limitations of Soft Power

In September 2007 Burmese monks took to the streets in their thousands to protest against the dictatorial rule of the generals and call for the introduction of democracy. The images of saffron-robed monks peacefully showing their disapproval of the regime were powerful reminders of Burma's plight and yet, despite the hope they awoke, they were unable to fulfil their aim. The protests were brutally put down and the leader of the democratic opposition put under house arrest. Soft power has its limits, especially when the settled order is exploitative or simply concerned with the maintenance of its power at any cost.

The methods of the Burmese monks are poles apart from those I will consider next. The monks protested peacefully and sought to project their message of defiance to the Burmese public and to the wider world. The media were key. One of the first actions of the Burmese military government was to close down communication, shutting down internet and mobile networks. For terrorists too the media are central to their strategy and, as we shall discuss next, they have become expert at adapting their tactics to the logic of a media age.

The Unholy Trinity: Politics, Violence and the Media

Is terrorism a form of political communication? This is novelist Martin Amis's view. He described the 9/11 attacks as 'political communication by other means' (September 2001). Here I will examine this question as well as the symbiotic relationship of terrorism and communication. I will examine these issues with particular reference to the Madrid 2004 bombings and the government communication response.

The Meaning of Terrorism

'Terrorism' and 'terrorist' are contested, value-laden terms which the media often use inconsistently. So, for example, the BBC would routinely refer to the IRA as a 'terrorist' organization while, in its coverage of the Madrid bombings, it described ETA as a 'Basque separatist group'. Definitions abound but one common element is that it involves violence or the threat of violence. A useful definition is that formulated by Nacos who describes terrorism as: 'violence for political ends against non-combatants/innocents with the intent to win publicity [...] for the sake of communicating messages to a larger audience' (2002: 19). A caveat should be entered here. Terrorism does not only seek publicity. It seeks a number of goals including (see Norris, Kern and Just, 2003: 7–9):

- Spreading fear and anxiety among the public
- Destroying opponents and symbolic targets
- Achieving publicity for a cause
- Advancing demands
- Undermining opponents
- Mobilizing and reinforcing support
- Polarizating of opinion
- Demonstrating of the movement's strength
- Underlining the weakness of the state

The Peruvian Maoist group *Sendero Luminoso* waged a campaign in Peru in the late 1980s and early 1990s aimed at spreading fear about the imminent collapse of the state and demonstrating their own strength. ETA's assassination of Spain's prime minister, Luis Carrero Blanco, in 1973 sent a message about their own ability to strike at the heart of power, reinforced their support and eliminated one of their most active enemies. The destruction of the Twin Towers in New York in 2001 was of enormous symbolic significance, while the kidnapping and murder of Israeli athletes at the 1972 Munich Olympics by the Palestinian Black September group brought spectacular publicity for the cause of an independent Palestinian state.

Post-9/11, terrorism scholars have pointed to what has been termed 'new' terrorism distinguished from 'old' terrorism in three areas (see Wilkinson, 2004). First, terrorist groups such as Al-Qaeda are transnational in ideology, aims and membership; terrorist groups such as the Tamil Tigers in Sri Lanka and the Kurdish PKK group have been typically focused on nationally or ethnically defined goals. Second, their organization is diffuse and networked through new media. Traditional terrorist groups also use new media but, again, their membership is strongly linked to a well-defined ethnic heartland and diaspora. Third, the scale and nature of the violence perpetrated by new terrorism goes far beyond that of past terrorist attacks. Previously it appeared to be the case that terrorists were interested not in how many were killed, but in how many people were watching. This no longer seems to be the case. As the Madrid (11 March 2004) and London

(7 July 2005) bombs showed, no warnings are given and bombs are positioned and timed to explode so as to cause the maximum carnage.[6]

The understanding of terrorism as directed against the state does not preclude the possibility that the state might involve itself in what might be called terrorist-like activity. The actions of the Argentine military regime (1976–83) against its political enemies or Russian actions against the Chechen population in the 1990s certainly share many of the elements that define terrorism. One crucial difference, however, is that they are not normally executed with the aim of garnering widespread media attention.

Terror, Communication and the Media

Late nineteenth-century anarchists were the first to refer to their acts of murder for political reasons as 'propaganda of the deed' (Graham, 2005). Their aim was to reveal the repressive nature of the state as it reacted violently to anarchists' own acts of violence. In direct contrast to the philosophy of peaceful protest, they sought to 'persuade' others of the rightness of their cause through violent, attention-grabbing acts.

The identification of terrorism's intrinsic communicative function, and thus of the public relations challenge it poses, is a common thread to scholarly discussions (see Louw, 2003: Nacos, 2002; Schmid and de Graaf, 1982; Tuman, 2003). Scholars have suggested that one of the main purposes of a terrorist act is to direct messages to specific audiences (Nacos, 2002; and Tuman, 2003: 18–23). As Wilkinson puts it: '[terrorism] has been a remarkably successful means of publicizing a political cause and relaying the terrorist threat to a wider audience [...] When one says "terrorism" in a democratic society, one also says "media". For terrorism by its very nature is a psychological weapon which depends upon communicating a threat to a wider society' (2001: 177). This was very well understood by Timothy McVeigh when he targeted the Murrah Federal Building as a political statement against the US Federal government and chose a location which would have maximum visual impact for media coverage (see Nacos, 2002: 12–13). The Oklahoma bombing in 1995 killed 168 people and was the first major terrorist attack on the US mainland. Terrorist incidents are fashioned in order to meet Western media's criteria of newsworthiness (Carruthers, 2000: 170). As Schmid and de Graaf put it: 'Since the Western media grant access to newsmaking events that are abnormal, unusual, dangerous, new, disruptive and violent, groups without habitual access to news-making use these characteristics of the news value system to obtain access' (1982: 217).

The 2004 Madrid bombings killed 191 people without warning travelling on early morning trains into Spain's capital city just three days before the country's general elections. Despite the government's initial declarations that ETA was responsible for the attacks, it quickly became clear that the bombings had been carried out by a group linked to Al-Qaeda. The bombs sent a stark message to the Spanish people and their government: indiscriminate death is the price for your government's unpopular support for the Iraq invasion. They also pursued a precise objective: to inflame Spanish public opinion to ensure that the country's troops would be withdrawn from Iraq (Aviles, 2004). For the terrorists, 'the immediate victim is merely instrumental, the skin of a drum beaten to achieve a calculated impact on a wider audience' (Schmid and de Graaf, 1982: 14). The death and destruction caused by the 11 March bombs were the means by which specific domestic and international audiences were addressed, including:

- The Spanish government
- Opposition parties
- The Spanish electorate
- The Spanish media
- Global media
- Other national governments, particularly those with troops in Iraq
- Al-Qaeda members and sympathizers
- Iraqis

The acts of terrorism erupted into what Nacos describes as the 'triangle of political communication' (2002: 11), formed by the media, decision-makers and the public and interest groups. Given the complexity of interaction in the global contemporary environment, the communication relationships might be more accurately described as a matrix rather than a triangle. Certainly, the global media were an important influence in how domestic public opinion and media reacted to the bombings, driving them away from the government version of events (see Canel and Sanders, 2004). Terrorism and its publicity imperative place severe responsibilities on both journalists and politicians: how can journalists ever avoid giving terrorists the 'the oxygen of publicity'?[7] How should politicians handle the task of informing the public about terrorist threats and how should they respond to attacks once they have occurred? I will examine some of these questions next, beginning with an analysis of the Spanish government's response to the 2004 terrorism attacks.[8]

Framing a Communication Response to Terrorism

Both politicians and journalists seek to frame public understandings of events, define them in their terms, emphasizing certain elements of the story at the expense of others to ensure their preferred reading of what is going on. Framing is first of all about selection, about the inclusion and exclusion of content. 'To frame', Entman explains, 'is to select some aspects of a perceived reality and make them more salient in communicating a text, in such a way as to promote a particular problem definition, causal interpretation, moral evaluation, and/or treatment recommendation for the item described' (1993: 52). Second, frames organize reality. They refer to the way things are understood or, more precisely, mentally organized. A frame has thus been associated with the notion of schemata: 'The schemata of interpretation which are labelled frames enable individuals to locate, perceive, identify, and label' (Goffman, 1986: 21). Frames are powerful for political communicators because they are means by which political language can be used:

- To define reality
- To create understandings of the past and future
- To provide interpretation and linkage
- To set the agenda
- To provide stimulus for action (see Graber, 1985).

The frames adopted by political sources are expressed in press releases, briefings, official statements, press conferences, interviews and speeches. These provide one element in the production of the news frames which dominate the interpretation of an event. Other central factors include the facts of the event itself and the views of dissident groups. International media too can play a part in challenging what has been described as 'one-sided' consensual framing of an event (Norris, Kern and Just, 2003: 12).

The news frame becomes a significant factor in the formation of public opinion which in turn feeds back into the public policy agenda. The frame for the Bush Government's response to 9/11 was that of a 'War on Terror'. There was an initial consensus about how the attacks should be interpreted by Americans 'with broadly similar patterns in framing responsibility and interpreting these events offered in the main outlets for the mass media as well as a broad consensus among political leaders' (Graber, 2003: 12). The adoption of a common frame promoted by the Bush Government and adopted by the news media made it considerably easier for Bush to achieve support for an aggressive foreign policy in Afghanistan and Iraq.

Although referring to presidential rhetoric, the Smiths' thoughts (1994) on governmental communication are a useful starting point for examining the Spanish government's communication response to the Madrid bombings. They point out that contemporary political leaders 'must construct and share a coherent explication or a justification of mutual values, needs and goals'. Furthermore, government communication orientates society by 'the definition of aims and problems in consonance with the narratives which integrate people, interests, values, traditions, power distributions and spheres of influence' (Smith and Smith, 1994: 19). To do this, governments must nurture and sustain: '(1) an image of trustworthiness, (2) a reputation for managerial competence, and (3) a consistent and coherent rhetoric that coordinates the political perceptions of diverse publics' (1994: 191–2). Trust, competence and consistency are the three dimensions of the space in which governmental communication operates. They are also three areas of potential weakness that governments face when there is a crisis: people begin to doubt the president's competence and trustworthiness.

The authors identify two strategies to react to a crisis. One is the 'strategy of division' which consists in identifying voters' prejudices, situating the message of the adversary in what is rejected and positioning one's own message at the opposite extreme. The other is the 'strategy of inclusion' where a message is addressed to a large audience in order to gain a broad coalition so that 'Presidential coalitions are built around both convergence and divergence. They can best be understood as unifying around and dividing from, as identifying with and polarizing against' (Smith and Smith, 1994: 231).

Government Communication and Terrorism

The scale of the attacks (this was the largest peace-time terrorist massacre in Western Europe), the apparent intention to affect the outcome of a democratic election and bring about Spain's withdrawal from Iraq ensured that the events received global media and political attention. The complex matrix of communication influences and the fact that the governing party was fighting an election meant that the PP was faced with an unusually challenging communication task.

The Madrid bombs blew apart the domestic political agenda. Having been four points ahead in the polls, PP lost the elections to the Socialists who won with 5 per cent more of the vote.[9] Compared to the previous general elections in 2000, there was a very high turnout and an extra million and a half people voted. Perceptions and evaluations of the Madrid bombings differed according to views on who was responsible for the attacks. The Spanish government's communication about the bombings came at the end of an election campaign in which it knew its future was tied up with how the Spanish electorate would assess both the responsibility and reasons for the bombings as well as the government's response to them. At the same time, the opposition media and political forces were active in pushing alternative frames with which to interpret the events of 11 March. In such circumstances – what have been described as 'two-sided' contexts – 'the process of political communication can become extremely controversial, as both communities dispute the meaning and interpretation of similar events' (Norris, Kern and Just, 2003: 14).

Government ministers loomed large in the communicative response to the bombings and very quickly seemed intent on promoting one particular interpretative frame for the attacks, namely the responsibility of ETA. Initially this not unreasonable view of events was shared by all political forces,[10] but it began to be undermined by leaks from security forces and information from foreign media and commentators suggesting an Islamist link. Despite the growing evidence, government ministers and the country's prime minister continued to press home this interpretation and appealed to all 'honourable Spaniards' to rally around the Constitution and reject terrorism. This could only act as a strategy of division: for Basque and Catalan nationalists the Constitution was a matter of controversy. On the final day before elections, the governing party was literally under siege. Their political opponents successfully mobilized protests outside PP offices in which the government was accused of lying.

As Entman states: 'Poor strategy creates a power vacuum that opposing elites and journalists may enter with their own interpretations. On the other hand, inventive presidential strategy can endow frames with extra energy needed to penetrate down the levels' (2003: 423). In the Spanish case, interpretations of opposing elites and journalists were more successful than a government strategy which reacted to the immediacy of events, and clumsily promoted a view calculated to favour it even as contradictory evidence became available. The government's communication lacked what Entman (2003: 423) has termed 'cultural congruence', where 'a news frame can cascade through the different levels of the framing process and stimulate similar reactions at each step.' According to this analysis, the more congruent the frame is with schemas that dominate the political culture, the more success it will enjoy. Part of the problem for the Spanish government's communication was its choice of culturally incongruent frames, relating to essentially divisive issues surrounding the Constitution and the identity of the Spaniards. This approach could only end in disunity.

In addition, the Spanish government failed effectively to define the problem: the issue became 'who lied?' rather than 'who carried out the murders?' This failure of problem definition ineluctably resulted in difficulties in identifying the causes, conveying moral judgments of those involved in the framed events and endorsing remedies for the situation. People cared about whether ETA or al Qaeda were responsible, but they also wanted to know who had apparently lied. Trying to frame those responsible for the bombings as 'terrorists' did not work and, while Bush was able successfully to use the strategy of framing those responsible for 9/11 as enemies, in Spain the government itself became the enemy.

8

The Political Persuasion Industry: Lobbyists, Pressure Groups and Think Tanks

Introduction

Political parties have traditionally been seen as the main actors in representative democracy and political communication (see Hague and Harrop, 2001). However, one consistent feature of the political communication landscape over the last 40 years has been the steady rise in the number and diversity of actors engaged in political persuasion. This chapter examines the development of what I call the political persuasion industry which now includes *lobbyists*, *pressure groups*, trade associations, charities, trade unions and, more recently, *think tanks*. My focus will be on the *ways they attempt to influence the policy process, the reasons for their development and growing importance* and, finally, *the issues raised for the integrity of the conduct of democratic politics*.

Lobbyists and Pressure Groups

On one view of democracy, the development of functional constituencies that mobilise particular interests apparently runs counter to the underlying rationale for legitimacy in representative democracies. In addition, only those groups that mobilise or can employ advocates will influence policy. As Rawnsley puts it:

> the idea of pressure groups acting as a channel of democratic political communication is an illusion because of the notable absence of a level playing-field for group competition. Governments will listen to some groups, and ignore others, depending on the issue, the resources that the group can mobilise, whether the group is considered legitimate on that particular issue, and the political and public mood. (2005: 103)

Table 8.1 Pressure group and political party membership

	1990s	Early 2000s	Mid/late 2000s
The National Trust (UK)	2.29 m (1996)	2.7 m (2001)	3.5 m (2007)
Amnesty International (UK)	125,362 (1998) 700,000 worldwide (1990)	154,611(2001)	176,000 (2008) 2.2m worldwide (2007)
Greenpeace	194,309 (1998)	193,500 (2001)	140,000 (2006) 2.8 mworldwide (2006)
Labour Party (UK)	400,465 (1996)	311,000 (2000)	248,294 (2004)

Sources: *The Guardian*, 29 January 2002; 10, 12 April 2004; and 25 July 2007; http://news.bbc.co.uk/1/hi/uk_politics/6209399.stm (accessed 10 January 2008); email communication of author with Greenpeace and Amnesty International, January 2008.

On the other hand, freedom of association and the right to petition (see below) are fundamental tenets of democratic politics and the number and diversity of groups and associations of all kinds can be taken as a measure of the civic vitality of a society (see Putnam, 2000). Certainly, if membership is taken as a sign of political engagement, pressure groups have become in that respect more significant actors in political communication than political parties (see Table 8.1). Both pressure groups and lobbyists, however, chiefly engage in political communication as persuaders (and often educators too) and it is on this characteristic that I will focus next.

Pressure Groups

A pressure group can be defined as 'any organisation that aims to influence public policy by seeking to persuade decision-makers by lobbying rather than by standing for election and holding office' (Coxall, 2001: 3). Pressure groups may of course do much more than this. Groups such as Greenpeace act as a rallying point for environmentalists, have a research capacity and undertake non-violent action to further their campaign aims. The Royal Society for the Protection of Birds provides high-quality science expertise in its chosen area. Trade unions bargain on behalf of their members for better wages and conditions. However, persuasion is at the heart of their mission. Pressure groups seek to inform and explain to others the issues relevant to their principal cause with the main aim of influencing policy-makers to make decisions in line with the group's views. This definition makes communication absolutely central to what a pressure group is and does.

Their *modus operandi* may vary – they may carry out protest politics (see Chapter 7), they may be insider groups such as chambers of commerce, considered legitimate and consulted as part of a policy network, or they may be considered outsiders, social movements such as the Women's Liberation Movement or the various anti-globalization groups, that cannot or do not want to be part of a government recognized policy network (see Grant, 1995). They all share the aim of achieving attention for their cause and bringing about peaceful political change.

Given the public distrust that exists of much conventional political communication, it is interesting to find that certain kinds of pressure group enjoy a high degree of trust (see Jordan, 1998). In part, this may be due to the fact they never risk getting their hands dirty with the responsibility of office. However, it may also be linked to the perception of independence from vested interests, buttressed by such principled measures as refusing to accept business donations and to adopt party political stances. For these reasons, their communication may be considered less contaminated by interests other than those declared as the chief cause of the organization. The same cannot be said for the group I shall examine next, the lobbyists.

Lobbying: The Oldest Profession?

From time immemorial, people have sought to influence the powerful, looking for ways to induce them to take actions and make decisions which would favour their cause or interests. The right to petition was recognized by monarchs across Europe. It was later guaranteed by the First Amendment to the US Constitution which specifically prohibits Congress from abridging 'the right of the people […] to petition the Government for redress of grievances'.

The lobbyist Michael Burrell spoke of this right in arguing for the legitimacy of lobbying:

> I feel strongly that what we do is central to the functioning of a healthy democracy. The right to petition for redress of grievance goes back to the *Magna Carta*. What we do is help people express their grievances as best we can. In a free society it is curious if people can spend their money on doctors, lawyers and accountants, but not on issues where the future of their business is at stake. (cited in Michie, 1998: 240)

As we shall see, these views are not uncontroversial. Before examining them, I will first explore what lobbying is and what its exponents do.

The Lobbyists' Work

In straightforward terms, lobbyists, or political or public affairs consultants (as many prefer to be known), seek to persuade policy-makers of the merits of a case for their client. The term 'lobbying' has been variously said to have arisen with reference to the lobby area of the Westminster Parliament where members of parliament would mingle with those seeking favours or to the Willard Hotel lobby in Washington during the presidency of Ulysses S. Grant (1822–1855), where legislators would be petitioned by diverse interests.

Some scholars have considered lobbying or public affairs to be a sub-field of public relations. According to White (1991: 55) public affairs is 'a specialist area of practice within public relations concerned with those relationships involved in public policy-making, legislation, and regulation that may affect the interests of organisations and their operations'. Cutlip, Center and Broom, (1994: 17) concur, defining lobbying as 'the specialized part of public relations that builds and maintains relations with government primarily for the purpose of influencing legislation and regulation'. In a practitioner's view, lobbying is 'any action designed to influence the actions and the institutions of government' (Miller, 2000: 4).

In short, lobbyists' work involves:

- Research, monitoring and intelligence gathering about relevant environmental features (these can include regulatory, economic, political, media, cultural and personal data).
- Formulation of strategy and tactics involving a range of target audiences (such as, for example, politicians, government, media, public, interest groups).
- Linkage into a consultation network (this may already exist by virtue of being a member of a trade association, trade union or non-governmental organization or may be engineered through the establishment of an interest group principally for lobbying purposes).
- Representation and/or advocacy of clients' case to decision-makers.

This set of practices is given coherence and purpose by the aims established by strategic or persuasive communication. It is the latter, I would argue, which fundamentally defines lobbying.

The Centrality of Communication

Lobbyists seek to persuade others through a variety of techniques including the development of relationships, the marshalling of evidence and concerned constituents, the mobilization of opinion formers and media as well as direct advocacy on behalf of the client. Lobbying is not just about seeking to influence politicians. This may be part of a long-term campaign strategy but, depending on the issue, the state of public opinion, the contingencies of the political situation and its context, short-term tactics may favour a different approach. In Britain, for example, according to one lobbyist: 'Lobbying Parliament is the most inefficient way to influence legislation – it requires the most effort with the least likely result.' (Michie, 1998: 243). It is more effective to lobby civil servants and become part of the consultative policy-making process. Senior and middle-ranking civil servants have a significant influence in setting the terms for legislation. By the time legislation has got to parliament, it is usually too late to have a substantial impact.

The mobilization of public opinion in order to influence policy-makers is also known as 'grassroots' lobbying' and where a mobilizing campaign is directed toward influential people in the community, it is known as 'grasstops' lobbying. 'Astroturfing' refers to the engineering of a simulated public clamour on any particular issue, usually by interested parties who prefer to disguise their true identity by establishing apparent grassroots organizations. An example of a successful grassroots strategy was the campaign devised by the UK public affairs consultancy, *Westminster Strategy*, on behalf of a Japanese company which made cassette audiotapes.[1] The government had proposed a levy on blank cassette tapes. The campaign's tactics were to galvanize the various constituencies of opinion which would be affected by more expensive cassette tapes including students and the blind. The 'Hands off reading' campaign proved successful in staving off the extra tax. However, as another lobbyist explained, even the best-planned campaign has its limits:

> The use of lobbyists doesn't give big companies as much edge as people think. What gives them their edge is their size and the quality of their case. A good lobbyist will optimize a case, but can't turn base metal into gold. You can't make a credible case out of one that is poor. (Miller cited in Michie, 1998: 244).

Most major corporations and pressure groups ensure they have a lobbying capability, effectively guaranteeing them a persuasive voice on issues that matter to them. This may be found in an in-house department, variously denominated as the corporate communications, public relations or public affairs department. The capability may be partially or entirely contracted out either to the appropriate trade association or to a professional public affairs company or, commonly in continental Europe, to lawyers' firms.[2] Lobbyists can be employed by special interest groups, charities, NGOs, corporate clients and even governments. The Kuwaiti government hired one of the largest public affairs companies, Hill & Knowlton, to mastermind the campaign to gain international support after Iraq's invasion of the country in 1990. The EU parliament roster of organizations acting as lobbyists includes groups such as *The Alliance for Beverage Cartons and the Environment* and the *Xerox* company.

The Growth of Lobbying

Lobbying is a multi-million dollar industry. In the United States almost one billion dollars was spent on lobbying by the top ten companies and organizations over six years (see Table 8.2). Tobacco, professional health interests and pharmaceutical companies were well represented.

Table 8.2   Lobbying costs in US companies and organizations – The Top Ten

Company/organization	Total lobbying costs 1998–2004	2004 lobbying costs
US Chamber of Commerce – association representing more than 3 million businesses	$204,614,680	$53,380,000
Altria Group Inc (formerly Philip Morris) – tobacco and food conglomerate	$101,220,000	$13,240,000
General Electric Co. – technology and services conglomerate	$94,130,000	$17,240,000
American Medical Association – association representing doctors	$92,560,000	$18,520,000
Northrop Grumman Corp. – defence and technology conglomerate	$83,405,691	$12,566,000
Edison Electric Institute – association of shareholder-owned electric companies	$82,866,628	$11,000,000
Verizon Communications Inc. – broadband and telecommunications	$81,870,000	$9,120,000
Business Roundtable – association of chief executive officers of leading companies	$80,380,000	$7,680,000
American Hospital Association & State Affiliates – association of hospitals and other health care centres	$79,205,772	$13,505,772
Pharmaceutical Research & Manufacturers of America – represents pharmaceutical research and biotechnology companies	$72,720,000	$15,520,000
TOTAL	**$972,972,771**	**$171,771,772**

Source: Data taken from the Centre for Public Integrity:
http://www.publicintegrity.org/lobby/top.aspx?act=topcompanies (accessed 17 July 2007).

According to *PoliticalMoneyLine*, a non-partisan organization that tracks such expenditures, in the first half of 2005, US corporations and interest groups spent a record total of $2.1 billion to lobby Washington (Mullins, 14 February 2006). In 2005 there were nearly 35,000 registered lobbyists for the US Congress alone, a number which had doubled in the five years from 2000 (Birnbaum, 22 June 2005).

In 2001, the largest PR firms, including public affairs capabilities and operating worldwide, were by revenue:

Weber Shandwick Worldwide	$426,572,018
Fleishman-Hillard Inc.	$345,098,241
Hill and Knowlton, Inc.	$325,119,000
Incepta (Citigate) (from 2005 Huntsworth)	$266,018,371
Burston-Marsteller	$259,112,000
Edelman Public Relations Worldwide	$223,708,535
Ketchum, Inc.	$185,221,000
Porter Novelli	$179,294,000
GCI Group/APCO Worldwide	$151,081,645
Ogilvy Public Relations Worldwide	$145,949,285

Source: Source Watch, Center for Media and Democracy:
http://www.sourcewatch.org/index.php?title=Public_relations_firms

Brussels is the second largest centre for lobbyists after Washington DC with approximately 3000 special interest groups of varying types. The European Parliament lists around 5000 officially registered lobbyists but registration is not compulsory and estimates of numbers vary from around 13,000 lobbyists up to 30,000 working in Europe's political capital.[3] The European Parliament estimates 70 per cent of these lobbyists represent corporate interests, 20 per cent NGOs, including trade unions and health and environment groups, with the remaining 10 per cent lobbying for individual countries.

These groups include:

- about 50 offices in Brussels representing countries, regional and local authorities (their work is not confined to lobbying activities)
- more than 200 individual firms with direct representation, and about 100 consultants with offices in Brussels
- about 100 law firms in Belgium specializing in Community law and performing an advocacy function

The prime targets of lobbyists are the more than 6000 Commission officials involved in policy-making and 785 parliamentarians. As the EU's regulatory significance has steadily grown since the 1970s so have the number of lobbyists. As in Britain and the United States, the scale and nature of lobbying activities have attracted the attentions of the EU regulators. From being an entirely unregulated activity, concerns raised by some aspects of lobbying have, as we shall now see, fuelled demands for tighter regulation.

Concerns about Lobbying

Ian Greer established one of the first lobbying companies in Britain in 1970. Twenty-five years later he found his company, Ian Greer Associates, embroiled in a major political scandal known as *Cash for Questions*. Accused of paying MPs to ask questions in parliament on behalf of such clients as Mohammed al Fayed, owner of Harrods, his company's activities helped place the spotlight on the lobbying world. As lobby executive Michael Burrell put it: 'Public affairs was little known until the Cash for Questions scandal. Now there is the widespread perception that what we do is illegitimate and the methods we employ are corrupt' (cited in Michie, 1998: 240). The concerns raised about lobbying are serious. They touch, on the one hand, on its very legitimacy. On this view, lobbyists simply exploit our ignorance of, and impotence before, the complex systems of the world and, in doing so, corrupt the democratic process. On the other hand, it is claimed that the practices associated with lobbying are often in themselves corrupt. This second view suggests that with tighter regulation and greater transparency lobbying may have a legitimate role. Three principal criticisms can be made.

Buying influence. The first and most serious criticism is that lobbying permits the rich and powerful to buy influence, and thus corrupts the democratic process by allowing special interests to prosper. The vast sums of money spent on lobbying activities suggest that, at the very least, companies believe that lobbying is influential. To take one example, in 2004 Hewlett-Packard, the Californian computer maker, saw an opportunity in the Republican-controlled Congress to achieve legislation which would allow it to repatriate profits at a lowered tax rate, allowing it to make nearly $14.5 billion in profit from foreign subsidiaries. It significantly increased its lobbying budget to $734,000. The legislation was approved and, as the company's head of government affairs put it: 'We're trying to take advantage of the fact that Republicans control the House, the Senate and the White House [...] There is an opportunity here for the business community to make its case and be successful' (cited in Birnbaum, 22 June 2005).

Groups, causes and companies who have the resources can get their side of the story heard, something not permitted to less advantaged groups. This could very well have the pernicious effect of undermining the assumed commitment in democracies of legislators and policy-makers to discharge a public trust for the common good, albeit with regard to their overarching ideological principles.

There seems to be considerable force to this criticism. To counter it, lobbyists and indeed civil liberties' groups appeal to the First Amendment argument that citizens have a right to petition and lobbyists are simply facilitating this basic right. However, there seems to be no getting around the fact that organized interests can, if they have resources, buy in advocacy services and steal an advantage. Lobbying makes true the variation of the Orwellian tenet that 'All citizens are equal but some citizens are more equal than others'; *de bono* work and commitment to community projects can ameliorate but not disguise this reality.[4] It is, however, one thing to have one's case heard and quite another for it to be influential. In other words, it is perhaps more correct to argue that money can buy the possibility of access and of having the best case put on one's behalf. These are significant advantages, but whether they translate into influence will depend on other factors. Indeed, some of the measures called for by critics of the lobbying industry, such as ensuring that all lobbying contacts are officially declared by legislators, may offset some of its perceived benefits.

The revolving door. In July 2005, the consumer advocacy group *Public Citizen* published a report detailing the increasing tendency for former legislators to move from Congress to 'K Street', the home of lobbying in the US capital. Lured by salaries as high as $300,000 and the growing acceptability of lobbying as a suitable job for former law-makers, research found that since 1998, 43 per cent of the 198 members of Congress who left government to join private life had registered to lobby. The concerns raised by this development were strongly put by *Public Citizen*'s president, Joan Claybrook:

> Now Congress has become a way station to wealth. Members use it for job training and networking so they can leave office and cash in on the connections they forged as elected officials. No wonder the public is cynical about whose interests lawmakers are protecting in Washington. Lobbying has become the top career choice for departing members of Congress. (27 July 2005)

Various proposals have been made to limit the 'revolving door' including a longer 'chilling off' period for congressmen and women than just one year and greater restrictions on their access to privileged areas such as Congress restaurants and gyms.

Corrupt practices. Gift-giving not only materially benefits the person who receives it, it is also a time-worn method for gaining psychological leverage over the recipient of the gift (see Cialdini,1993: 17). In 2005 a scandal broke in Washington about the fraudulent and gift-giving activities of Jack Abramoff, lobbyist and Republican activist. He showered congressmen and administration officials with sports and concerts tickets and golfing trips to Scotland. The resulting criminal investigations convicted nine people, including Abramoff, and added to the pressure to introduce tighter regulation of the US lobbying industry.

Making Lobbying Respectable

Transparency is the great enemy of special interests and, often in response to scandal and media and pressure group activity, at the beginning of the twenty-first century politicians began to establish more effective mechanisms to ensure transparency. Scandals in London and Washington prompted action to regulate lobbying by their respective legislators. In Britain, Cash for Questions produced the Committee for Standards in Public Life and a raft of measures to clarify the relationship between parliamentarians and lobbyists. An independent parliamentary ombudsman was established who, for example, could oblige 'Tony Blair to reveal his pattern of meetings with commercial lobbyists' (Evans and Leigh, 16 March, 2004).

In the United States, the Lobbying Disclosure Act requires lobbyists to be registered and to file reports on contacts twice a year unless they represent an elected official or an organization of elected officials. In early 2007 both Senate and Congress approved further lobbing and ethics legislation with rules which include:

- Ban on gifts from lobbyists and organizations that employ lobbyists.
- Value tickets to sporting events and concerts at real face value for purposes of the gift limits.
- Prohibit organizations that employ lobbyists (other than universities) from arranging or financing trips for members and staff, except for one-day trips.

A more controversial proposal is the Executive Branch Reform Act that would mandate executive officials to list all oral and written communications with anyone who contacts them in order to try to influence them. It is opposed by a number of pressure groups on the grounds that it interferes in citizens' First Amendment right to petition, invading their privacy by making any approach to public officials a matter of public record. At the time of writing, the proposed legislation had not been passed into law.

EU regulation of lobbying has a more patchy record. Lobbyists themselves have organized as the *Society of European Affairs Professionals* (SEAP) created in 1997 (it merged with the *European Federation of Lobbying and Public Affairs* in 2000). SEAP's aims are to unite the profession and better promote its interests but it has only 140 individual members, representing perhaps as little as one per cent of the total number of lobbyists.[5]

Concerns about lobbying transparency in the EU led to the launch in 2005 of the *Alliance for Lobbying Transparency and Ethics Regulation* (ALTER-EU), a coalition of academics and groups such as Greenpeace and Corporate Europe Observatory. It lobbies for more stringent regulation along American lines of the EU lobbying industry. On 21 March 2007, the EU approved a communication on the European Transparency Initiative which showed that, for the moment, they have decided on a more permissive, self-regulatory route, preparing the launch of a voluntary register as well as a code of conduct for relations between interest representatives and the EU institutions. Addressing Belgian business associations, a senior EU Commission official set out the justification for this approach:

> Through cooperation on the register, we can resist any campaign to outlaw or discredit legitimate interest representation, and we can ensure a solid, sustainable foundation for the credibility and legitimacy of the business.
>
> We can keep the EU institutions open and accessible without daily contacts between us being subjected to bureaucratic hurdles.
>
> And by acting now, in the absence of a lobbying 'scandal', we can help to prevent scandals and we can address the ever increasing level of lobbying of EU institutions in a cool-headed analytical state of mind.
>
> We can work calmly with the profession to set out the rules of the game, instead of reacting defensively and under media pressure in a crisis. (Kallas, 18 June, 2007)

Transparency did not appear to be the most prominent concern in the official's mind. The issue of transparency is, however, of increasing concern to parliamentarians. In 2007 British MPs called for more transparency among lobbyists. In particular, they expressed concern that there is no mandatory requirement for lobbyists to reveal the identity of clients (see Coates, 31 March 2007). Without appropriate mechanisms to ensure a high degree of transparency, it will be difficult for EU lobbyists to shake off the suspicion that they have something to hide.

The Think Tank Industry

On a parsimonious definition of 'think tank', there were estimated to be over 4000 think tanks around the world in 2000 (see Stone and Denham, 2004: 5). Most of them have been founded in the last 40 years. The term itself is taken from the Second World War when it was used to describe a secure room where military plans and strategies could be discussed. It was first used in 1949 to refer to contract research organizations such as the RAND Corporation which gave defence and security policy advice to the US military. The huge growth in their number in and beyond the United States, their traditional heartland, suggests common structural features that have facilitated their development, some of which are linked to the twenty-first-century communication environment and its impact on the conduct of politics and policy development. In this section I will discuss these issues after first establishing what we mean by the vast array of organizations which go under the name of 'think tanks'.

The Ever-Expanding Think Tank

The proliferation and ubiquity of organizations either describing themselves as or appearing to have think tank characteristics makes definition a fraught issue. Depending on one's definition, Britain's left-wing Fabian Society founded in 1884 could lay claim to being the world's oldest think tank. Hames and Feasey described the think tank as 'a non-profit public policy research institution with substantial organizational autonomy' (1994: 216). Think tanks have also been described as 'universities without students', contract research organizations, advocacy tanks and vanity organizations (see Ableson, 2004: 221). None of these terms, however, would accurately describe the Chinese and French functional equivalents of the think tank. Nor are the latter characterized by the relative political autonomy found in think tanks in the Anglo-American context. As Stone and Denham put it, 'the line between both French and Chinese policy intellectuals and the state is blurred to such an extent that to talk of independence as a defining characteristic of think tanks makes little sense in their respective cultural contexts' (2004: 2).

All think tanks can be said to be concerned with the analysis of policy issues. However, they vary considerably in two crucial aspects. The first concerns their degree of autonomy in relation to their economic sponsors. There are think tanks which enjoy a high degree of economic independence in that their funding sources are diversified and they may benefit from an endowed funding base. Others rely on one exclusive source of funding from government, for example, or from one benefactor.

The degree of autonomy from the state and political parties in policy development and analysis is a second key area of difference between think tanks. Some may be constituted in such a way as to be able to have considerable autonomy and independence in establishing their policy agenda within a broad policy remit. University-based think tanks, frequently found in Germany, would be an example of this kind of organization. Using these two dimensions – the degree of economic dependence and the degree of policy dependence – we can construct a typology of think tanks (see Table 8.3) ranging from government think tanks, such as the China Institute for Economic Reform with a high degree of economic and policy dependence, to

Table 8.3 Think tank typology according to economic and policy autonomy

		Degree of dependence in relation to political/policy agenda		
		Low	**Medium**	**High**
	High	Non-partisan policy agenda but revenue streams not stable; e.g., FIEL (Argentina)	Broad policy agenda dictated by funders; e.g., EUI-Robert Schuman Centre (Italy)	Fixed partisan policy agenda by funder; e.g., China Institute for Economic Reform
Degree of dependence in relation to economic sponsorship	**Medium**	Non-partisan policy agenda with diverse revenue streams; e.g., Conference Board (Canada)	Inspired by specific political principles with diverse revenue streams; e.g., IPPR (UK)	Linked to political party policy agenda with diverse revenue streams; e.g., FAES (Spain)
	Low	Funded mainly by endowment and non-partisan; e.g., Hoover Institution (US)	Funded mainly by endowment and inspired by specific political principles; American Enterprise e.g., Institute for Public Policy Research (US)	Funded mainly by endowment with strong policy agenda; e.g., Heritage Foundation (US)

those such as the Brookings Institution (US) with a substantial degree of economic and policy autonomy. In the middle-range of policy and economic dependence are organizations such as *Demos* (UK) which are broadly inspired by a specific set of political principles and rely on a mixture of revenue sources.

Think tanks come in many guises. Some have formal political party affiliations such as the *Friedrich Ebert Stiftung* associated with the German Social Democratic Party; others belong to universities. All are in the business of the analysis of the assumptions underlying policy, the documentation of relevant policy information, the generation of policy ideas and proposals, the consideration of long-term trends rather than immediate events and, increasingly, the marketing of these ideas so as to bring about policy change.

The Ubiquitous Think Tank

Think tanks were once considered principally an American phenomenon partly because very few were to be found outside the United States and partly because the country's specific economic and political conditions were thought to be uniquely favourable to their development (see Denham and Garnett, 1998: 4). The US constitutional separation of powers favouring legislative power and initiative and enhanced by a weak party structure, the openness of its public administration staffed in its upper echelons by political appointments, the multiple publics available for policy analysis and advice, all contributed towards creating an environment in which think tank expertise could find a ready audience. Benign economic conditions and a philanthropic culture were also key in fostering their growth. Certainly these conditions have meant that think tanks have prospered in the United States as nowhere else. However, their proliferation around the world indicates that the peculiarities of the American political soil are not the only reasons for their success. Think tanks are common in many parts of Europe. In Germany, for example, there are over 100 with the oldest going back to the beginning of the twentieth century (Thunert, 2004). Many receive public funding and all of the major political parties are loosely associated with research foundations that play some role in proposing policy, but generally are more involved in providing research to support policy-makers.

Since the decline and eventual collapse of communist regimes in the early 1990s, think tanks have developed in Russia and Central and Eastern Europe. There are, for example, 12 in both Poland and Slovakia. In China think tanks have been developed by the party-state apparatus with a fixed political and policy agenda and without the capability for independent policy generation and analysis typical of non-communist institutions (see Ming Chen-Shai, 2004: 142–3).

Explaining Think Tanks' Success

How can we account for the global spread of think tanks? There are probably several factors at work of variable importance depending on the context. Here I set out six.

First, we are living in information saturated times, with a dizzying array of sources with which to make sense of the complex issues of our times. Policy-makers often do not have the luxury of time to work through and formulate medium- and long-term policy in all areas. Think tanks can perform a useful ordering function, providing perspectives on long-term trends and gathering together expertise to analyse specific issues.

Second, think tanks have the capability to generate the kind of blue skies thinking that bureaucracies operating to routines or parties to ideological dogma rarely can. They can convene diverse voices and views and provoke fresh thinking on the major issues of the day.

Third, think tanks claim to offer expertise in their field of specialization. Whether this is the case or not varies considerably from think tank to think tank. Some employ top-flight academics. Former Stanford professor, Condolezza Rice, worked at the Hoover Institution, for example. However, other institutions running on tighter budgets tend to use young researchers or are often vanity projects for displaced politicians.

Fourth, the media demand for experts or pundits and for the stories generated by think tank reports is insatiable. An 'expert' view, however well-founded or not the claim is, immediately bestows legitimacy on the opinions being expressed. The politics of expertise is also found in government. Think tanks can provide valuable cover for governments setting out on unchartered policy paths.

In fifth place, think tanks can provide the appearance, if very frequently not the reality, of having a degree of detachment from government and immediate partisan debate. This again lends their views greater legitimacy than those known to emanate from clearly partisan sources. Of course, this factor does not apply when the think tank concerned is principally engaged in advocacy. Although, as we shall see, 'advocacy tanks' are not always as transparent as they should be in making clear their partisan starting point.

Finally, the increase in numbers of the partisan think tank suggests that they are increasingly seen as an important vehicle not just for public communication on policy but also for political communication, that is to say, communication directed at political persuasion. I will examine next what kind of impact and influence think tanks may have.

Impact and Influence

In social science research questions regarding the direction and nature of influence as between social agents or sets of stimuli and responses are extremely difficult to answer. This difficulty is compounded when one is setting out to examine the impact and influence of ideas. Broadly speaking, think tanks seek to influence what is sometimes called 'the climate of opinion' and to have an impact on policy decision-making and the policies adopted by government. The notions of 'climate of opinion' or 'public opinion' are in themselves highly complex (see Chapter 10). Attempts to disentangle the causality of changes in opinion through studies of media effects, for example, have produced limited results (see Chapter 12). For think tanks there have been no systematic studies of their impact and influence partly because the issue of influence is so difficult to operationalize (see Abelson, 2004: 231).

Think tanks themselves often refer to media citations or opinion pieces published, evidence provided to official committees and the number of reports and studies published. However, while these may be useful performance indicators, they cannot provide a reliable map of influence.

As Ableson puts it (2002: 140): 'Think tanks try to create the impression that they play a critical role in injecting new and innovative ideas into the public arena.' The UK think tank, *Demos,* bears this out in its website description of itself: 'As an independent voice, we can create debates that lead to real change. We use the media, public events, workshops and publications to communicate our ideas.'

The British conservative think tanks, the *Institute of Economic Affairs* (1957), the *Centre for Policy Studies* (1974) and the *Adam Smith Institute* (1977), are credited with shifting the prevailing ideological consensus with regard to economic policy, helping to usher in Thatcherism. Again, however, without the development of an effective methodology to map influence in policy-making, researchers can do no more than speculate about the truth or otherwise of these claims.

Deep Lobbying

Think tanks are operating in a highly competitive ideas market so that it could be argued that 'developing effective marketing techniques to enhance their status in the policy-making community, rather than providing decision-makers with sound and impartial advice, had to become their main priority' (Abelson, 2004: 225). Certainly, communicational intent, focusing on issues known to attract media interest, organizing events with celebrity speakers, does appear to be a growing tendency in some areas of the think tank world. Denham and Garnett (2004) point out that in the British context, newer generations of think tanks have been strong on ideological advocacy and weak on empirical research as compared to the older generation of think tanks which focused on independent research.

This development is one which has led some critics to argue that think tanks are in fact no more than vehicles for propaganda, promoting the ideological arguments of their founding organization. Groups such as SpinWatch argue that they are facades for 'deep' lobbying to form opinion in favour of private interests and that they are just public relations under another name. This is certainly true of some groups which, in allowing ideology or the search for quick headlines to contaminate their research, devalue 'the think tank currency' (Denham and Garnett, 2004: 246). These developments narrow down the range of the democratic conversation and undermine its integrity. However, the notion of an institution producing soundly based research, even when this is within declared ideological parameters, that contributes to policy discussions is one which, I would argue, is not only defensible but also possible and desirable. Being 'a kind of intellectual pressure group' (Coxall, 2001: 75) is a legitimate role in democratic societies. The challenge, as for others engaged in political persuasion, is to ensure that operational terms and conditions are made clear and that intellectual integrity is not compromised by skewed research.

Conclusion

In 2006, Washington lobbyist Jack Abramoff was convicted on charges of corrupting public officials and defrauding American Indian tribes. He worked for a top lobbying company, was a Republican activist and the director of a conservative think tank. His story encapsulated the potential for corruption of the political persuasion industry. The potential operates on three levels. First, there is the straightforward temptation to win arguments and persuade others not on the merits of one's case, but by material means. At its crudest, this involves the literal purchase of support through bribery and corruption. On a marginally more subtle level, it involves the deployment of vast resources to engineer consent and to privilege certain points of view. Third, the potential for corruption exists at the level of communication itself. Persuasion, as has been pointed out elsewhere, is a perfectly legitimate mode of communication. However, where the methods used and the resources deployed mislead – in astroturfing, for example – persuasion becomes manipulation.

Technological, political, economic and media developments in the twenty-first century have contributed to the massive expansion of the political persuasion industry, to its enhanced capacity for corrupting the grounds of political communication and to the capacity of other organizations to scrutinize its behaviour and practices. In the last 20 years a virtual industry has developed to examine critically the activities of lobbyists, pressure groups and think tanks. These include the various projects of the US-based Center for Public Integrity (LobbyWatch, for example); PoliticalMoneyLine which provides information about money in American politics; Sourcewatch–Wiki which collects information about lobbying; projects by *Public Citizen* including CleanupWashington; and in Europe Spinwatch and the Corporate Europe Observatory (CEO). These provide a very necessary but, by themselves, insufficient counterweight to the large battalions of the professional persuaders. Structural measures including adequate regulatory and ethical frameworks can help ensure that openness and transparency drive out the worst kinds of practices. This is the role of governments, undertaken with more seriousness in the US than by the EU, and the professional persuaders themselves. Ultimately it is in the latter's interests to create a communicational context of integrity.

Lobbyists, pressure groups and think tanks have one shared aim: they seek to persuade and influence others. The terms under which this aim is exercised can, however, turn what is a legitimate goal and activity into a force for injustice. Getting these terms right is still very much a work in progress.

9

Global Political Communication

Introduction

Since the inception of political communication studies over 50 years ago, nation or national states have provided the principal framing context for research and discussion. Researchers examine national election campaigns, national political news practices and organizations and national public opinion. There are good reasons for this: political, cultural, economic and media systems have had not exclusively but principally national borders. However, the predominance of the 'national' in political communication has had three important drawbacks. First, it has meant that the supranational and especially the sub-national contexts for political communication have been neglected areas of study.[1] Second, the concept of the 'national' itself has been widely and sometimes uncritically adopted as the unit of analysis without consideration of the theoretical limitations of this approach. Third, as I noted in Chapter 1, the United States' pivotal place in communication studies has meant that its scholars' findings and research paths – rooted as they are in a specific cultural context – have often set the agenda and shaped the direction of political communication research, entrenching a particular national environment at the heart of theory-building.

However, a number of developments in the latter half of the twentieth century helped shift scholarly interest towards complementary frameworks for the analysis of political communication. Technological, political and economic change has contributed to a simultaneous expansion and fragmentation of public space. Political actors in post-industrial democracies have less control than ever of the temporal and spatial dimensions in which their power is exercised. A casual remark or unfortunate stumble can be seen around the world in the time it takes for a CNN news feed to be transmitted or someone to upload the images onto YouTube. Tailoring specific messages for specific audiences becomes more complicated, especially where messages lack consistency. Politics has gone global and political communication has had to follow.

In this chapter I will examine three related developments. First, the *emergence of global media power* dominated by largely Western news organizations, potentially bringing us news from everywhere as it happens with allegedly significant consequences for international politics, summarily expressed by what has been called the 'CNN effect'. However, the dominance of the Western gaze upon the world, of its cultural conventions and ways of understanding, have been increasingly challenged by the establishment of news organizations such as the Arab satellite channel, Al-Jazeera. In second place, I will examine the implications of these *challenges to the Western gaze* together with, finally, the most recent thinking about the *principles and practices of public diplomacy* as pursued in a multi-polar world in which neither the verities of nation states nor the assumptions of globalization are clear (see Hafez, 2007).

The Emergence of the Global?

Visiting a remote Peruvian village in the mid-1990s, a mother told me that her recently born child had been christened 'LadyDi' in honour of the British princess. At the time the phenomenon of 'globalization' was on the lips of every commentator and little LadyDi seemed to be a graphic example of the reach of global celebrity culture and of the economic, cultural and political processes transforming our world. While few would doubt that global level transformations have taken place across the world in the last 20 years, it is less clear what they mean. In particular, what do they mean for the field of political communication? Can we speak of the emergence of a global public sphere? I will discuss these issues next with particular reference to the news media.

The Nation and the Globe

The nation or nation state is, for many, one of those taken for granted, natural categories that seem simply to exist in the same way as the ground beneath our feet. The United States, Japan, Russia have an existential weight that makes the fact of their historical contingency almost inconceivable. However, a cursory examination of any national history, or indeed national present, alerts us to the possibility of alternative national histories and futures, depending on the stories we choose to tell about who we are and where we want to go. The British national story subsumes many local, regional and national ones: Londoners, the Cornish and the Scottish have their own categories for establishing who they are. Often these categories are compatible like a Russian doll, fitting neatly one inside the other. Sometimes they are not. Versions of Basque nationalism, found mainly in Spain, make Basque identity entirely incompatible with a Spanish one.

Of course, the nation has never been the only and exclusive category of identity. Religion has been equally if not more important for many. Religions such as Islam and Christianity have fashioned non-national-based understandings of their identities, directing Muslims and Christians to a sense of belonging to potential, if not in fact, global communities. However, the nation has long been a pre-eminent vehicle of identity and the nation state, despite constant reports of its imminent demise, continues to be the basis of legitimacy for the exercise of political power and for the understanding of identity. So, for example, notwithstanding enormous international sympathy for the Burmese monks and ordinary people calling for democracy in their own country in September 2007, the international community stood by the principle of non-interference in the internal affairs of sovereign states as the protests were brutally repressed. Nation states continue to matter and the practice of political communication continues to be bounded by them.

However, these boundaries have begun to look ever more porous. At the end of the twentieth century, the term 'globalization' became a buzz word used by political and business leaders alike to refer to the changes sweeping the world that appeared to undermine national systems' capacity to deal with the world's economic, political and ethical challenges. This process of globalization was driven in part by economics. Growth in levels of world trade and the flows of capital, goods and services around the globe intensified towards the end of the twentieth century, facilitated by developments in electronic communications. Every day vast quantities of capital can be transferred around the world at the click of a mouse, with the potential to fuel a country's growth or devastate its economy. By 2007 the major computer companies such as IBM had built super-computers capable of processing 478 trillion calculations per second. Corporate behemoths like Wal-Mart ($35.11b) and BP ($27.43b) have larger revenues than the gross domestic products of many nation states (Panama's is $26.16b, for example) with the ensuing power that such financial muscle bestows.[2] Anti-globalization activists have long pointed to the negative economic, political and cultural consequences that the overweening concentration of resources and untrammelled action of the market can have for less advantaged parts of the world. What does seem clear is that the nation state cannot hope to be the exclusive master of its destiny nor control the terms of its own self-understanding. Environmental change, possible pandemics and trade conditions are global matters.

Human consciousness of the global, one of the defining features of globalization is, like other aspects of globalization, a process of *longue durée*. Political, cultural, technological and economic processes have been in train for many centuries, contributing to greater global interrelatedness and the compression of time and place. However, the intensification of consciousness of the world as a whole, where issues are conceived of in global terms and national reference points are made relative to more general and supranational ones, is a notable development at the beginning of the twenty-first century. As we shall see, the media have played a significant role in these changes.

Global News Media: Technology, Regulation and Convergence

The current global communications network came into being in the last 30 years, powered by developments in technology as well as in the regulatory and market environments. Take technology. It is not *the* determinant of political and economic change; politics and economics are key to the development of technology.[3] However, it is no exaggeration to say that twenty-first-century communications technology is transforming the ways we relate to time and space, with significant implications for politics and society. Nineteenth-century developments such as the introduction of the telegraph in 1837, the telephone in 1876 and the laying down of oceanic cables from 1857 onwards contributed to these processes, expanding our ability to conduct global transactions and to conceive of the world as a whole. However, at the end of the twentieth century the sheer velocity and take up of technological change have been unprecedented. The reach of media technologies has grown with each wave of innovation. For example, it took 40 years for radio, introduced in the 1920s in the United States, to gain an audience of 50 million. The same number was using personal computers only 15 years after the PC was introduced. After four years of public availability, the internet was being used by 50 million Americans. By 2007, 1.71 billion were using the internet worldwide, a growth of 225 per cent between 2000 and 2007. The internet and the mobile phone, integrating cameras and recorders, have opened up the spaces and sources of communication, as the images and messages transmitted from the Burmese democracy protesters in September 2007 showed.

However, as Burma also demonstrated, technology is not a sufficient condition for political change. All social relations are marked by governance mechanisms. As Scholte says 'there is no such thing as an unregulated social context' (2000: 101) and here again the continued relevance of the nation state is shown. Regulation is principally created and administered by state, regional and global institutions, all of which are established by states.[4] In the 1980s Anglo-American communications policy pursued a liberalizing agenda. Ronald Reagan and Margaret Thatcher deregulated their country's respective communications industries, a trend that was followed by most liberal democracies. Some states have sought to limit the impact of Western free-market ideology and its attendant political and cultural implications. The King of Bhutan, for example, banned television and the internet until 1999 in an effort to conserve his country's unique cultural heritage. The

Chinese government strictly limits unrestricted access to the internet. Global operators such as Google and MySpace have agreed to restrictions in the Chinese market including, for example, filters on news and discussion of the religious group, Falun Gong, the Dalai Lama and the Tiananmen Square killings. National borders may have become more porous in the twenty-first century, but governments continue to find effective means of policing and controlling information environments in ways that belie over-optimistic accounts of the democratizing impact of new technology.

A third feature of the international scene in the last 20 years, facilitated by the deregulated international trading regime and the free flow of capital, has been the convergence and concentration of the media industry. In 1998 mergers and acquisitions reached an all-time record with more than 12,500 deals totalling over $1.6 trillion. The trend accelerated in 1999 and the twenty-first century opened with the world's biggest merger between Time Warner and AOL. Deregulation and relaxation of cross-media ownership have allowed the creation of global media empires. Before late twentieth-century convergence, most media businesses had their distinct areas of speciality. Disney was known for its cartoons, Rupert Murdoch as a newspaper publisher. In the twenty-first century, the communication industry is global and media groups span several areas of the communication business. Take Murdoch's business empire, perhaps one of the best documented of all those that dominate the communications industry. His interests spread across newspapers, television, cinema, book publishing and the internet, and are found throughout Europe, Latin America, the United States, Asia and Australasia.

Between them the top eight communication companies (see Table 9.1) provide US citizens with practically all their television news: NBC (General Electric), ABC (Disney), CBS (Viacom), Fox News (News Corporation) and CNN (AOL-Time Warner). They also provide much of the world's most popular entertainment.

Table 9.1   Eight top US communication organizations, 2006

---

* General Electric (owner of NBC, market value: $390.6 billion)
* Microsoft (market value: $306.8 billion)
* Google (market value: $154.6 billion)
* AOL-Time Warner (market value: $90.7 billion)
* Disney (market value: $72.8 billion)
* News Corporation (market value: $56.7 billion)
* Viacom (market value: $53.9 billion)
* Yahoo! (market value: $40.1 billion)

Source: *Mother Jones* magazine, 2006.

The Global Village through Western Eyes

National identities are partly imagined and shored up by the stories we tell about our past and this bestows power on the story-tellers, the producers and disseminators of symbolic products in news and fiction. Their contribution to the shaping of the moral, political and cultural order can help build or erode alternative communities of identity not based solely on national lines. Furthermore, instantaneous, 24-hour electronic communication does not just convey news and entertainment more quickly. Its apparent fusion of the real and the represented alters the fabric of our lives. The extraordinary becomes part of our everyday experience; the image of Tiger Woods or Queen Elizabeth II may be more familiar to us than the face of our next-door neighbour. Celebrity and the phenomenon of the global celebrity of entertainers, sportsmen and women and, less frequently, politicians is itself largely a product of new communications technology. In the 1960s, the Canadian media theorist, Marshall McLuhan (1911–1980), predicted that the effects of electronic communication and improved transportation would be to create a 'global village' where, in the same way that members of a tribal village are aware of their interdependence, members of the global community are conscious of human society in its entirety.

However, as we have seen, on various measures global communication has been dominated by the West: technology and content, and thus values and narratives, have been theirs so that even though the world might be in the process of becoming a global village, it is one seen through Western eyes. This has particularly been the case in relation to the news and information marketplace.

Global news agencies such as Reuters and Associated Press (AP) continue to maintain the most complete transmission networks and capacity for widespread, rapid coverage of international events. They provide the pictures and words for much of what we take to be international news. Joined by 24-hour news channels from the 1980s onwards, channels such as Reuters TV, CNN, Associated Press TV, CBS International and BBC World have provided much of the vocabulary, conventions and substance of global news.

From Victorian times, provision of world news had been dominated by mainly Western-based, news agencies that between them carved up world coverage, shadowing the imprint of empire. Agence France Presse (AFP), the successor to Havas (founded in 1835), is a non-profit making news agency that receives indirect subsidies from the French government. It has a strong African presence and employs around 4000 people with journalists in 165 countries. The US, non-profit making cooperative, Associated Press (AP) founded in 1846, has around 3700 employees. Describing itself as 'the essential global news network', it is the world's largest supplier of video news, has 243 bureaux in 97 countries and claims that on any given day, half the world's population sees AP news. The UK-based Reuters began as a news agency in 1851. In 2007 its international multimedia news agency employed 2400 staff in 196 bureaux serving 131 countries.[5]

Several thousand media workers are responsible for gathering and conveying information involving the lives of the more than six billion people who live on the earth. Global information flows continue to be dominated by the West. Criticism of this situation was at the heart of the 1970s debate about the worldwide system of collection and distribution of news and information that took place at the UN agency UNESCO, (see Taylor, 1997: ch. 1). It was strongly criticized by countries from Africa, Latin America and Asia for maintaining a situation where communication power and control lay along an East/West axis linking the United States and Europe, marginalizing newly independent nations of the former colonies. It was argued that the major Western news agencies dominated news flows, primarily one-way from North to South.

Much of the debate was strongly conditioned by the political and technological conditions of the time. However, a number of issues continue to be relevant for understanding constraints to the development of a global village.[6] I will highlight four. The first concerns the gate-keeping role of Western news-gatherers, controlling the flow and content of news and information. This can result in those countries that make up nearly 85 per cent of the world's population being, on the one hand, at best under-represented or at worst absent from the global conversation; on the other, it means that non-Western countries are represented to the world and to each other through Western eyes. As the Pulitzer prize-winning Nigerian journalist, Dele Olojede, put it, there is no African conversation about Africa. South Africans learn about what is happening in the north of the continent from overseas news agencies (conversation with author, 20 October 2006). In second place, it is claimed that the West is able to set the global news agenda, not telling us what to think but certainly telling us what to think about and in doing so, they act, in third place, as 'primary definers'. The process of primary definition plays an important role in determining our understanding of the world since the first and earliest definition of an event tends to stick. Finally, Western news is criticized for the negativity of its reportage of many parts of the globe. The dynamics and nature of conventional news values ensure that a great deal of news is indeed about the unusual and the negative. However, various aspects of the West's coverage of other parts of the world appear to make death, disease and disaster synonymous with the lives of whole communities (see, for example, Stevenson, 1999). These communities, understandably, object.

State-driven remedies offered in the 1970s, such as, for example, the establishment of regionally based news agencies, foundered on the reefs of insufficient resources and lack of respect for journalistic autonomy and freedom.

However, a number of late twentieth- and early twenty-first-century developments are contributing to the opening up of public space.

Opening Up Public Space

Western public space has, in international terms, been dominated by the big Western news agencies. This continues to be the case for the West at the beginning of the twenty-first century. In other parts of the world, similar patterns prevail. The Chinese population's world-view, for example, has been chiefly supplied by the government dependent Xinhua press agency founded in 1931. Challenges, however, have emerged. Western hegemonies and Eastern hermeticism now encounter globally distributed news that is adding new voices to the global conversation.

Challenging the Western Gaze: Al-Jazeera

The Middle East Broadcasting Corporation (now known as the Middle East Broadcasting Centre, MBC) was established in 1991 with Saudi funding during the Gulf War to provide Middle East viewers with an Arab account of the war. The well-respected news channel Al Arabiya, founded in 2003, is part of its stable of channels. However, it was the launch of Al Jazeera in 1996 that really challenged the dominance of the Western gaze and, to a certain extent, the Arab state perspective.

Established and funded by the Qatari government, it was the first Arab TV channel in the Arabic language prepared to cover sensitive political issues. Its founding ethos was heavily influenced by the large number of journalists recruited from a failed BBC Arabic service project, where impartial news and representation of all viewpoints had guided coverage. This was unknown on Arab television news, which would not show, for example, representatives of the Israeli perspective or, in the case of conservative Arab states like Saudi Arabia, radical Islamic views such as those of Hezbollah, the Shia Islamic political and paramilitary movement. Al Jazeera aired controversial political shows calculated to spark fierce debate. Complaints poured in from Arab governments, displeased with the channel's iconoclastic coverage of Arab politics and culture. Saudi Arabia, Kuwait, Jordan and Morocco were among those who complained about coverage and attempted to restrict the channel's activities (see Miles, 2005).

Al Jazeera's commitment to reporting the news as it saw it brought criticism from all sides. In particular, its relative independence from the state was an entirely new feature of the Arab media environment. Media freedom had long been tightly controlled by Arab governments. Even at the beginning of the twenty-first century, newspapers must adhere to strict rules about what they may or may not publish. In Bahrain, for example, one of the region's least repressive regimes, photographs of the country's leaders must be published in appropriately prominent positions regardless of the news value of the story. Failure to do so can lead to the newspaper's temporary closure (Arab journalist, interview with the author, 15 February 2004).

Understanding this context makes Al Jazeera's foundation and success all the more remarkable. For the first time, an Arab-based media organization sought to establish its credibility on the basis of independent reporting and debate, challenging if necessary the cultural and political sensitivities of the Arab world and the wider Western world. In doing so, it opened up for Arab audiences the terms of discussion, airing issues never covered before and revealed to Western viewers how Arabs and Muslims saw and understood events affecting their region's politics and culture.

Al Jazeera first came to international attention in its coverage of the US/UK operation against Iraq in 1998 known as Desert Storm, when it was the only news channel in Iraq able to get pictures of events out to a wider world. However, as a number of studies show (see, for example, El-Nawawy and Iskandar, 2002; Miles, 2005), the channel really made its name among Arabic speakers in its coverage of the second *intifada*, the Palestinian uprising in 2000. The channel's showing of the shooting of Muhammed al-Durra, a 12-year-old Palestinian boy, by Israeli soldiers enraged viewers and galvanized Arab audiences in support of the Palestinians. According to Miles (2005: 91), the television coverage of the *intifada* shown in homes, cafes and offices across the Muslim world, helped 'forge a new Arab political awareness', where for 'the first time Arabs made their autocratic leaders defend their decisions and policies'.

Al Jazeera emerged as a major world media player in the events following the 9/11 attacks on the United States, exemplified by its exclusive broadcast on 7 October 2001 of Osama bin Laden's statement about the attacks. Its unrivalled access to the Arab world allowed it to 'scoop' the Western media heavyweights. Al Jazeera's transmission of this and future Bin Laden footage was strongly criticized by the US and UK governments, who asked their broadcasters not to retransmit it for security reasons.

Al Jazeera has added a new perspective to the news-telling mix. In 2006 it launched an English language version of its service, extending the reach of its view. However, we should be cautious about overstating its impact or its distinctiveness. In the Arab world its authority has been challenged in some quarters by accusations that it has failed to champion the Palestinian cause, tried to divide and rule Arabs, and is the result of an 'American-Zionist plot' (see Miles, 2005). More accurately, one can state that it has adopted much of the broadcasting conventions and grammar pioneered in the West, including the BBC's substantive notion of news and the CNN's presentational techniques of providing raw, breaking stories, an emphasis on 'liveness' and 'seeing' news as it happens, In other words, Al Jazeera has followed fairly closely a mainstream Western model of news. Ironically, this is at a time when, as we shall see next, this model is undergoing radical change and is being challenged by alternative global views.

Alternative Networks

In November 2007, the BBC launched an audience-driven version of one of its flagship radio programmes, *PM*. Known as *iPM*, the interactive programme asked listeners to 'Share what you know' by shaping the running order of the Saturday programme through the internet. This bold new mission was accompanied by the BBC website's somewhat nervous statement that 'It might not work but if it doesn't we can at least blame you, the listener. It's your programme.' The experiment was an acknowledgement that, as we will see in Chapter 13, news is not just what happens as decided by the correspondents of Reuters or Al Jazeera.

As we have noted throughout this book, developments at the beginning of the twenty-first century are allowing the emergence of dispersed, 'contrapuntal', alternate and, perhaps, alternative media environments with as yet uncertain consequences for the conduct of politics. Anti-globalization activists turn the tools of a globalized world against itself as they plan their WTO protests online; Jihadi websites help radicalize young Western Muslims; Mac users support each other through internet fora. These networks criss-cross nations and the globe, helping to create a range of public spaces which, using Edward Said's musical metaphor, Roger Silverstone describes as 'contrapuntal' to express the empirical reality of the multiplicity of voices in our contemporary media environment and also a 'way of seeing the world as defined and only understandable through the relationship of self and other, of similarity and difference' (2007: 101). The idea of counterpoint underlines the melodic rather than harmonious relationship between voices and is a useful metaphor for modelling the diverse and at times dissonant global commons in which we find ourselves.

Global Communications and International Affairs

Winning friends and influencing people have always been the stuff of diplomacy. Relationships between states have been nurtured, negotiated, caricatured or terminated as long as there has been an international state system.[7] However, for a significant period of its existence, foreign diplomacy was almost exclusively the preserve of elites, carried out behind closed doors away from the public eye. This continues in part to be the case, but the emergence of the *mediapolis* and thus of the importance of 'soft' power have changed the terms of the diplomatic game. 'Public diplomacy' was a term introduced in the 1960s to reflect the growing recognition that diplomacy was no longer simply an elite activity. It is no coincidence that this occurred at a time when the media's ability to affect public opinion and influence foreign policy was being increasingly debated in the United States. In particular, the media's coverage of US involvement in Vietnam (1959–75), was held by some commentators to have undermined the war effort, even though subsequent research showed that journalists largely reflected political consensus about the war, only becoming critical when Vietnam became a subject of political controversy (Hallin, 1986).

I will examine next three questions raised by the emergence of the twenty-first-century global communication network and the conduct of international affairs: first, the *relationship between media and their impact on the conduct of foreign policy*; second, *the contentious character of political communication during times of conflict* (a subject also explored in Chapter 4); and finally, *emerging re-understandings of public diplomacy* in the twenty-first century.

The CNN Effect

In Tony Blair's valedictory speech to the Reuters Foundation about the media, he reflected on how the changed media environment affects the conduct of politics:

> You have to respond to stories [...] in real time. Frequently the problem is as much assembling the facts as giving them. Make a mistake and you quickly transfer from drama into crisis. In the 1960s the government would sometimes, on a serious issue, have a Cabinet lasting two days. It would be laughable to think you could do that now without the heavens falling in before lunch on the first day. (2007)

Communication technology makes it possible to know a government action or decision the moment it occurs and allows the news media to provide a constant flow of global real-time news. The pioneer of 'live', 24-hour news channels was CNN (Cable News Network). Founded in 1980, it broke through into global public consciousness in its coverage of the 1991 First Gulf War. The only foreign broadcaster left in Baghdad, its journalists showed the world – including the US president and Pentagon generals – the impact of the Allied bombardment of Iraq's capital city.

The speeding up of, and potential impact on, the quality of policy decision-making as a result of the contemporary media environment is an undoubted fact. Among policy makers and journalists in the 1990s, however, the notion that the broadcast media somehow affect the substance of foreign policy – the so-called CNN effect – became an untested 'fact'. It was argued that foreign policy decisions at times of crisis and conflict were increasingly being driven by television coverage: horrific images of famine in Ethiopia in the 1980s, the atrocities in Bosnia or a murdered American soldier being dragged through Somalian streets in the 1990s were enough to place public pressure on policy-makers to 'do something' (see Taylor, 1997).

Examined from the perspective of the twenty-first century, however, these claims seem overly simplistic. Research has shown (see, for example, Robinson, 2002) that any media effect on foreign policy is highly contingent on elite policy uncertainty and media framing of the issue in either a critical or empathetic way. In other words, where there is elite consensus about a for-eign policy position the media are unlikely to have an impact. And even when cracks appear in this consensus, leadership commitment to a policy will also be a key factor in its implementation. Take the US invasion and presence in Iraq from 2003 until the end of the Bush presidency in 2008. For most of that time, daily stories and images told a terrible tale of suffering and death and yet President Bush refused to bend to pressure to withdraw American troops. In retrospect, the notion of the 'CNN effect' – while useful in alerting us to ele-ments of media power in a changing communication environment – failed to do justice to the continuing weight of structural and systemic factors that limit media power, *especially* in times of conflict as we shall see next.

Conflict and Political Communication

For liberal democracies, waging war successfully is as much about deploy-ing effective communication strategies as military ones. 'Information war', the use of black and white propaganda during, before and after times of conflict, is nothing new (see Knightley, 2004). Peace-time efforts to 'manu-facture consent' (see Herman and Chomsky, 1988) are intensified at times of war as governments – unsurprisingly – seek to ensure that the news indus-try reads global events in the ways they want them to and that coverage conforms to the government agenda.[8] This process is fuelled by the conven-tions of reporting that tend to 'index' coverage to elite views and can at times encourage second-rate journalism, more interested in peddling stereotypes than seeking the truth. Even at the best of times, news gathering and reporting tend to show conflicts as zero-sum games: there are only win-ners and losers; villains and victims. Extremely complex situations such as that of the Congo during the late 1990s and early part of this century are presented in black and white terms and audiences are none the wiser, even if they wanted to be, of what is happening.

There are, however two important caveats to be made to this rather bleak view of how political communication operates at times of conflict. The first concerns the place of misinformation and deception during wartime. Where the war is just,[9] it is hard to maintain that misleading one's enemy is not legitimate. If I am being threatened with death, I can argue that the communicational context of a mutual commitment to truth-telling has effectively broken down. This does not, however, justify all and any deception. There are certain symbols and conventions – driving a truck with a cross or crescent symbol to indicate a medical purpose, a journalist's commitment to veracious reporting – that are preserved and should be respected even in wartime.

The second caveat concerns the performance of journalists and media companies. Just as some of the conventions of journalism may work against the grain of providing a full and adequately truthful account of conflicts, it is also the case that its conventions of scrutiny, investigation and challenge to power provide many examples of journalists seeking to alert the public, despite governments' best efforts, to critical views and alternative perspectives at times of conflict and war. The BBC's world editor, John Simpson, was attacked by the Labour government for his allegedly pro-Serbian stance when he wrote an article in April 1999 suggesting that the NATO bombing to protect Albanian Kosovans did not seem to be working. In his diaries, Blair's media chief, Alastair Campbell, stated that the UK government 'had a real problem with the BBC'. In his view, 'They made no effort to balance the fact that they were reporting democracies and a dictatorship, virtually taking the dictatorship propaganda at face value while putting everything we did through a far more intense scrutiny' (2007: 371). Military and political leaders may have the power to employ the full panoply of PSYOPS (psychological operations)[10] but, in liberal democracies, this will, and should always be, subject to the intense scrutiny of their citizens.

The Kosovo war in 1999 was the moment when media management techniques developed by the Blair governments – what I called the Millbank model (see Chapter 5) – were exported into the international arena. NATO's bombing campaign against Serbia to force it to cease military operations against Albanian Kosovars had initially received widespread public support in the West. Public opinion was primed to accept the bombing. Having watched and read the reporting of the wars between the various nations of the previous Yugoslavia in the 1990s, 'Milosevic' and 'The Serbs' were definitely seen as the 'other', the villains of the story.[11] British newspapers, for example, were almost unanimous (the *Independent* was the only exception) in their support for a NATO bombing campaign against Serbia and, with NATO describing the Serbian actions in Kosovo as 'the worst genocide since WW2' (Campbell, 2007: 371), public support was assured.[12]

Journalists were expelled from Kosovo in March 1999 when bombing began and only a few were allowed to remain in Belgrade. The bombing lasted 80 days. During this time, blunders as well as Serbian reluctance to accept NATO's terms began to weaken public support. The Chinese Embassy was bombed, killing a husband and wife and another journalist. A line of escaping Albanian refugees was also mistakenly attacked and, a month into the bombing campaign, Serbian TV headquarters was deliberately targeted, killing 16 media workers. Fears that NATO was losing the communication war, that public and media support were slipping away, prompted the revamping of the NATO communication operation under the leadership of Alastair Campbell. As a British minister put it, NATO's media staffers needed 'some good old-fashioned Millbank discipline instilled in them' (Jack Straw cited in Campbell, 2007: 377). The confusion and lack of clear messages that had previously reigned were replaced by an efficient, fast, coordinated communication effort. Mistakes were quickly admitted and NATO staff worked hard to get their story out first. Journalists, however, were largely unable to gain access to the field of conflict and, like their colleagues stuck in Belgrade, were highly dependent on official sources for their stories.

This was to change for Operation Iraqi Freedom, the name given to the invasion and occupation of Iraq in 2003 by coalition forces (mainly the United States, Britain, Spain, Italy and Australia). Six hundred journalists were 'embedded' with coalition forces and a number were allowed to operate outside the control of the military (see Tumber and Palmer, 2004). Information was provided by the military to a media pool based in Qatar. The invasion's success – despite the Iraqi information minister's increasingly risible attempts to affirm the contrary – was succeeded by the dark days of terrible civilian casualties, torture of Iraqi prisoners by American forces at Abu Ghraib prison, and the revelation of the inadequacy of reconstruction plans in the immediate aftermath of the invasion. In these circumstances, together with the non-appearance of weapons of mass destruction (WMD), message control became a far distant memory for government communicators.

Public Diplomacy

In 1999 the Clinton administration created the post of Under Secretary of State for Public Diplomacy and Public Affairs in the US Department of State. In 2002 the UK government launched the Public Diplomacy Strategy Board to bring together the British agencies engaged in communicating Britain to overseas' publics. The Foreign Office, the British Council and the Tourist Board were charged with promoting the United Kingdom as a land of 'dynamic tradition' and of being a country that is 'principled and professional'.

These developments were signs of the coming of age of 'public diplomacy'. There is no one accepted definition for this diffuse set of activities that can include government-sponsored television or radio (BBC World Service and the Voice of America, for example), educational exchange programmes, art exhibitions or tourism campaigns. The actions are undertaken to influence favourably public attitudes in ways that will support foreign policy goals in political, military or economic affairs. Sovereign states are the main protagonists of public diplomacy, although other multilateral actors such as the United Nations and business corporations seek to influence public attitudes on a whole range of foreign policy issues.

'Public diplomacy' could be considered as yet another euphemism for propaganda and its definition is close to that of 'PSYOPS' (see note 12). Certainly, in the days of the Cold War between the United States and the Soviet Union (see McNair, 2007: 170–9) there appeared to be little to differentiate the two. However, contemporary thinking about public diplomacy suggests that rather than seeking to capture hearts and minds, it is, or should be, more orientated to building 'personal and institutional relationships and dialogue with foreign audiences by focusing on values' (Van Ham, 2003: 431).

One key assumption in this thinking is that the new political environment is characterized by transnational publics and that, therefore, the distinction between domestic and foreign policy becomes ever harder to make. The 2007 declaration of a State of Emergency in Pakistan not only affected Pakistanis at home and in the diaspora, but had consequences for states involved in Afghanistan and in combating terrorism.

From an emphasis on effective message delivery, the new global political environment suggests that new approaches are required. In the view of one policy analyst, twenty-first-century public diplomacy should be characterized by a focus on building 'trust and mutuality', an integration into policy and 'a continuous, concerted attempt to develop a parallel "people-to-people" conversation that works through NGOs, diasporas, political parties and other non-governmental avenues' (Leonard, Small and Rose, 2005: 8). This approach is fleshed out in the British government's proposals set out in *Public Diplomacy in the Middle East*. According to the summary by Leonard, Small and Rose:

- It recognizes that an overt PR style 'campaign' is unlikely to be successful and may even be counterproductive.
- Its short-term aims are limited, focusing on correcting mistaken impressions, without any expectation of 'winning hearts and minds'; its more modest goal was to get people 'to hate us for the right reasons'. It recognizes that trust can only be built over the long term.
- Its longer-term goals are designed as a partnership with people in the region, with as much focus on their interests, aspirations, fears and sensitivities as on narrow British interests.

▪ It recognizes the importance of domestic audiences in reflecting messages out to the region – dealing with anti- Islamic prejudice at home is
important, both in its own right and if Britain is going to be seen as a
credible interlocutor, facing up to failings and prejudices. (2005: 41)

This model is far removed from either straightforward propaganda or efficient PR operations that effectively deliver messages. It also goes beyond
concerted efforts at explanation, useful as these are. Instead it focuses on
'mutuality', on long-term trust-building rather than short-term image-
building. In other words, this new model of public diplomacy suggests that
political communication in global times requires listening as well as speaking, together with the practical work of developing shared activities that
can generate the trust necessary for any communication to take place at all.

Part Three

Getting the Message

10

The People: Opinion, Polls and Participation

Introduction

Politics, as we saw in Chapter 3, refers to the realm of the public. This seemingly straightforward statement is so rich in meaning that understanding its implications will occupy much of this chapter. A consideration of the shifting boundaries of the private and the public provide a necessary backdrop to a discussion of the emergence of the concepts of the 'people' and 'public opinion', key issues in understanding the communication of politics.

Political communication in constitutional democracies is predicated on the existence of the public despite signs that this public is less than eager to engage in formally programmed politics (as declining election participation in some countries suggests) and the notion of the 'public' is more difficult to conceptualize in an internet age.

Notions such as the 'public' refer, as we shall see, to abstract entities, in some senses fictions. The 'public sphere' and 'public opinion' do not exist in the way in which 'my brother's car' and 'my opinion' do. It was for this reason that Margaret Thatcher's infamous statement that 'There is no such thing as society' is, despite its apparent harshness, strictly speaking true.[1] A moment's reflection reveals that much of our taken for granted political language is metaphorical: the nation speaks; the public's right to know; the country expects. All these phrases are devices of our imagination and they show that it is certainly true that many political and, indeed, social phenomena are only elusively captured by language. However, while Thatcher could say that there is no such thing as society and Bourdieu stated that 'Public opinion does not exist', both 'society' and 'public opinion' can still be useful indicators of shifting and imprecise realities that social and political scientists seek to understand and politicians and journalists seek to use.

This chapter will examine first, notions of *the public* and *the private* and the historical background to the *emergence of public opinion*. The relationship between the *public sphere* and *civil society* will also be explored in this context. This discussion will set the stage for the consideration of *four models of public opinion*, the last of which is explored in the development of opinion-polling. *Opinion polls* and their strengths and limitations are examined. Finally, debates about *the public's engagement*, or lack of it, in formal politics are discussed.

Understanding the Public

The 'public', its views, rights and interests, is perhaps one of the most bandied about terms in the political and journalistic vocabulary. Precisely what it means requires a careful examination of various currents of thought, some of which would argue that the public, as we broadly understand it today, dates its existence from the eighteenth century (see, for example, Habermas, 1962/1989). A number of thinkers suggest that the 'public' is the prerequisite for political life. This is the view of the political theorist Hannah Arendt (1958) and one I shall first explore before addressing the more commonly accepted understandings of the term.

The Public and the Private

The urge to shield the expression of the basic needs and conditions of our humanity from public gaze appears to be fairly constant across time and place: the moments of birth, death and sex are all acts traditionally hidden from view. However, cultural and historical manifestations of what is meant by the private realm have varied considerably. Today what we understand as 'private' refers to a sphere of intimacy unknown to the ancients and to many contemporaneous inhabitants of the planet: having one's own room to sleep in is still a luxury for the few. The notion of privacy arises in contrast to the notion of the public. In the ancient world the sphere of privacy was, as Hannah Arendt put it, 'the other, the dark and hidden side of the public realm, and while to be political meant to obtain the highest possibility of human existence, to have no private place of one's own (like a slave) meant to be no longer human' (1958: 64).

Modern notions of privacy have moved far from those of classical Rome. They owe much to eighteenth-century Romanticism's emphasis on the self, on the individual. Jean Jacques Rousseau's (1712–1778) *Confessions* heralded the importance of the intimate realm where privacy was no longer equivalent to a state of deprivation. After the depredations of twentieth-century totalitarian states who tried to eliminate privacy, privacy's importance to human well-being was recognized in various human rights conventions.

The good of privacy is no longer in question even though its boundaries might be (see Sanders, 2003).

The Rise of Society and the Possibility of a Public Sphere

Arendt considered Romanticism's exaltation of the intimate as a reaction to its attempted colonization by what she called the social sphere which in time would also come to undermine the political realm (1958: 22–78). Although criticized for its lack of clarity (Pitkin, 1998), Arendt's definition of the social (1958: 28) can be said to refer to the realm of activities linked with the household and necessity. In Western history the category of the social has, suggested Arendt, transformed the public sphere into 'society', the family writ large, whose modern political form is the nation, with dele-terious consequences for the truly public and political. In this situation political economy becomes the dominant science and mere living rather than living well the principal preoccupation.

In Arendt's view of the public realm, politics is considered an end in itself and a sphere of freedom, where human beings can act, can initiate change. This sense of the 'public' is well expressed by one of Nixon's aides in Joe McGinnis's classic account of media campaigns, *The Selling of the President*: 'The whole thing about politics, even at the fringes, is that what you do and say suddenly affects the world' (1969/1988: 58). However, where the political realm is replaced by the economic one – by the market – where politics is bureaucratized, politics and politicians are not highly thought of. There is no longer a public space in which individuals can speak and be recognized; the good life has been privatized.

A more optimistic reading of the post-Enlightenment world can be found in the work of social theorists such as Jürgen Habermas.[2] His account of the development of the 'public sphere' from the eighteenth-century periodical press and coffee shop society suggests that the personal opinions of private individuals can evolve into public opinion, through a process of rational-critical debate open to all and free from domination. The key principle of *Öffentlichkeit*, publicity or publicness, is provided, according to Habermas, by the press. The existence of a public sphere is defined not only by the degree of public participation but also by its rationality and quality: it is social discourse and dialogue of political relevance.

Both Arendt and Habermas explore the related issues of how human arrangements should be for there to be a public that matters and what it means for the public to matter. Their theoretical accounts of the grounds and conditions for the existence of the public contain obscurities and it is not always easy to understand how they translate in practice into twenty-first century society. Nevertheless, both thinkers elucidate key themes for our times. Their thinking illuminates discussion about such practical issues as the regulation of public service media, the role and mission of politics and why many inhabitants of post-industrial democracies feel alienated by the activities of contemporary politicians.

Civil Society

As the newly elected President of a re-born Czechoslovakia after 42 years of communist rule, Vaclav Havel, declared in 1990: 'People, your government has returned to you!' The fall of communism in Central and Eastern Europe at the close of the twentieth century witnessed a renewed interest in the notion of civil society (see Seligman, 1995). The concept has a centuries' old tradition in European social thought and political philosophy. It marked a distinction between the state and the individual, between the public and the private and was often used as a counterpoint to the notion of the state. Civil society referred neither to the individual, nor the state, nor the market. Cohen and Arato (1992/1997) examined it as an area of social interaction situated between market and state. Characterized by a plurality of forms of social life and by publicity in forms of culture and communication and also by degrees of privacy and legal frameworks, civil society is distinct from political institutions and economic organizations, and could be said to include:

- the sphere of the intimate (particularly the family)
- the sphere of associations
- social movements
- the many forms of public communication

Only certain kinds of arrangements of civil society allow a public sphere and public opinion to exist. In pre-constitutional times, the monarch was the only public person, the source and principle of unity among particulars. The development of civil society gave rise to the possibility of the public and, as absolutist monarchical power broke down, also to the notion of the 'public' standing as a reference for the people. Until French revolutionary times, the 'people' had little political content. After the Revolution (1789–99), the people increasingly became the depositary of authority and legitimacy and their opinion, the public's opinion, began to matter.

The Emergence of Public Opinion

What is public opinion? It is sometimes considered to be the sum total of opinions held on a particular subject by individual members of society or a mood or emotion that suffuses a society. The first conception underlines the practice of opinion polling, the second the analysis of collective behaviour. It has been described as 'one of the most difficult topics in democratic theory', its meaning 'often dictated by the tools we have on hand to measure it at any given historical moment' (Herbst, 2001: 451). Bourdieu trenchantly declared that public opinion did not exist. In this section I will examine the emergence of political opinion and the dominant models for understanding and devising ways of knowing what it is. It is a complex picture and my, necessarily synthetic, approach draws one possible map. Key underlying themes are those of the understanding of influence and, as discussed in Chapter 1, agency.

Some Historical Background

The historiography of public opinion is largely a European and North American affair (see, for example, Habermas, 1962/1989), a story told as being closely linked to the development of printing, democracy and free speech and association. Anderson's (1983) account of the emergence of what he calls the 'imagined community', the nation state, tells a story of public opinion's emergence in the embryonic national states of Latin America. These communities of opinion were bound together by shared interests expressed in the first newspapers of the American continent.

Pinpointing times and places for the emergence of any human phenomena – let alone one as elusive as 'public opinion' – is an extremely risky enterprise. Bearing this warning in mind, one common starting point for the emergence of public opinion is the milieu of late seventeenth-century Europe and, in particular, English society after the decisive victory for parliamentary rule struck by the 1688 Revolution. Europe's seventeenth-century wars of religion and the religious divisions within nations were the backdrop for an increasing interest in tolerance, free speech and the rules governing human behaviour. The English philosopher, John Locke (1632–1704), identified in Chapter 28 of *An Essay Concerning Human Understanding* three general laws that govern human conduct: divine law, civil law and the general regard of others, 'the law of opinion or reputation'. Opinion here is equated with the regard of others, one's reputation and the esteem in which one is held as determined by other people. The condition of public-ness is implicit in this understanding of 'opinion', a word which, in epistemological terms, distinguishes fact from something uncertain and denotes a lower state of knowing.

Rousseau is credited with the first use of the term 'public opinion' (see Monzón, 1996: 47–9), using it to refer to social customs and the manners of society. In France the term was often equated with the republic of letters, the world of the *philosophes* and literary salons of eighteenth-century

Enlightenment Europe. The nineteenth-century utilitarian model of society as being formed of individuals who seek to maximize their own benefits proved an alternative and influential approach to the 'public sphere' perspective. The utilitarian outlook – found in the works of the English philosophers, Jeremy Bentham (1748–1832) and, in more nuanced manner, John Stuart Mill (1806–1873) – underlines the way in which majority rule works to maximize the benefits for individual interests. This suggests that majority opinion is truly the key to establishing the most advantageous course of action for a community.

Four Models of Public Opinion

An increasing interest in public opinion in the nineteenth century was intensified in the twentieth from both a normative and social-scientific perspective in the works of Walter Lippmann, John Dewey and Harold Lasswell. Together with the utilitarians, these three thinkers provide archetypal ways of thinking about public opinion.

Lippmann had strong objections to the very possibility of public opinion. He raised two issues which became perennially debated and researched in subsequent opinion studies. First, he expressed his scepticism about the public's ability to possess informed, sensible opinions about the great and small political questions of the day. Second, and in part related to the first point, he noted the media's role in shaping public opinion in ways which skew views and attitudes: 'Public opinion is based on a fragmentary, often incomplete and distorted, set of pictures.' (Lippmann, 1922: 29). His transmission model of journalism and his poor view of the public's capacities led him to argue that government by elites was the only option in representative democracies. In his bleak view of the media's distorting role, he anticipates the work of those like Herman and Chomsky (1988) who consider public opinion formation as the 'manufacturing of consent', the control of the many by the powerful few. However, unlike Lippmann, they use this analysis to argue for a radical transformation of media and society.

An alternative approach to thinking about public opinion was developed by the American philosopher, John Dewey. His *The Public and its Problems* (1927) was written as a defence of democracy in response to Lippmann's *The Phantom Public* (1925). He suggests that public opinion will truly exist where there is 'free and full intercommunication' (1927: 211) enabled by the press. His model envisaged a public existing in interaction with politicians and elites, with journalists acting as mediator. In terms reminiscent of the public journalism movement and more recently citizen journalism (see Chapter 12), no longer would the public be the audience and passive consumer of news, but instead its user and real instigator as citizens actively participating in public life.

Finally, a more empirically based approach to the understanding of public opinion was developed in the first part of the twentieth century. As founder members in 1947 of the *American Association for Public Opinion Research*, communication researchers Harold Lasswell and Paul Lazarsfeld (see Chapter 2) were apostles of the application of quantitative social scientific techniques to gauge public opinion. Their wartime studies of the effectiveness of propaganda alerted them to the malleability of public opinion and to the role of media influence.

To summarize, we can define four ways of thinking about public opinion (see also Herbst, 1993):

- the majoritarian principle where the opinions of the greatest number of people are those that matter (Bentham and Mill)
- the denial either of the existence or the possibility of public opinion (Lippmann and Bourdieu)
- the discursive/consensual definition based on the notion that public opinion evolves through communication so that the public becomes a community (Dewey)
- an aggregated, measurable set of data found in opinion polls and surveys (Lasswell and Lazarsfeld).

Gauging Public Opinion

The growing acknowledgement of the importance of public opinion has ensured intense political and media interest in understanding what it is and how it can be measured. These interests have spawned a veritable industry of focus group and opinion poll experts, the two leading approaches adopted in the last 70 years to gauging public opinion.

Polling

Public opinion existed long before opinion polls existed, although in the minds of many – and perhaps particularly the media at election time – the two have become synonymous. Political opinion polls based on the questioning of a representative, systematically drawn sample of voters started in the United States in the 1930s. In 1937 the *Public Opinion Quarterly* was founded, the year after George Gallup had conducted a poll using statistically constructed sampling techniques to predict correctly the outcome of the US presidential election. Against the *Literary Digest*'s unscientific but massive 10 million readers' poll predicting a win for the Republican candidate, Alf Landon, Gallup's poll foresaw the Roosevelt landslide victory.

Gallup demonstrated that it was not the size but the representativeness of the sample that mattered. He used the technique with similar success to predict, against all prevailing opinion, the 1945 Labour win in the British general elections. As politicians and journalists increasingly sought more precise information about public attitudes to allow them to fine tune campaigns and the reporting of them, pollsters' successes made them necessary members of election teams.

Until polling became established, the taking of the public temperature was often done intuitively. British prime minister Stanley Baldwin (1867–1947) was said to consult his railway station manager. And even when polling had become long established, intuitive measures were often favoured for gauging the public mood. The wife of Labour's leader, Glenys Kinnock, is said to have believed her husband had lost the 1992 general election – which they had – when voters avoided eye contact with her as she canvassed their vote.

However, the accuracy of election polling ensured that systematic sampling of aggregations of individual opinions became the dominant model for representing public opinion. As politicians began to understand that an effective election strategy requires accurate information about voters, an industry of pollsters developed. Many were commercial companies commissioned by parties, and increasingly by the media, to chart public opinion. Independent foundations and state agencies also established regular polling programmes on a range of public attitudes.

In the twenty-first century, it is hard to conceive of any contemporary political party refusing to commission or consider the evidence of polls in devising electoral, opposition or governing strategies. Polls are also now a fixed feature of the media and political persuasion scene. Companies such as YouGov are regularly commissioned to run internet polls – the company's speciality – on a range of issues upon which the media will then hang a story and pressure groups seek leverage.

Focus Groups

Developed to fine tune 1950s' American marketing research, focus groups provide a complementary technique for gathering information on public opinion. In British Labour's successful 1997 campaign, they were used extensively by Philip Gould (1998). His findings showed that the Conservatives' campaign message of 'New Labour, New Danger', in emphasizing Labour's newness, committed a cardinal strategic error, underscoring Labour's own effort to get across the message that it was indeed new.

Surveys of voters' values using multivariate techniques were again developed in the United States. They seek to probe more deeply below the surface froth of voters' preferences and views of candidates to discover what are considered to be their more stable, underlying values. Campaigners use findings to identify and develop strategies to shape these values. Ronald Reagan's chief strategist and pollster, Richard Wirthlin, is credited as one of the architects of this approach. He worked with Reagan from the time of his gubernatorial campaign for the State of California in the 1970s, where he pioneered the use of the computer to analyse complex demographic data in order to create voter target groups and tailor political ads accordingly. Wirthlin's techniques are now part of the common stock of weapons in the politician's armoury, contributing in part to the huge inflation of campaign costs.

How Do Pollsters Do It?

The standard question for political polling, which seeks to gauge levels of support for political parties, is 'how would you vote if there was an election today?'

To get an accurate response, opinion polling techniques have become progressively more sophisticated as pollsters have learnt from past errors. However, there are basically two approaches to sampling:

Random probability. The pollster selects every nth (say, 14th) name from, for example, the electoral register for a number of areas or sampling points.
Quota sample. The pollster finds respondents who match the social characteristics of the population.

For the second method, around 40 per cent of people approached refuse. Pollsters seek to substitute with people with similar characteristics but it can be a moot question as to how representative these samples can be with such a high drop out rate.

Polling methods include *face-to-face interviews*, *telephone surveys* and, increasingly, *internet polls*. Telephone surveys are commonly used in the United States. Here pollsters have to be aware of the distorting effects of, for example, the percentage of those who are ex-directory. The most frequently used form of self-administered survey was until recently the postal survey. It is has now been largely replaced by internet polling which provides an economic alternative.

Election studies also often include *panel interviews* in which a representative small sample of voters is interviewed at regular intervals to track changes before and during an election campaign with the drawback that results can be skewed because of the effect of increasing political interest through the interviews.

In Britain, polling companies claim that 95 per cent of a predicted Labour or Conservative vote in a sample of 1000 is right to within a margin of 3 per cent, although this will only be in the relatively rare circumstances of having achieved a random sample. Margins of error could mean the difference between victory and defeat in specific conditions: this proved to be the case in the US 2000 presidential elections where media exit polls wrongly predicted a Democrat victory for Al Gore. The British first past the post voting system for national elections can also offer hostages to fortune for pollsters. In 1992 the election result – where John Major won for the Conservatives against his Labour rival, Neil Kinnock – severely dented confidence in the pollsters' work. They had predicted a narrow Labour lead of between 0.55 per cent and three per cent. In fact, the Conservatives won with a lead of 7.6 per cent. Subsequent studies concluded that the following factors were to blame:

- **Unrepresentative selection of respondents**. Pollsters set quotas which allowed too few interviews with, for example, two car owners (traditional Conservative voters) and too many with council (public) housing tenants (traditional Labour voters).
- **Late swing**. External factors including campaign mistakes by the Labour team such as their flamboyant and over-confident Sheffield pre-election rally resulted in voters moving away from Labour.
- **Spiral of silence**. Polls consistently underestimated Conservative support (spiral of silence – see below) and overestimated Labour support (spiral of fashionability).
- **Selective participation**. Labour supporters were under-registered.

After 1992 UK polling companies agreed to a number of changes including an increase in phone polling; changes to quotas and taking more account of 'don't knows' (DKs) and 'won't says'.

Problems with Polls

The 1992 British election result provided evidence for what the German researcher, Elizabeth Noelle-Neumann, had identified as one major challenge for pollsters, namely what she termed 'the spiral of silence' (1984; Noelle-Neumann and Petersen, 2004). This refers to the interplay between mass media, interpersonal communication and social relations and how individual perceptions of prevailing climates of opinion can impact upon individual expressions of opinion. Her studies of German public opinion in the 1970s found that people tend to conceal their views if they think they are in a minority and are more willing to express them if they think they are dominant. This then produces a spiralling effect whereby those views considered dominant gain ground and alternatives retreat.

To a certain extent, pollsters can take account of potential spiralling effects in their sample modelling and in their interpretation of DKs. However, there are some more fundamental problems with polls which have been thoroughly explored by a number of researchers (see Bishop, 2005) and can be summarized as follows.

Public knowledge and ignorance. Polls generally assume that respondents have views on matters they may know nothing about. Surveys commonly include leading questions such as 'You may have heard about the president's policy on [...].', and proceed to ask for a view. There is evidence, however, to suggest that American voters at least are uninformed about public affairs and may never have heard about an issue for which they are asked for an opinion. However, when prompted, people seem to prefer to offer an opinion even when they are asked to provide responses to fictitious issue questions (see Bishop, 2005).

The significance of words, questions and order. The words used, the forms of questions (open-ended/free choice or closed-ended/forced-choice) and question order have all been found significantly to affect poll results (Bishop, 2005). Take one of the most commonly used polling questions: 'What do you think is the *most* important problem facing this country today?' When faced with a closed list of issues, respondents provide significantly different responses to when given *carte blanche* to provide their own unconstrained views. Questions which cue politically partisan responses ('The prime minister has proposed [...]' instead of 'It has been proposed [...]') will also provide substantial response differences. Pollsters can also prompt more black and white maps of opinion by filtering out DKs or allowing only a binary yes/no response on issues. Asked, for example, whether one opposed or supported the 2003 Iraq invasion permits no possibility for uncertainty. Question context and order also affect response. In telephone surveys, a 'recency' effect has been found where respondents tend to choose the last response whereas in internet surveys the opposite tends to occur, the so-called 'primacy' effect (Bishop, 2005: 64–6).

Problems with polls extend to other areas of opinion research. As Herbst points out (2001: 454), agenda-setting research, for example – despite its undoubted contributions to the field – is based on the premise that media content and public opinion, as measured by content analysis and surveys, can be separated out as two distinct elements in the process of opinion formation. It hypothesizes that interaction exists and suggests that the direction of that influence is from the media to the public. In reality, however, journalists and editors are members of the public too, and it would be improbable in the extreme to suppose that there would be no interaction between the two. Disentangling the direction of influence is no easy matter.

The Uses and Misuses of Polls

Polls are an imperfect simulacrum for understanding what the people think. They can provide misleading evidence which either disguises public ignorance of public affairs or skews opinions in directions dictated by the pollsters. And yet, because of their status as scientific artefacts – providers of quantitatively attested, hard facts – polls are immensely popular among many politicians and most journalists. They provide a continuous popularity test for incumbents and cues for voters and campaigners for the supposed climate of opinion. Opinion polls, then, become more than a supposed reflection of public opinion; they are transmuted into major influences on the conduct and interpretation of campaigns and on the conduct of policy. Bill Clinton used them as a matter of course to 'triangulate' policy positions. Intense publicity given to negative polls may deter a minister from doing what he or she believes is the right thing to do. But they may also mislead politicians about what people care about. In the British 1992 elections, it appeared that the electorate wanted more spending on public services. Even though this might have been the case, the final Conservative victory showed that they cared even more about not being taxed more heavily.

What about evidence that polls influence voters? Only 2 to 3 per cent of voters say they are influenced by polls, but there is some evidence to suggest that this may not be the case. In France, for example, because of concern about media reporting of polls, and their potential impact on election results, polling is banned in the 24 hours before voting and exit polls cannot be reported until after voting has ended at 8 P.M. Banning the reporting of polls seems rather drastic and unrealistic in a globalized, internet age.

The media's role is easily abused. Headline poll results can be published without context or caution giving highly misleading impressions of the real state of public opinion. The media's agenda-setting or 'priming' effects – that is, the way in which they can make aspects of an issue more salient (see, for example, Weaver, McCombs and Shaw, 2004) – are significant in shaping public views in unexpectedly subtle ways. Bishop (2005: 148–57) makes this argument in exploring the apparent paradox of high approval ratings for Bill Clinton at a time when the media were full of news about his extra-marital affair with Monica Lewinsky and a possible impending impeachment. The approval rating poll question, 'Do you approve or disapprove of the way [president's name] is handling his job as president?' was interpreted in the context of Clinton's personal problems and the high approval ratings related to the public's view that 'he was doing the best job that could be done under extremely trying circumstances' (Bishop, 2005: 156).

Bishop makes a number of proposals (2005: 188–202) for improving the way opinion polls represent public opinion including: the breaking down of poll results according to the level of public awareness and attention to the issue; the random probing of respondents' replies to understand what they had understood by the questions; additional questions to assess the volatility of the opinions held; adopting Gallup's five-dimensional question design plan (respondent's [R's] awareness/knowledge of an issue, R's spontaneous overall views of issue, R's views on the specifics, R's reasons for holding that opinion, R's intensity of feeling on the issue). It may also be preferable to explore public ignorance or to provide deliberative public opinion polls (see, for example, Fishkin, 1995) on such complex issues as the European Union Constitution, submitted to referenda in a number of EU member states. Media organizations too are urged to be more responsible in the way they present polling information. However, a more radical question is whether the entire approach of the media to representing public opinion is conducive to citizen's participation in public affairs. In their study of media representation of public opinion in the 2001 UK elections, Brookes, Lewis and Wahl-Jorgensen conclude that there is 'an overwhelming emphasis on the horse race' (2004: 77) and that 'the discursive construction of the apathetic electorate works ideologically to legitimize a situation in which media and political elites are the key players' (p. 78). This analysis smacks a little of blaming the messenger. However, it poses significant questions about how the public participates in public affairs and to what extent the media and politicians work with or against the grain of a vigorous, healthy public sphere. Certainly Dr Gallup would not be pleased with the current media use of the polls as a means to predict election results. He considered them devices to improve democracy by improving feedback to the politicians.

Public Participation

In Britain and the United States, the question of the people's participation in public affairs as measured by voting in elections, membership in associations and consumption of mainstream political news was the subject of scholarly, journalistic and political concern in the first decade of the twenty-first century (see, for example, Putnam 2000; Patterson, 2003; BBC, 2002; Lloyd, 2004; Power, 2006). Their work points to the following five trends:

1. Declining participation in civic associations (Putnam).
2. Increased privatization of leisure time through technological developments, particularly of television and, more recently, the internet (Putnam).
3. Declining voter turnout (Patterson, BBC, Power).
4. Declining trust in formal politics (Patterson, Lloyd, BBC, Power).
5. Declining consumption of political news particularly among the under-45 age group (BBC).

These data are used by the authors to formulate explicitly and implicitly a number of hypotheses about the state of contemporary political participation. At the risk of being accused of over-simplification, I would state their central theses and assumptions to be as follows:

- Rich social capital, as represented by dense associational networks that generate trust and cooperation, is a necessary condition for a healthy democracy (Putnam).
- The displacement of face-to-face social networks by privatized mediated networks emphasizing entertainment values undermines social capital (Putnam, Lloyd).
- The provision of political news by the media is necessary for the existence of a well-informed citizenry empowered to participate in public affairs (Patterson, Lloyd, BBC).
- News about politics emphasizing division, negativity and trivia increases public distrust in politics (Lloyd).

These arguments are made in specific cultural and political contexts but the implication is that, given similar conditions and developments, other post-industrial democracies would develop similar patters of behaviour. I will examine these claims next.

Political Engagement

Putnam's analysis of trends of American civic disengagement include decreasing voter turnout and attendance at public meetings, as well as declines in aggregate membership of associations such as bowling clubs: since the 1950s the number of bowlers in the United States has increased, but their membership of local leagues has decreased. American bowlers increasingly bowl alone. However, two issues should be borne in mind when considering whether these measures provide evidence for decreasing political engagement. First, as Norris (2000) has pointed out, there are considerable difficulties in producing reliable data on structural indicators such as association membership quite apart from the fact that contemporary associations such as the StopTheWar coalition tend to be unbureaucratized, informal associations without the membership lists and party dues typical of older forms of association such as trade unions and political parties. A second, more fundamental problem is how to measure the cultural norms of cooperation, trust and toleration that Putnam considers essential for healthy democracies. Clearly, not all associations foster these norms and associations are not the only places they are nurtured.

Norris's preliminary cross-national study examining a number of data sets concluded that: 'The results of the comparative research to date means that the case for a widespread erosion of associational life and social trust essentially remains 'unproven', based on the available evidence' (2000: 8). She finds that high social capital, characterized by high trust and strong membership of associations, is found in Nordic countries and most Anglo-American democracies while these characteristics are least common in post-Soviet Central European and South American societies, concluding that high social capital may be strongly related to 'long-standing cultural traditions and historical legacies, which may relate to religious backgrounds' (2000: 16).

The British Power Commission, established in 2002, takes the fact of political disengagement in the United Kingdom as its starting point and sets out to find how it can be reversed. The report cites research evidence to explode the myth of political apathy (2006): participation in campaigning groups, online referenda, mass street protests,[3] consumer action, community and charity work engage large numbers of citizens. Nonetheless, it acknowledges that there is general disengagement from formal politics as shown by voter turnout, party membership and public attitudes. However, it rules out some of the explanations proffered including 'the low calibre and probity of politicians' or an 'overly negative news media' (p. 16). Its basic conclusion is that Britain is operating industrial age politics for post-industrial age citizens (see pp. 18–19). Greater educational provision and achievement, increased affluence and decreased deference have created a citizenry out of kilter with a political world which refuses to address its electorate as grown ups and to reform its institutions and practices.

To summarise, the evidence suggests that there are high levels of public political engagement across the world but a significant degree of formal political disengagement, particularly in post-industrial democracies. Its causes are varied and, in the case of Britain at least, do not appear immediately attributable to a more corrupt political class or corrupting media (see Canel and Sanders, 2006; Power, 2006). In any case, a lack of interest or attention to political news and analysis understood as coverage of policy does not necessarily equate to a lack of interest in politics per se. There are many forms of non-institutional political participation and these are now greatly facilitated by electronic mediated forms including participation in phone-ins, text messaging, blogging and online discussion groups. The question remains, however, whether without major institutional and cultural reform, the added activity and opportunities for engagement result in any real shift of power to the people.

Trust and 'But' Politics

One of the overriding issues in contemporary politics is the question of trust. In a poll published in the British *Observer* newspaper in April 2007 people were asked, 'Which of the following words or phrases do you associate with Tony Blair the politician?' From the list offered, the highest scoring were: 'Too concerned with spin' 49 per cent, 'Out of touch with Britain' 45 per cent, 'Not trustworthy' 43 per cent, 'Tired, run out of ideas' 40 per cent, 'Insincere' 38 per cent. The lowest score was for 'Trustworthy' which only 6 per cent associated with Blair (see 'The Blair Poll', *The Observer*, April, 2007). In part, these results reflect the people's weariness of a leader who was about to step down, after having been in power for ten years and having led the country to an increasingly unpopular war.

However, trust is not just a Blair problem. A 2005 BBC poll found that 87 per cent of those interviewed did not trust politicians to deliver what they promised (18 March 2005) and EU-wide Eurobarometer surveys consistently find that politicians are among the least trusted professional groups.

One possible approach to rebuilding trust is to pursue what has been called 'but' politics'. Formerly, political leaders such as Thatcher or Bush have followed what might be called 'or politics', where citizens are presented with stark alternatives: it's either him or me; either you are with the terrorists or you are with the war on terrorism. Political analyst, Daniel Finkelstein, suggests that the time might have come for 'but' politics, where the people are taken into the conversation of politics as fellow adults:

> In an era where politicians lack credibility, why not try something unthinkable? Why not try the whole truth? Why not try saying that a new policy has a cost, that a fresh law may not work, that a reform has some risks? Why not share all the advice, the upside and the downside?' (4 April 2007)

This new politics is one which would take seriously the idea of public participation, of interactive, deliberative politics where politicians 'imagine the public as a set of relationships and as an adverb – people doing things publicly, facing the wider world together' (Eliasoph, 2004: 300). In some ways, the cat is already out of the bag. People across the world are finding ways to converse, work and act together, often facilitated by technological developments. The bigger question, perhaps, is whether people want to be part of the conversations taking place about their world and if they don't, why not.

Electronic Meeting Places

When Madrid suffered the worst civilian bombing casualties in post-war Europe on 11 March 2004, Spain's citizens were not cowed into silence. In the days that followed, mass demonstrations opposing terrorism and street protests outside the governing party's offices took place across the country (Canel and Sanders, 2005). Much of this spontaneous public action was activated by text messaging of dates and times of the demonstrations (see Sampredo, 2005). Earlier in the decade, the internet had been the effective meeting point for those wishing to protest against globalization in Seattle and Genoa.

In this final section I will examine some of the potential offered by twenty-first-century technological developments (ICT-Information Communication Technology) for increased citizen involvement in public affairs, attempting to avoid the Scylla of e-pessimism or the Charybdis of cyber-utopianism.[4]

Digital Connections

The discussion about the potential of digital communication and information technologies for enhancing the 'public sphere' should take as its starting point one essential fact: the unequal distribution of electronic resources across the planet. In 2004 at the bottom of the United Nation's Development Index, Niger had two telephone lines per 1000 people compared to Norway's 669 at the top of the list. In 2003 that country had 390 Internet users per 1000 compared to two in Niger at the bottom of the list (see UNDR, 2006). However, one positive indicator of growing interconnectedness is in mobile phone use, which in Africa grew by 5000 per cent between 1998 and 2003, even though the proportion of people using mobile phones remained low at around an average of 6 per cent throughout Africa (BBC, 9 March 2005). For most people around the globe, radio is still the most widely used medium.

The internet, however, continues to extend its reach and its connecting potential flows from three characteristics:

- **Accessibility**. The internet is accessible in two senses. First, it is materially speaking an accessible medium, relatively cheap and straightforward to use. Secondly, the absence of barriers to entry means that it is open to everyone with the necessary material resources. Unlike the Greek *polis*, women as well as men, young and old, can use it. Furthermore, the possibility of anonymity allows users to express views they may otherwise feel uncomfortable about stating. Citizens in paternalistic or authoritarian states can be more unconstrained in expressing their views through the internet than through other media and as ICT becomes more mobile and connected, control over access and information diffusion becomes ever more difficult.
- **Information**. The internet's connectedness and hypertextuality have created a treasure trove of information, made more accessible by the development of effective search engines such as Google. The availability of vast swathes of information empowers schoolchildren, journalists, academics,

citizen groups, all who seek to know. But, there is a dark, Faustian side to this search for knowledge: some use it to make bombs and others to view child pornography. The development of information management systems has also allowed a number of governments around the world to make available information for two purposes: first, for citizens to engage in the routine transactions of, for example, submitting tax returns, requesting official documents online. A second purpose, is to enable citizens to engage in policy development, increasing government accountability and transparency. Both purposes form part of the drive in a number of regions and countries around the world towards e-democracy or e-government.

- **Interactivity**. One of the premises of the e-democracy being developed in places such as the State of Minnesota in the United States is the dialogical or interactive relationship of user and provider of information. ICT permits dialogue and deliberation, and these characteristics are increasingly features of relationships where they were once absent: educators, journalists, business leaders and now politicians find that, like it or not, they must at least provide the means to engage in conversation with a public which was once simply talked at.

Of course, all advances in our mastery of the material environment that allow us to extend communication and diffuse knowledge have democratizing potential. The invention of the printing press was one of the crucial steps in wresting away control of the word from the entrenched powers of the fifteenth century. However, entrenched powers are often quite adept at adapting to find ways of re-establishing their hegemony. The Chinese government's success in controlling the internet is a sobering reminder of this. However, certain features of ICTs give grounds for hope; first, that such control will become ever more problematic, and second, that those who exercise power will understand that the nature of that power cannot but change in an increasingly networked environment. The implications of this second point are still to be worked out, but a number of politicians seem at least to be considering what they might be. Before becoming British prime minister, Gordon Brown spoke in a television interview of the need for a 'new kind of politics'. He continued: 'If you believed in the past that you could have a top-down approach and a government that simply pulled the levers, that is not how it is going to work in the future. [...] you have got to listen and [...] be prepared to talk, consult and debate' (cited in Ashley, 8 January 2007). This is still to be accepted by a number of governments around the world. There are signs of hope: the People's Republic of China aims to have all ministries, provinces, autonomous regions and overseas embassies connected to the internet by 2010, although it still seeks to control and monitor citizens' access (see Rawnsley, 2005: 181–2; 188–90).

To conclude, there is evidence that ICT developments are not simply extending the possibility of 'politics as usual'. Advocacy and 'lifestyle' or identity politics on the internet attest to the partly upbeat assessment by Dahlgren that 'The Internet is in the forefront of the evolving public sphere, and if the dispersion of public spheres generally is contributing to the already destabilized political communication system, specific counter public spheres on the Internet are also allowing engaged citizens to play a role in the development of new democratic politics' (2005: 160).

However, there is a final question here – the 'elephant in the room' – regarding what the people want. There is an assumption in democratic theory that a vibrant democracy requires communicative spaces where politics are discussed, shaped and decided; the more universally open and accessible the better. A common position flowing from this assumption is that people want to be citizens, that they wish to participate in the political worlds they inhabit. This is the view of political scientist, Gary Rawnsley who considers that 'current cynicism is misplaced and that people throughout the world – from different societies, cultures, religions and political systems – want to participate in politics' (2005: 197). It is true that there are now thousands of politically related websites: blogs, discussion groups, chat rooms, NGOs and so on. But the research literature tells us that most users of the internet seek out other kinds of material; pornographic sites are some of the most commonly looked for locations on the internet. There are, then, more fundamental questions still to be answered about how and why engaged publics are formed.

11

Political Campaigns

Introduction

In this chapter I examine political campaigns, and, in particular, election campaigns, the principal historical site both for political communication practice and scholarship. The chapter tackles four main themes. First, it explores *the purposes of political campaigns*. In second place, the chapter examines *the realities of election campaigns*, the role of resources and in particular the role of strategy. The third theme focuses on *the campaign message* and *what makes a message or candidate persuasive*. Finally, the chapter examines some of the ways the message can be communicated, the tactics employed by contemporary electioneers, the use of *political advertising*, the projection of *candidates' images and policies in free and paid for media* and *the significance of the internet* for campaigners.

What Are Campaigns For?

Essentially all political campaigns apply strategy and tactics to win a position, be it an actual political position such as that of president or senator, or a policy or issue position such as the adoption of global standards on carbon emissions. Campaigns were originally exclusively military actions, the word itself taken from the French 'campagne' (Latin, 'campus') to refer to the open country suitable for military manoeuvres. The transference to the political domain occurred at the beginning of the nineteenth century in the United States, a time when the opening up of suffrage made it worthwhile to expend effort in organizing public support for political platforms. Political campaigns reflect the truth that, paraphrasing the military thinker Carl von Clausewitz (1780–1831), politics is war continued by other means.

Most frequently associated with the organized effort to gain election to a public position,[1] one of the earliest organized political campaigns was primarily directed not at winning an election, but at changing government policy. Known as Ireland's Liberator, Daniel O'Connell (1775–1847) campaigned in nineteenth-century Britain for Irish home rule and the repeal of laws penalizing Catholics because of their religion, including legislation debarring them from election to parliament. A noted orator and respected for his integrity, O'Connell's mixture of strategies and tactics included the mobilization of the Irish peasantry through the founding of the Catholic Association in 1823, funded by just one penny a month per person; the enlistment of the country's influential Catholic clergy to the cause; huge 'Monster Meetings' of ordinary people; and his own election to Parliament. He was also supported by a Catholic press that faithfully reported his speeches and spread his message across Ireland. His aims were partially achieved by the passing of the Catholic Emancipation Act in 1829 and fully accomplished by the creation of the Irish Free State in 1922.

O'Connell's broad objectives were those of any political campaigner, namely to inform, persuade and mobilize his audience, using the people and the media peacefully to influence political priorities and achieve specific political goals. I will examine next some of the evidence regarding the media's role in engaging, mobilizing and influencing the public in political campaigns.

Civic Engagement and the Media

Civic engagement, one of the principal purposes of political campaigns, is made up of two separate processes. The first refers to what are called the possible cognitive and attitudinal affects of campaigns: questions related to how and what we learn about issues and leaders – their competence and trustworthiness – from campaign groups, parties and candidates, from our friends and from the media. The second process involved in civic engagement is related to political mobilization and explores measures such as voter turnout, interest in public affairs and participation in political parties and causes.

Research in the area has concentrated on the media's role in the public's knowledge of and attitude to politics, particularly during election campaigns and more specifically in the context of American presidential campaigns (see Kaid, 2004a). Some scholars have pointed to what they consider to be a 'media malaise' effect; in other words, a diet of negative news and concentration on the 'horse race' by the media discourage people from civic participation (Patterson, 1994). This may or may not be true for the United States where there is no public service requirement for mainstream broadcasters to provide information about elections so that the various forms of political communication – 'spots' (short 30-second adverts), debates and interviews – provide the main forms of candidate information.

However, as we saw in the previous chapter, the evidence for the impact of media use on civic engagement and persuasion presents a complex picture. In their work on the British 1997 general election, Norris and colleagues (1999) examined cumulative long-term cognitive effects of media use and short-term campaign effects.[2] Their analysis showed that 'long-term levels of political knowledge and participation are significantly associated with patterns of media consumption' so that those who most regularly and most attentively watch TV news or read the press are 'significantly more knowledgeable than the average citizen about party policies, civics and the parliamentary candidates standing in their constituency' and are also more likely to turn out to vote (Norris et al., 1999: 113). Their findings suggest that there is insufficient evidence in the British case to blame the media for civic disengagement.

Setting the Agenda

Most people learn about issues from the media. However much campaign groups, candidates and parties might push their slogans and messages, the media are the principal framers of political discourse. Not surprisingly, then, campaign groups spend considerable time and resources in attempting to set or build the media agenda. Campaign groups, especially where the issue is off the public radar, will engineer 'media events', calculated to appeal to prevailing news values. Britain's Fathers 4 Justice, campaigning for fathers' rights of access to children, provided a number of notorious examples including members' of the group dressed as 'superheroes' such as Batman and Superman scaling public buildings (Buckingham Palace among them) or sparking a security alert at the House of Commons in 2004 by throwing purple powder onto Tony Blair. Faith-based charity groups and other organizations, campaigning for changes in Third World aid policy, very effectively harnessed people power and rock glamour in their Make Poverty History 2005 campaign, garnering massive media interest, using a popular BBC comedy series and a white wristband to publicize aims.

Election campaigns very deliberately choreograph events and photo ops to promote their chosen themes, although this can backfire. In December 1991, the UK Conservative Cabinet endorsed the Near Term campaign in preparation for the forthcoming 1992 elections. The campaign was to run for 11 weeks with a new theme each week. The first week was 'Leadership', second 'tax'. After the fourth week, the strategy ran out of steam as the media became increasingly resentful of the politicians' attempts to stage-manage coverage. According to its architects: 'By February, the process had become something of a joke in the press' (Hogg and Hill, 1995: 167) as it appeared that the Conservatives had become over-fixated on winning the battle of the campaigns, rather than concentrating on persuading people to vote for them.

Media Influence

The importance of image making through the media was firmly imprinted on the public mind with the publication of McGinniss's *The Selling of the President*, chronicling Nixon's transformation from an apparently grumpy politician to smooth presidential candidate. As Weaver put it: 'by making more salient certain issues, candidates, and characteristics of candidates, the media contribute significantly to the construction of a perceived reality that is relied on in making decisions and for whom to vote' (1996: 216).

The media are influential in campaigns in three significant ways:

1. They 'prime' voters. By focusing on certain policy or candidate attributes they make them more salient – for better or worse – in voters' assessments (see Scheufele, 2001).
2. They set agendas. In the 1997 UK campaign, John Major made last minute decisions reacting to media pressure about sleaze and the European single currency.
3. They frame issues and candidates. Despite campaign strategists' best efforts, the media are often the chief artificers of the campaign frames.

Mainstream news media have dominated these three levers of influence. However, the 1992 US presidential campaign marked the moment in election campaigns when talk shows and the internet became a venue for political communication. The internet only came of age in the 2004 US presidential campaign. Appearances on entertainment-focused programmes as an attempt to bypass traditional media and influence voters on candidates' own terms became a more notable feature of political campaigns from Bill Clinton's 1992 saxophone-playing performance on the *Arsenio Hall* show. As I shall discuss in the next chapter, the media are not the only purveyors of influence. Influential citizens matter in how we think about politics and the rationale for their influence lies at a deeper level, explored by psychologists who examine the dynamics of persuasion and the principles that can act as powerful triggers for compliance, often without our realizing it.

Campaigning for Election

Around 64 BC Quintus Tullius Cicero (102–43 BC) wrote for his more illustrious brother, Marcus Tullius Cicero (106–43 BC) *Commentariolum Petitionis*, apparently the first account in Western history of electioneering practice.

Conditions in the late Roman Republic were clearly different to those of twenty-first-century constitutional democracies but constant features persist. Cicero is encouraged to mobilize his friends, persuade his enemies, attack his opponents, campaign on his record and avoid detailed policy discussion. Here we can discern some of the enduring goals of political campaigns discussed above and the key differentiating feature that distinguishes elections from issue campaigns namely, the seeking of public office.

Election campaigns are critical periods in democracies. They 'select decision makers, shape policy, distribute power and provide venues for debate and socially approved expressions of conflict about factional grievances and issues, national problems and directions, and international agendas and activities' (Swanson and Mancini, 1996: 1).

In 2007, presidential and general elections took place in Nigeria and Kenya, Australia and Russia, and, in 2008, in Spain and the United States. Notwithstanding their many differences and the disappointing corruption of the democratic process in some of these countries, their election campaigns shared a number of characteristics: they all operated within the structure of constraints and opportunities created by what might be called the *electoral force fields*; second, they all employed *strategy and tactics* to achieve their ends; and, finally, they were each subject to that set of developments loosely known as *Americanization*. I shall discuss each of these features next.

Electoral Force Fields

Campaigns may persuade, inform or mobilize the public, but how they do so depends on an intricate network of three sets of structural, environmental and resource variables in which long- and short-term processes play their part. If we take first *structural factors* these include:

- The regulatory context – is paid for political advertising permitted? Are there statutory requirements regarding television coverage of politics?
- The political system – presidential or parliamentary?
- The voting system – first past the post or proportional representation?
- The political culture and tradition – attitudes to gender, race and religion.
- The media ecology – is there a highly partisan press? Commercial or public service television? Wide internet access?

In second place, *environmental factors* refer to those events, processes and issues that combine to make the political weather at any given time and shape voters' concerns and interests. The 2004 Spanish election campaign was transformed by the bombing of Madrid's suburban trains three days before the election. France's economic stagnation made Sarkozy's message of the need for change highly effective in that country's 2007 presidential elections. In the 2004 US presidential elections, at a time when the country was at war in Iraq and Afghanistan, the candidate with the greatest credibility as commander-in-chief was more likely to win.

In third place, *resource variables* refer to the arsenal of assets and identifiable liabilities that campaigning parties and candidates have to manage, including financial resources and symbolic ones such as celebrity endorsements. The interplay between structural, environmental and resource variables gives each campaign its particular form and content and to a great extent determines the strategy and tactics employed.

Campaign Strategy and Tactics

The science and art of strategy have been the subject of study since the writing of the sixth-century Chinese military treatise *The Art of War* by Sun Tzu. This celebrated work underlined several factors that were considered essential for military planning and have since been applied to the worlds of business and politics. These include:

- The competitive nature of the theatre of operations
- The role of positioning which depends on mission, climate, terrain, leadership and methods of the campaign
- The need for flexible planning, involving knowing how to respond to changing conditions
- The significance of unity
- The importance of building trust in the leader

Strategy involves developing game plans much as a coach does for a football team. Game plans have to be well understood, have clearly distributed roles and tasks and be open to modification according to the circumstances.

In the view of another New Labour proselytist, Peter Mandelson, the 1997 Conservative campaign failed because it 'lacked a strategy, message and discipline' (Butler and Kavanagh, 1997: 239). Post-election analyses concluded that they could have had 4 per cent or 40 more seats with a better campaign. However, they also concluded that superior campaign strategy and tactics did not ultimately decide the election. 'The Conservatives, eighteen years in power, provided the opportunity. Labour seized it' (Butler and Kavanagh, 1997: 253).

Early planning is vital. In many countries the campaign period is regulated. Four weeks of campaigning are permitted in Spain and France, with up to two days before the election set aside for 'reflection'.[3] However, the realities of the electoral cycle tend to concentrate political minds rather earlier (see Figure 11.1): to have any chance of success candidates and parties

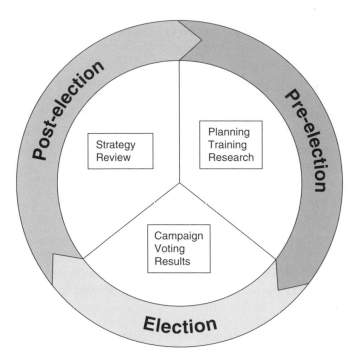

Figure 11.1   The electoral cycle

should begin preparing electoral strategy and operations long before the commencement of the official campaign. According to Theodore White's classic study of Kennedy's campaign, *The Making of the President 1960*, work began three years before the election.

Long-term planning involves staff recruitment, information gathering including constituency, voter and opposition profiling and various kinds of surveying (see Table 11.1), fund-raising, media planning and message development.

The near or pre-campaign involves the rolling out of the candidate's or party's main messages. To take the example of the Conservatives' 1997 campaign, the first phase ran from the beginning of 1996 up to the summer 1996 with the theme, 'Yes it hurt; yes it worked.' The attack phase was initiated on 1 July with the slogan, 'New Labour, New Danger.' The only trouble was a coherent approach was never achieved on this as Major himself would often talk about Labour's stealing of Tory policies. From the previous winter and spring the Conservative Party had held a series of discussions with representatives of sympathetic think tanks. Government ministers attended seminars to develop ideas for the manifesto. However, according to one commentator: 'The quality and range of the Tories' polling, focus groups

Table 11.1 Campaign surveys

Type	Function
Focus groups	Explore attitudes/emotions below the surface
Benchmark polls	Provide comprehensive map of voter profiles and chart name recognition, attitudes, knowledge and issue preferences
Tracking polls	Follow voter trends on a regular basis
Push polls	Persuasion tool to 'push' voters away from opponents ('How would you feel if you knew candidate x supports the death penalty?')

and other electoral arts [...] lagged some way behind Labour' (Seldon, 1997: 660). Even though strategy meetings had begun over a year and a half before the general election and there was some preparation from March 1995 of the 'War Book', the failure of the Conservatives to position themselves successfully and lack of party unity meant that, quite apart from the formidable opposition they faced, there was little prospect that the Conservatives would win the 1997 election.

The election campaign itself is at the same time both strongly structured and highly contingent. The best-laid plans can all too easily be knocked off course. Writing about the Conservatives' 1992 campaign, two of its organizers described its atmosphere of organized chaos (or chaotic organization) and how, of the 19 press conferences scheduled after the party's manifesto launch, only four followed the pre-election plan (Hogg and Hill, 1995: 214).

Despite the Conservatives' organizational difficulties, they won the election with 43 per cent of the vote and a majority of 21 seats. It had been a long campaign (six weeks). Clever tactics including negative adverts emphasizing Labour's tax plans, an underestimate in the polls of the Conservative vote disguised as 'don't knows', a populist press hostile to Labour and an unconvincing challenger brought about a detectable late swing to the Conservatives.

Five years later Labour was in the strategic driving seat, conscious in that and subsequent elections of the importance of trying to control the ever more frantic media agenda. As Blair explained (2007): 'When I fought the 1997 election – just ten years ago – we took an issue a day. In 2005, we had to have one for the morning, another for the afternoon and by the evening the agenda had already moved on.' US-style, media-dominated elections had well and truly arrived.

The American Way of Electioneering?

The US presidential elections of 1896 saw one of the first uses of a political campaign consultant in American history (see Shea and Burton, 2006: 1–2).

Republican candidate William McKinley hired Marcus Hanna to run his campaign on business principles. Hanna proceeded to mastermind a slick operation that directed printed campaign material at America's main ethnic groups, raised money from industry and brought voters on 'pilgrimages' to meet the candidate in the days when direct touting for votes was seen as a sign of weakness. Dwight D. Eisenhower's 1952 campaign for president 'hired an advertising team that produced some of the first television campaign commercials. Using the product-tested technique of name repetition, Eisenhower's jingle went, 'Ike for President, Ike for President; You like Ike, I like Ike. Everybody likes Ike' (Shea and Burton, 2006: 3).

It is arguable whether the practice of using marketing techniques to 'sell' candidates and package presidents is as new as has sometimes appeared. However, the view that an election campaign is chiefly a marketing challenge (see Maarek, 1995) and the emphasis in electioneering practice on money, marketing techniques, television and image have been particularly intensively cultivated in the context of the US presidential elections, leading to campaigns being dominated by a 'media logic'.

But the question needs to be asked as to whether the adoption of US campaign practices favouring the predominance of image and electronic media, of horse-race and personalized media coverage, of negative and personalized campaigning, and the employment of battalions of communication and marketing consultants to conduct surveys and focus groups amounts to *Americanization*, understood as a unidirectional process of cultural convergence, and to what extent this *Americanization* is simply the professionalization of campaign practices responding to structural changes. The latter view is taken by a number of scholars (see Negrine and Pathanassopoulos, 1996). It is argued that growing similarities flow, for example, from the insertion of the medium of television. This is not to suggest a deterministic model, but rather to accept, as Marshall McLuhan first pointed out, that new media enable new forms of social interaction. The development of the *mediapolis* could be described without any reference to Americanization.

This is not to deny the pre-eminence and influence of US campaigning practice, spread throughout the world in the 1970s and 1980s. Campaign consultancy is now, however, an international business. Initially dominated by the United States, the industry has globalized: Spanish consultants work on campaigns in Latin America (various campaigns in 2006), Australians in Britain (for Conservative Michael Howard in 2001) and the British in South Africa (Mandelson helped the ANC in 1999). In their global survey of election campaigning, Plasser and Plasser concluded that, while there are a number of common macro-trends, there is 'strong evidence for a hybridization – or a merger of traditional country- and culture-specific campaign practices – with select transnational features of modern campaigning' so that 'globalization of campaigning does not lead to a standardization of campaign practices' (2002: 350–1).

Campaign Money and Machine

About 600 professional consultants were paid $1.78 billion for 2003–4 political campaign work in the United States. Media consultants, who handle advertising and give strategic advice, received 67 per cent of all money spent – roughly $1.2 billion. Direct mail consultants had the second-largest amount, nearly $298 million (17 per cent of all spending). Fundraising consultants cost candidates at least $59 million (http://www.publicintegrity.org/consultants/). For the 2008 presidential elections, all candidates had already raised $420 million by the end of 2007.

The role of money is perhaps the greatest differentiating factor between US campaigns and those in much of the rest of the world. In every US presidential election since 1976, the top fundraiser at the end of the year preceding the election has become his party's nominee for the general election. Resources matter and in political environments where funding caps are generous or easily circumvented, the role of money in winning elections is a major and understandable concern.

This problem is obviated where funding is limited by law. In the United Kingdom, for example, parties and candidates must abide by the Political Parties, Elections and Referendums Act 2000 (PPERA). Individual candidate campaign spending is strictly limited, varying according to constituency voter numbers but usually amounting to around £9000. Political parties are restricted to spending limits that amount to around £18 million where all seats are contested. In the 2005 general election over £42 million was spent by the political parties and third parties such as campaign groups, and £14 million by individual candidates, amounting to an average of just under £4000 per candidate. The largest proportion of money was spent by parties on advertising (37 per cent), followed by sending material to electors (22 per cent) and rallies and events (10 per cent) (see Electoral Commission, 2006).

The Message

When leader of the Conservative party, John Major, was told he was going off-message in the UK general elections, he replied: 'I am the message' (Seldon, 1997). In fact, particularly in non-presidential systems, the message is rather more complex than this, consisting in the candidate, issues, the party and the manifesto. Consultants spend a great amount of time and energy crafting messages that will deliver the necessary votes to their candidate and party. They know that just small effects in voter preferences, if delivered in the right place, can have significant consequences for election results. Messages are made up of representations of issues, parties and candidates. Much research has focussed on voters' perceptions of issues on the one hand and image on the other (see Hacker, 2004); however, this dichotomy has clear limitations as image perceptions can shape issue judgements and vice versa. I will discuss some of these issues here.

Candidates and Images

As Iyengar put it, 'image is everything' in politics (2005: 1). But what is meant by image? There is no one definition. Political communication scholars have thought of it in two ways (see Hacker, 2004): first, image has been defined as the set of stimuli projected by the party or candidate; second, it has been associated with the attributes perceived by the electorate. In fact, it is increasingly clear that images are formed by the interaction between the two. Images are formed at the intersection of specific communication acts – a speech, an appearance on a chat show – performed by the candidate and our own perceptions filtered through pre-judgements and knowledge (Hacker, 2004).

Image is not character. Character refers to the amalgam of traits, dominant sentiments and habits, who we are, our personhood. Aristotle considered good character to be one of the most effective means of persuasion possessed by a speaker, for it wins trust and bestows credibility. In one way or another, all politicians seek to project 'good character', despite the apparent disdain for image professed by politicians like former Spanish prime minister, José María Aznar (see Sanders, 2004).

Projection of character inevitably requires image-making since the presentation of the self in the public realm involves choices about clothes, haircut, language selected from a repertoire of possibilities. The inevitable element of artifice involved can lead to accusations of manipulation and lack of authenticity. However, as I discussed in Chapter 4, we are all in one way or another performers. For politicians the performance, and what it purports to show, is core to their professional vocation: it does not matter so much if our postman presents himself as a good huntsman, but turns out to be squeamish at the sight of blood; if we were to discover this to be the case for Russian leader, Vladimir Putin, however, his credentials as a strong and trustworthy leader, would be badly affected, especially in Russian eyes.

Discovering credibility gaps undermines trust in politicians. Journalists' unveiling of image-management strategies is a favourite sport during election campaigns: was Al Gore's uxorious kiss an attempt to shrug off his stiff image in the 2000 campaign? Was Ségolène Royal really as angry as she seemed in her debates with 2007 French presidential rival Nicolas Sarkozy, or was this to show she would be tough enough for the job? Image strategies seek to promote those attributes considered necessary for the job, but in doing so they must take into account the personal attributes of the candidate and play to his or her strengths and turn weaknesses into positives.

How Images are Formed

Our images of politicians are formed in four main ways:

1. **The communicator's record**. This is particularly important for incumbents but any credible record of public leadership can be used to win voters' support, given that voting is at times an act of reward or punishment. Hilary Clinton underlined her record of public service and experience in contrast to Barack Obama's relative inexperience in her bid to win the Democratic presidential nomination for 2008.
2. **Facts about the communicator**. Biographical information regarding, for example, the candidate's war service (Yitzhak Rabin and John McCain), modest background (John Major), outsider status (Jimmy Carter, Nicolas Sarkozy), experience of family suffering (Bill Clinton and Gordon Brown). Policy positions are supposedly the red meat of elections. They are what the elections are all about. However, it is frequently the case that candidates attempt to 'square the circle' in their policy announcements in order to alienate as few voters as possible. For example, Angela Merkel, campaigning for the German chancellorship in 2005, spoke a great deal about the need for truth-telling and political courage but little about specific policies. Candidates frequently frame policy positions in ways that appeal to 'motherhood' values and avoid the risk of precision.
3. **Endorsements of the communicator**. Discovering that someone we admire and respect backs a particular candidate is a powerful form of social proof and a tried and tested technique in commercial advertising. Candidates use it to persuade us they are the one as Barack Obama did when he received the imprimatur of Oprah Winfrey in 2007.
4. **Communication actions**. Psychologists estimate we have less than ten and perhaps nearer four seconds to make a first good impression (see Hogan, 2005: 15). Candidates can attempt to rebuild their images through the range and number of the communication actions they perform, but matters as fundamental as non-verbal communication (twitches, voice pitch, facial expressions), physical appearance (height, attractiveness, age, clothes) the medium used (debates have more credibility than adverts), and mistakes or gaffes made (falling from a collapsing platform as occurred to Republican candidate, Robert Dole, in 1982) all go into the mix of what makes an image.

Attributes of the Ideal Candidate

Credibility is key to persuasion and in politics top attributes include trustworthiness, competence, expertise and likeability. Credibility relies both on subjectively and objectively determined elements. Trustworthiness – the belief that someone warrants our trust – is a prime component of credibility. On one view of trust, political candidates are considered to be trustworthy when we have strong reasons to believe that they will act in our best interests. This understanding of trustworthiness may explain the apparent anomalies in polls that show leaders such as Australia's John Howard, criticized on a number of occasions for a lack of truthfulness yet scoring highly on levels of trust. Honest John Major consistently did better in the 1996 focus groups than Tony Blair on trustworthiness and sincerity yet failed miserably in the polls. Generally, politicians are probably held to a lower level of truth-telling than other professions and often voters will make their decision on the basis of the least-worst choice.

Expertise, a component of credibility, can be established by objective measures. It is related to knowledge and ability and is often claimed on the basis of someone's past record. Greater credibility can be gained by transparency and apparently acting against one's own self-interest by, for example, confessing faults or mistakes.

Dynamism and charisma are also attributes associated with successful political leadership. Leaders like to be shown jogging, fishing, playing football as symbols of their vigour and dynamism. Charisma, from the Greek for 'gift' or 'divine favour', is associated with those who provoke strong emotions in others, have excellent communication skills and the ability to project unusual confidence and authority. Politicians such as Pakistan's assassinated opposition leader Benazir Bhutto project the sense to others that they understand their concerns, that they identify with their sufferings, hence their strong populist appeal, particularly in populations with low levels of political knowledge.

Likeability is also key. As Iyengar stated, describing the US case: 'For the 25 percent of the electorate that lacks a partisan identity, voting is really about "likeability quotients" rather than issue positions' (2005: 4).

Previously, gender weighed heavily against women (see Hellweg, 2004: 28). This appears to be shifting as presidential results in Latin America showed: Michelle Bachelet was elected as the first woman president in Chile in 2006 and Cristina Fernández de Kirchner in 2007 became Argentina's first elected female president.[4]

In the United States all campaigns carry out extensive research into their opponent's voting record and personal life. 'Oppo research' involves searching databases and talking to those who know and preferably dislike the candidate. The research helps candidates craft strategies that can play to their strengths and underline their opponents' weaknesses, as Bush's campaign did in 2000 by focusing on Gore's penchant for bravado.

Developing the Message

Research and polling information is used to ensure that messages are tailored for different groups of voters, especially the undecided or 'swing' voters.

The finessing of voter segmentation was turned into a high art by the Clintons' pollster, Mark Penn. The UK Labour Party adopted his approach and Britain's 1997 election was remarkable for its degree of focus on particular electors and constituencies. The Labour Party used a 'Programme for Identifying Key Voters' as well as direct mail surveys to select 40,000 key voters in each target seat. They were canvassed by telephone and direct mail with the bulk of the party's resources thrown into these marginal constituencies. Of the 100 most vulnerable seats, the Conservatives lost all but one.

Framing messages is a key art in campaigning. In his *Moral Politics* (2002) George Lakoff combines cognitive science and political analysis to develop arguments about how politics should be conducted in the twenty-first century. In *Don't Think of an Elephant! Know Your Values and Frame the Debate* (2004), he argues that politicians have continued to use an unsuitable seventeenth-century understanding of the mind – where thinking is considered a purely rational process – to conduct twenty-first-century politics. Politicians are wrong, he suggests, to think that if they just explain themselves better, people will accept their argument. This approach ignores the existence of deeply embedded frames of understanding, 'world-views' of politics, that profoundly influence our response to political messages. In the United States, argues Lakoff, these 'worldviews' revolve around the notion of 'nation as family' so that the notion of a 'nurturing parent' guides the liberal worldview, while the 'strict father' model guides the conservative one. He argues that politicians must find a 'principled' rhetoric where policy positions can be situated within these overarching frames, something he considers the Republicans to have managed quite successfully. He suggests that Democrats, on the other hand, fail to integrate their policy positions with values or find the right metaphors to trigger a positive response from voters.

Lakoff's analysis has three serious shortcomings: first, it reduces our understanding of politics to just two psychological types; second, it neglects the importance of political and economic context for election outcomes; most importantly, it assumes that elite political discourse is largely able to frame the election debate, a questionable claim in our media-saturated times. However, his work makes a significant contribution in underlining the key roles of narrative and semantics in communicating values and emotion in campaigns.

Keeping it Simple

The reality of campaigns is that the media are one of the primary framers of political discourse. Media priorities call for simple, short messages. Easily understood narratives encapsulated in slogans, images, metaphors and sound-bites act as the communication kernel of the campaign. Even in political environments where election communication has a protected status, with television time given for party and candidate communication, audience figures increasingly dictate a shorter, snappier format (see Electoral Commission, 2003: 31–2). These formats also force definition, however limited this may be. In effective campaigns, verbal and visual shorthand are integrated to provide strong and meaningful messages.

Challenger slogans often refer to the 'time for a change' theme such as Eisenhower's 1952 'IT'S TIME FOR A CHANGE', Kennedy's 1960 'LET'S GET THIS COUNTRY MOVING AGAIN' or New Labour's 1997 'BECAUSE BRITAIN DESERVES BETTER'. Or to the failures of the incumbents such as the UK Conservatives' 'LABOUR ISN'T WORKING', which brought Margaret Thatcher to power. Slogans are not new. Cato the Elder rallied support for his policy advocating the destruction of Rome's great rival, Carthage: 'Carthago delenda est! – Carthage must be destroyed!'

Slogans are not trivial. When they work, they resonate with what people care about and with an emerging political and social landscape. Roosevelt's New Deal' spoke to Americans' desire for economic and social stability. Memorable slogans become the signposts for their times.

The Medium is the Message

One of the main tasks of campaign strategists is to think through the campaign narrative and decide how, when and where messages should be communicated. These decisions relate to strategy and to tactical matters such as the targeting of key voters, carefully profiled and identified by pollsters. They are highly dependent on the resources available, the strengths and weaknesses of the candidates and the electoral context. Direct or telephone voter canvassing, campaign songs, speeches, slogans, interviews, TV or internet candidate debates, advertising, direct mailing, rosettes, pins, streamers and websites provide a rich panoply of communicational possibilities available to campaigners who, through their choices, also affirm the kind of message they wish to communicate. I will next examine some of the most effective media for campaign communication.

Communicating the Message

Getting attention is one of the key goals of any election campaign. Politicians are competing in a very crowded field and usually at a clear disadvantage compared to more expert competitors: sportsmen and women, singers and actors are generally more attractive communicators. Campaigns need to be vivid, attractive and, paradoxically, repetitive. An added challenge for campaigners is to overcome the well-attested human tendency to seek out information that confirms our already established views and decisions.

Election campaigns, then, must use a range of communication options to shape and frame, to the extent they can, the campaign 'reality'. These options can be classified into three categories according to the degree of party or candidate control exercised: first, there are actions largely under campaign control. These include canvassing, meetings, rallies, invited appearances, targeted visits, photo ops, speeches, websites, policy documents (manifestos, war books) and all kinds of paid for and free political advertising. Second, there are communication actions undertaken by campaigns which, despite their best efforts, are not entirely under their control. These include participation in debates, call-in programmes, chat shows, interviews. Finally, campaigns may also seek to take advantage of or co-opt to their cause sympathetic groups and commentators who, while apparently independent, can act as campaign proxies. I will next examine examples of these different kinds and styles of campaign communication focusing on:

- political advertising
- negative campaigning
- candidate debates
- Internet and proxy campaigning

Political Advertising

Paid for or free political advertising provides candidates and parties the opportunity to present their message directly to the public without the mediation of journalists. This can be relayed in all kinds of media – billboards, posters, television, press, radio and, from the 1992 US presidential elections, the internet.[5] Television advertising continues to be the most significant form of political advertising and eats up the greatest proportion of campaign budgets although trends in other areas of advertising suggest that this may change in the future.

Political television advertising can be defined as 'any message primarily under the control of a source used to promote political candidates, parties, policy issues, and/or ideas through mass channels' (Kaid, 2004b:156). They are useful in that they:

- communicate issue information to voters
- contribute to name recognition
- influence voter recall about specific campaign issues and candidate issue positions
- affect voters' evaluations of candidate images

Research has also shown that US voters learn more from television adverts than from television news or from televised debates (see Kaid, 2004b).

The type, quantity and content of television advertising is strongly influenced by national regulatory environments. In India and Mexico, for example, it is banned. In the United States, on the other hand, the First Amendment to the country's Constitution ensuring freedom of speech, guaranteeing political candidates the right to buy broadcast time for political advertising, greatly inflates campaign costs.

In Britain, before each election a committee of broadcasters and party representatives (the broadcast liaison group) agree allocations of radio and TV broadcasts, taking account of party support in terms of seats and votes in previous elections. By convention, the governing party and the main opposition party are allocated the same number of broadcasts and the maximum number of slots given to any party is usually five. A legal requirement to show Party Election Broadcasts (PEBs) was laid down for the first time in the 1990 Broadcasting Act and it has provisions governing the length, frequency, content and timing of PEBs.[6]

Three arguments can be made for replacing PEBs with paid for advertising:

- They are outmoded in a multi-channel, cable, satellite and internet world.
- They are ineffective; they are too long and people switch off; 30- or 60-second slots could provide a greater array of political information to the voter.
- Human rights' provisions regarding freedom of expression undermine the state's right to ban broadcast political advertising.

The UK's Electoral Commission reviewed evidence regarding the effectiveness and desirability of PEBs after the 2001 general election. It reported findings suggesting that 35 per cent of respondents had some interest in PEBs and 22 per cent considered that PEBs had influenced their decision on election day. Only two per cent said they found them persuasive. Despite this evidence for their limited impact, it was still considered greater as compared to other sources of influence: 14 per cent of respondents thought PEBs to be influential compared to views of local candidates (13 per cent), campaign leaflets (6 per cent), opinion polls (four per cent) and billboard posters (2 per cent) (Electoral Commission, 2003: 12–13). The Commission concluded that PEBs continued to be useful and that the main argument against paid for political publicity would be the US-style inflation of campaign expenditure and the subsequent prejudice to less well-funded political platforms. This view was buttressed by public survey research carried out after the 2005 election on behalf of Britain's broadcast regulatory body, OFCOM. It found that approximately seven in ten respondents thought that PEBs were either 'very' or 'quite' important. 62 per cent said they had watched at least one PEB during the 2005 campaign and that it had influenced how they would vote either a little (39 per cent) or a lot (16 per cent) (see OFCOM, 2005).

Negative Advertising

Trashing the opponent has a long history. The US presidential campaign of 1828 was one of the most vitriolic ever held: an opposition pamphlet asked of the Democratic candidate, General Jackson, and his wife: 'Ought a convicted adulteress and her paramour husband to be placed in the highest offices of this free and Christian land?' Jackson considered that the relentless abuse was responsible for his wife's early death just before he took office.

Negative advertising uses a number of strategies to undermine opponents. One is to play to fear. In 1964 Democratic candidate, Lyndon Johnson, implied that the election of Barry Goldwater as US president would bring about nuclear war: in his presidential campaign ads a child picked petals from a daisy, followed by a countdown to an explosion and a looming mushroom cloud as Johnson intoned 'we must love each other or we must die'. In 1996 the UK Conservatives' attempt to provoke fear of New Labour backfired when the Advertising Standards Agency declared that their 'Demon Eyes' PEB, depicting Tony Blair with devilish eyes, was offensive. Labour were also accused of unacceptable images redolent with anti-Semitism in their campaign targeting the Conservative leader and his economics spokesman, both from a Jewish background.

More effectively, the Republicans used symbolic issues to depict Michael Dukakis, the 1988 Democrat presidential candidate, as a crazy liberal who polluted Boston Harbour and refused to require the Pledge of Allegiance in school. The nadir of this particular negative campaign played on racial fears and suggested that Dukakis's 'softness' on crime had been responsible for the parole of a dangerous Afro-American criminal who subsequently raped and murdered a young woman.

Negative advertising can be countered by getting in one's defence first (sometimes known as 'pre-buttal') – using a strategy of inoculation – where a candidate or even a party admits past mistakes or weaknesses. Alternatively, campaigns can respond rapidly to negative messages or attack ads with their own rebuttals; although often a necessary strategy, as Dukakis found to his cost in 1988, its weakness is that it allows one's opponent to define the terms of the debate.

'Going negative', questioning one's opponents' credentials or character, showing up holes in policy proposals, is a logical rhetorical strategy in the persuasion battle: elections seek to persuade voters of a candidate's or party's strengths in contrast to those of an opponent. They seek to define the debate in their own terms on the basis of the campaign mantra that 'if you're responding you're losing'. Positioning implies comparison and elections mean choices. However, campaign strategists can at times use disreputable means. In the 2000 presidential Republican primary in South Carolina, 'push polling' was used to spread a smear about John McCain that he had an illegitimate mixed-race daughter. Voters were called by 'pollsters' and, once it was established they were McCain supporters, were asked if they would be more or less likely to vote for McCain if they knew he had fathered an illegitimate child who was black. In fact, McCain and his wife had adopted a Bangladeshi child. McCain lost to Bush after having had a strong lead.

Negative ads that play down their negativity either through implicit attacks or avoiding *ad hominen* frontal assaults may be more effective and are certainly more respectful of the voter. Overly negative campaigning can backfire. Kaid's review of negative advertising in the US showed that electoral losers used more negative advertising and winners used more words indicating activity and optimism (2004b: 162–75). Evidence from experimental studies suggests that negative ads do enhance negative attitudes to those attacked but that there is also the associated risk of a backlash effect where people may think badly of those who use negative ads. The evidence for the impact on the political system is mixed with some work showing that it can demobilize voters (see Ansolabehere and Iyengar, 1995).

Candidates' Debates

In 2004, 62.5 million Americans watched the first of the televised US presidential debates. Following the first presidential and vice-presidential debates of the 2000 election, the Vanishing Voter Project found that the percentage of adults reporting having campaign-related conversations more than doubled to more than 50 per cent. Candidates' debates approximate to a gladiatorial contest where rivals are pitted against each other to show their mettle before an audience. Their unpredictable character is a large part of their appeal. Voters get to see not entirely scripted performances, even though the reality is that the rules of the encounter will have been carefully negotiated and the contestants endlessly rehearsed.

Perhaps the most famous debate was that which initiated the tradition in the US presidential race. The 1960 encounters between John F. Kennedy and Richard Nixon passed into campaign folklore as audience surveys suggested the importance of image in politics: television audiences gave victory to the youthful, handsome Kennedy instead of the jaded Nixon; radio audiences, on the other hand, considered that Nixon's superior command of the issues had won the day (Hellweg, Pfau and Brydon, 1992).

Research into the impact of debates has been greatest in the United States. It shows that they are significant in that, as I have mentioned, they attract large audiences and media interest; evidence also suggests that they both reinforce voting preferences and influence undecided voters (McKinney and Carlin, 2004). For example, during their first debate, Gore walked into Bush's personal space as Bush was talking. This was perceived as discourteous and aggressive by many and may have lost him thousands of crucial votes (see Pfau, 2002).

A number of countries with presidential systems such as France, Mexico and Peru have adopted candidates' debates. Germany, Spain, Canada and Australia have also used the debate format with modifications, such as the absence of an audience and the presence of a moderator who poses themes rather than asks questions. Despite many attempts and a consensus that they could increase voter interest, debates have not yet been adopted in the United Kingdom. In 2005 a modified format was used where the three main party leaders appeared consecutively, for about 30 minutes each, in a special edition of the regular programme *Question Time* in which a representative audience put questions to them.

The Internet and Proxy Campaigning

Negative advertising is not liked by voters but can be effective. An alternative way of going negative without compromising the candidate or party is the co-option or promotion of proxy or delegated criticism. This occurred to devastating effect for the US Democrats in the 2004 presidential elections. The Swift Boat Veterans for Truth group ran ads questioning the Democrat candidate's truthfulness about his war record and succeeded in reinforcing doubts about John Kerry's credibility, already dented by accusations of 'flip flopping' on his support for the Iraq war.

The development of internet political communities and social networking websites such as YouTube are also effective not only for mainstream campaigning but also for the building up and mobilization of grassroots (or 'webroots') political support. In 2004 Joe Trippi masterminded Howard Dean's internet-based campaign which had 'Blog for America' at its heart, a repository and venue for hundreds of comments and suggestions each day. The campaign succeeded in raising over $40m and signing up 500,000 supporters in less than a year and, until the candidate's Neanderthal scream (diffused across the internet), looked as if it could win Dean the Democratic presidential nomination. The 2004 presidential campaign showed, however, that 'political bloggers' principal practical effect lay in mobilizing the base and the activists within each party (Kline and Burnstein, 2005: 21).

This limited campaign impact is likely to change in the future. One of the main effects of the internet is to level the campaign and media playing field: it is now not only technically easy for bloggers, makers of spoof political ads and activists to get in on the act, it is also increasingly easy for them to shape the terms of campaign discourse. This, as Drezner and Farrell point out, happens because significant blogs become reference points for mainstream journalists and commentators and the 'rapidity of blogger interactions affects political communication in the mainstream media through agenda setting and framing effects' (2004: 17).[7] To this I would add that in a way, unlike mainstream media business models, user numbers are less important. So, while part of the influence of the top political blogs depends on the thousands of hits they receive, size is not the only determinant of influence. The blogosphere's multiplicity of opinion venues, however small the numbers coalescing around them, can provoke 'opinion storms' (see Hewitt, 2005) about issues that may have passed the mainstream media by because they are essentially networked, linked communication sites.

Conclusion

I have focused on election campaigns in this chapter, but much of what has been discussed applies to issue campaigns too. Sufficient resources, the understanding of context, strong and consistent messages and media friendly tactics can all add up to a successful campaign. Added to this, despite the concerns about money buying success, there are a number of developments that may be heartening for those who consider themselves the advocates of lost causes. These include the possibility of:

- **Choice over uniformity**. Based on his 'mining' research into US public surveys, the Clintons' pollster, Mark Penn, examines how the world is increasingly fragmented into niche groups whose identities are defined by specific habits and interests. In his view, choice has prevailed over uniformity, opening up new possibilities for groups who know how to organize themselves. Penn famously identified 'Soccer Moms' as swing-voters crucial to Bill Clinton's 1996 campaign. In 2007 he identified groups such as the self-explanatory 'internet marrieds', 'working retired' and 'extreme commuters' as new kinds of groups capable of triggering 'microtrends'. According to his book of this name (2007), just one per cent of Americans, three million people, can launch a social, cultural or political trend that can lead to significant change. Penn, however, has his critics, who consider that his use of polling data to develop 'small bore' politics has a narrowing effect on political leadership.
- **The blogosphere**. 'Small is the new big', says Glenn Reynolds of instapundit.com, whose book *An Army of Davids* (2007) suggests that technology is empowering ordinary people to challenge the large organizations that

have monopolized business, media and politics. He points to how blog-gers can challenge mainstream media.

- **Savvy audiences**. The opening up of options, the challenge of the small, the difficulties of control mean that audiences can know more, that secrets are more difficult to keep.

Of course structural power and the force of inertia in politics are still very strong. For it is also true, returning to elections, that political communica-tion can rarely upset a settled consensus. Political campaigners everywhere may have reasons to doubt the efficacy of their work where not blessed by considerable resources and a favourable *Zeitgeist*; but there are reasons too for hope.

12

Campaign Effects: Is Anyone Ever Persuaded?

Introduction

The US presidential campaigns are the highest spending political campaigns in the world. Presidential candidates and conventions spent and raised over $1 billion in 2004, with the lion's share taken by the two principal contenders, George W. Bush and John Kerry.[1] This figure was up by 56 per cent compared to similar activity in 2000. For the 2008 elections the top three candidates for the Democrat and Republican Parties had already raised more than $452 million by January 2008 and were on course to break previous records.

Driven chiefly by television advertising costs, campaign expenditure in the Unites States is the most extreme case of a worldwide phenomenon in democratic societies. Those who want to get elected expend time and money in the belief that by doing so they can persuade others to vote for them. Are they right? This is the principal subject of this chapter. I will examine the *effects of electoral campaigning*, one of the principal venues of political communication as well as *the notion of 'effect'* and *whether anyone is ever persuaded*.

The Long Search: Identifying Effects

As I discussed in Chapter 11, the purposes of campaigns can be summarized in three goals: first, they seek civic engagement, that is cognitive and mobilization effects so that voters learn about the issues and candidates and are moved to go out and vote; second, they aim to have public and media agenda-setting effects; and third, they seek persuasion effects, shaping and perhaps changing voting preferences. I will look at each of these kinds of effects in more detail.

Before considering contemporary thinking on campaign effects, it will be useful to sketch in some of the background to effects research in political communication. As we shall see, early work focused on voter persuasion and it is this I will examine in more detail.

Bullets, Needles and Strong Media Effects

The question of whether campaigns win elections and the issue of voter persuasion was at the heart of the earliest studies of political communication. Pioneers in the field such as Paul Lazarsfeld and Bernard Berelson had strong personal and scholarly reasons for wanting to understand what were the key elements in persuading someone to support one party or candidate as against another. They had seen political leaders such as Hitler and Mussolini first persuade their peoples to support them before installing themselves in power. Hitler's Nazi Party had risen from winning three per cent of the national vote in 1924 to 43.9 per cent in 1933, the year Jewish scholar Paul Lazarsfeld left his native Vienna for the United States. Propaganda studies, as they were known, were not only of theoretical but also of prime practical importance.

Social psychologists and political scientists sought to understand three related, yet distinct processes in the context of the development of mediated mass communication. First, they wanted to examine whether or not the new forms of mediated communication – radio and television broadcasts, advertising content – had effects. Second, they wished to understand the nature of these effects and third, they were interested in the impact of these developments on the conduct of democratic politics.

Metaphors can be highly revealing of the basic assumptions we bring to an issue or subject. Politicians speak of 'staying the course' or 'roadmaps to peace'. These navigational metaphors imply that there is indeed a way to follow and politicians have the means and commitment to take us down the necessary route. In the earliest days of communication research, scholars used phrases such as the 'hypodermic needle' and 'magic bullet' to characterize what they took to be the nature of media effects. The listeners' reaction of panic to Orson Welles's 1938 radio broadcast of the Martian invasion recounted in the novel *War of the Worlds* was taken to be paradigmatic of strong media effects. The transmission of media content would 'hit' those who received it in a similarly powerful way causing similar effects, much as being shot by a bullet or injected with noxious or curative substances would produce commonly experienced effects in the targets.

The combative nature of the metaphor indicated, on the one hand, a characterization of mass-media content as enormously powerful and, on the other, a distinct and unflattering understanding of human beings as uniform, passive creatures, highly prone to manipulation. As I have already noted, the early interests and concerns of communication research owed much to the social and political context of its time. The experience of the impact of propaganda efforts during the First World War, and of the Nazis' success in stirring up anti-Semitism in the interwar period, appeared to provide strong evidence for the 'magic bullet' approach to understanding media effects. However, as we shall now see, later research related specifically to political campaign effects demonstrated that the picture was less straightforward than had been earlier thought.

Examining Voting Decisions

Early voting studies paid great attention to examining the impact of campaign information on voters' decisions. According to the 'magic bullet' theory, political campaigns would involve the communication of strong, clear, targeted messages which would persuade voters to vote for the candidate who had been most successful in getting his or her message across. However, the first methodologically rigorous, empirical research to examine voters' decision-making found this not to be the case. Researchers at Columbia University's Bureau of Applied Social Research, led by Paul Lazarsfeld, examined the formation of the voting decisions of the citizens of Erie County (Ohio) in the 1940 election that renewed Franklin D. Roosevelt's presidential term (see *The People's Choice*, Lazarsfeld, Berelson and Gaudet, 1944/1948). Using an innovative panel research design, they conducted interviews with a representative sample of voters and found that radio and press had limited effects on voting decisions compared to the interpersonal communication effects of conversations with peers.[2] Community opinion leaders acted as a significant filter of mediated information, and political communication 'flowed' in a two-step process rather than being directly transmitted from candidate and/or media to voter as envisaged by earlier researchers. They noted the more significant impact of social factors on the act of voting and opinion formation rather than the effect of the media's transmission of campaign information. Family voting habits (primary group), party allegiances (secondary group) and religious identity (reference group) as well as *influentials* – those people who tell us what to buy, which politicians to support and where to go on holiday (see Keller and Berry, 2003) – were found to matter greatly in voting decisions.

Lazarsfeld, Berelson and Gaudet's work appeared to show that campaign effects were minimal and that mass media, for example, tended simply to reinforce partisan attachments rather than change them. Social and party alignment were found to be more important in deciding your vote than anything campaigners could say or do, although the latter were important in ensuring the 'activation' of already committed voters. In other words, campaigns could activate and sustain interest and commitment, reinforce voting intentions, but seldom persuade someone to vote differently from their declared party affiliation because of a campaign message. Work at the Survey Research Center at the University of Michigan buttressed the conclusions about the importance of partisanship, examining it from the perspective of predispositions affecting attitudes and opinions of issues and candidates (see Campbell et al., 1960). Both the Columbia and Michigan perspectives minimized the role of campaign communication in persuading voters.

The Return of Campaign Effects

The notion that campaigns have minimal effects dominated communication research from the 1940s. Political science research contributed to thinking which attributed voting decisions largely to structural factors such as class and party affiliation. Campaigns were regarded as fundamentally symbolic events, rituals, whose results had been preordained by prior incidents and accumulated impressions. However, from the 1960s onwards, evidence from elections in the United States and Britain showed that these factors were increasingly of less significance in predicting election outcomes. Voters' volatility was replacing voter stability. As the Power Commission put it for the British context: 'the changes of the post-war era have gradually created citizens who are better educated, have a higher sense of self-esteem, enjoy and expect to make decisions for themselves, and either lack or choose their own geographic, social and institutional bonds' (2004: 103).

These signs of voter de-alignment contributed to the development of an alternative school of thought that focused on theories of 'pocket-book' voting. Work influenced by Downs's economic theory of democracy (1957) and the decline in party identification suggested that the role of campaign communication was greater than supposed by early voting studies, conducted, it should be noted, in a much less media-saturated environment. Downs's approach suggested that voters act as self-interested agents who seek to maximize benefits. 'Pocket book' issues, those affecting our economic interests, would figure strongly in any voting decision. 'It's the economy, stupid', the 1992 campaign mantra established by Clinton's chief campaign strategist, James Carville, was considered the key factor in deciding one's vote. It was argued that on the basis of key economic variables as well as factors such as the incumbent's image and major political events, election results could be accurately predicted apart from the campaign (see, for example, Abramowitz, 1996). This model appeared to work well for the 1992 British general election, for example, where pollsters predicted a Labour victory, partly attributable to what was considered an excellent campaign, and political scientists correctly predicted a Conservative victory on the basis of a number of economic variables. It is worth noting too that the rational choice model provides a plausible explanation for various kinds of voting behaviour. For example, voters who decide not to vote may do so on the perfectly rational calculation that the remote likelihood of their vote changing the result does not outweigh the effort involved in going to cast their ballot.[3] Protest and tactical voting can also be partly explained by this model.

Thinking more broadly about campaign effects, in the last 20 years, a number of researchers have come to affirm that campaigns do matter. Iyengar and Simon, for example, have suggested that in media democracies (2000: 151) 'the consequences of campaigns are far from minimal' and that researchers need to adopt new conceptual and methodological vantage points from which to assess campaign effects. The decoupling of ideology from party and the general rush to occupy the centre ground by political groupings across the world have also served to underline the importance of symbolic politics as explored in Chapter 3. Where there are a greater proportion of unaligned volatile voters, campaigns seek to offer symbolic rather than material gratification to potential voters, crafting strong narratives and powerful images, and emphasizing personality rather than policy. In a number of South-East Asian democracies, for example, actors and singers have been favoured political candidates. This was particularly marked in the Philippines in the 2004 presidential elections when two former actors stood for election without any clear political platform.[4] However, it would be wrong to underestimate the continuing importance of the fundamentals of partisanship and ideology. They still matter but, as one scholar put it, 'these factors are made more or less salient through campaign communication, and many of the independent or swing voters are likely to be more influenced by the processes of campaign persuasion than simple party identification' (Hacker, 2004: 238). Take one example of why campaigns matter. We know that between 1876 and 2000, eight US presidential elections were decided by roughly a margin of 1.5 per cent of the popular vote (see Shea and Burton, 2006). If the net effect of campaigns is to mobilize, reinforce or persuade citizens within that degree of difference, then campaigns must matter and the questions become how and when they do.

Thinking about Effects

The pinpointing of an 'effect' is highly complex. I shall discuss this before considering election campaign effects with particular reference to the role of the media. However, the media are not an exclusive source of influence. There is a large body of research examining the role of the *influentials* and the nature of the persuasive process itself, the psychological principles that trigger compliance: we are affected not just by what we read, hear and see but also by the conversations we have; 'effects' themselves operate in the context of significant cognitive and affective processes.

Methodological and Theoretical Challenges

Unravelling the pattern of causes that may result in, say, physical illness requires the identification of a large array of variables, often interrelated in unexpected ways. Scientific method requires the execution of experiments to test hypotheses about the relationships of causes and effects. This is not such an easy proposition when applied to human beings. Laboratory conditions in which randomized experiments can be conducted are not so easily replicated when the subjects are humans.[5] For this reason, a great deal of effects research has been conducted on the basis of surveys and interviews. However, 'like all scientific techniques, survey methods have weaknesses, of which the logic of treating respondents' self-reported exposure to campaign communication as a reliable surrogate for actual exposure is particularly dubious' (Iyengar and Simon, 2000: 151). Research shows that we regularly under- or over-report exposure to various types of campaign communication. To avoid these difficulties, the best effects research will examine diverse streams of evidence including, for example, surveys, experimental studies and content analysis.

Identifying campaign effects involves methodological challenges, but there is one further, more basic question related to what is meant by an 'effect'. Attempting to understand how mediated communication affects human conduct, phalanxes of researchers have examined issues such as whether violence on television has an impact on behaviour or what we learn from negative political advertising and whether it makes us less likely to vote (see Chapter 10). In other words, effects can be conceptualized in terms other than those of straightforward persuasion outcomes and it is not unreasonable to assume that putative campaign effects are not limited to persuasion. Indeed, one of the clearest goals that campaigners may have is to get out the vote.

More profoundly, however, we can ask whether the underlying approach of much communication research to understanding the impact and influence of campaigns is the correct or only one. Its governing paradigms make two assumptions about human behaviour, each of which is extremely narrowly focused. First, human conduct is considered as primarily rational and the roles of emotion, of ethnic and religious identity – not irrational features of human beings – are often understated. This point is made by Westen, who describes the political brain as being 'emotional' and not a 'dispassionate calculating machine, objectively searching for the right facts, figures, and policies to make a reasoned decision' (2007). This has consequences for where we attempt to locate the sources of campaign effects. News coverage, candidates' speeches, debates, press conferences are all important sites, but they could be extended to include popular entertainment, jokes and comedy shows (see Berrocal, 2003).

Second, notions of value and meaning generation fail to make much of an appearance in analysing campaign effects. As we saw in Chapter 11, cognitive linguist, George Lakoff (see 1996 and 2004), argues for the importance of incorporating core values into political rhetoric as a way of ensuring that supporters and those in the centre will be motivated to vote for you. He suggests that US Democrats must learn from the Republicans about how to frame messages in terms of values since most people vote along the lines of moral identity rather than self-interest. Although Lakoff refers to overarching value frameworks – the big issues – the questions of values on a personal level may also be significant in assessing image and character.

Third, the focus of analysis for effects – individual attitudes and perceptions or aggregations of these – leaves aside the impact of larger contextual issues related to culture, history and political economy. John Street wisely encourages us to look to the contributions of cultural studies in ensuring that communication is not conceptualized as a stimuli-response model. He suggests that in thinking about media influence, it may be more fruitful to look at the way 'media shape powers and capacities, rather than have "effects"' (2001: 93). If we apply this suggestion to the analysis of campaign effects, it will alert us to the importance of examining them in the multi-layered and historically situated environments in which campaigns take place. Interpretation and reception of messages – as Stuart Hall showed us – do not take place in a uniform manner. The kind and source of the message – is it a political ad? A news report? An election speech? – and the context of reception – the characteristics of the receiver, what they are doing when watching a presidential debate – all affect the nature of political communication's influence.

Education and Mobilization

Election campaigns are, on the face of it, one of the great occasions in democracies for citizens to learn about policy issues and engage in the political process. They offer the opportunity for civic engagement at a time when, according to the Power report, 'the problem of disengagement from formal democracy is one afflicting most of the established democracies in the world' (2004: 119). Politicians race around the country giving speeches, attending rallies, feeding policy announcements to the media, devising internet strategies to get their messages out. Voters can access manifestos online, watch political ads, listen to the pundits and read newspaper election coverage. But what is learned from all this and how does it engage the voter? It sometimes appears to be the case that citizens are alienated by campaigns which shed more heat than light, by political processes which seem arcane and remote and by media that are more concerned with audience figures than civic duties. Certainly, a substantial tradition of communication research and commentary has suggested that this last factor – 'media malaise' (see Chapter 10) – has played a key part both in emphasizing trivia and image at the expense of substance and, at the same time, fostering voter apathy.

And yet the evidence would seem to suggest a more complicated picture. Even though the Power inquiry found 'very high levels of alienation from formal processes, particularly the main political parties and elections – on the part of the British people', it also found that the media could not be considered responsible and that the more pressing issue was that 'today's citizens feel they have a right to be listened to and taken account of but that the formal processes and institutions of democracy – voting and parties – do not offer a genuine opportunity for that' (Power, 2006: 107). Blaming the messenger alone for claims that citizens do not vote or do not learn from campaigns is, it seems, too simple. This is not, however, to absolve the media from responsibility in shaping the environment in which campaigns are conducted and, therefore, influencing voters' perceptions. As we shall see, most of what we know or perceive about candidates and parties is mediated through the press, radio, television and, increasingly, the internet. However, the Power inquiry showed that the challenge of generating civic engagement involves more than telling people to switch off their televisions: the nuts and bolts of political systems, the context of political culture and politicians themselves all play their part in shaping a vibrant and open civic world where citizens can believe that they have a role.

Iyengar and Simon's review of the available evidence about the educational value of US campaigns concluded that:

> campaigns are information-rich events. Contrary to the prevailing wisdom, the information they yield is multifaceted, encompassing the candidates' chances of winning, their personal traits and mannerisms, and most important, their policy and ideological bearings. Media campaigns may appear superficial, but they do educate citizens. (2000: 156)

'Media campaigns' designate the key area where campaigners seek to obtain influence in order to affect voters' perceptions of candidates. The media are the battle-ground where parties fight for voters' attention, seeking to mobilize and reinforce supporters and neutralize or undermine opponents' communication strategies. Their aim is to control the media agenda.

Agenda Control

As a permutation of media effects research, the agenda-setting hypothesis has been key in media and political research for over 40 years. The idea that the press influences public opinion was clearly formulated in the 1920s by Walter Lippmann. In 1963 Bernard Cohen argued that 'the press may not be successful much of the time in telling people what to think, but it is stunningly successful in telling its readers what to think about' (1963: 13). Thus, he reasserted the idea of media power in shaping public opinion and the agenda-setting research tradition brought scholarship back to the idea of powerful media.

Empirical confirmation of the hypothesis came in McCombs and Shaw's benchmark study of the 1968 US presidential elections (1972) which examined the relationship between the public's ranking of issue importance – *the public agenda* – with the media's ranking of issue importance in terms of frequency of coverage – *the media agenda*.

The key hypothesis they tested was that the media's agenda becomes the public's agenda: if the media give most coverage to the issue of crime, crime will be perceived as the most important issue facing the nation. McCombs and Shaw's work found a strong correlation between the newspaper agenda and the public's.

Dozens of agenda setting studies conducted since in a number of countries tended to support the McCombs/Shaw finding and their interpretation that the media impacted on the public's views of what is important. Concern for civil rights in the United States from 1954–74, for example, mirrored the news coverage of those years. The percentage of Americans naming civil rights as the most important issue facing the country ranged from zero to 52 per cent in 27 Gallup polls and strongly reflected news coverage in the weeks immediately preceding each of the polls (see Winter and Eyal, 1981). It would appear that the public use salience cues from the media to organize their own agenda. A caveat should be entered here, however, about differential agenda-setting effects according to the media context and the regulatory and cultural framework in which they operate. A study examining television's effects on the public agenda during the 1997 UK general election used both panel survey and experimental research (see Norris et al., 1999). The latter, where participants were randomly divided into seven groups and shown differing compilations of news stories to test afterwards their perception of issue salience, did demonstrate a media agenda-setting effect. This was not, however, the case for those in the panel survey.

The agenda-setting role of the media is one of the principal reasons why candidates and parties seek to control the media agenda, organizing themed campaign days with photo opportunities that will appeal to television, crafting sound bites or political advertising that will dominate the headlines and the conversation of the blogosphere. Politicians know that the public agenda has limited capacity. Many issues compete for attention, but only a small number make it onto the public radar screen, mainly put there by the mainstream media and increasingly by users of the internet. Hillary Clinton's online spoof of popular mafia television series, *The Sopranos* during her 2007 nomination campaign showed her and Bill Clinton discussing the campaign song. This candidate-inspired mini-video very successfully grabbed the free media's attention. Here the strategy was not about focusing attention on an issue or topic, but more about shaping the perceptual environment, showing a candidate in touch with popular culture and able to smile at herself. In spring 2007 a video appeared on YouTube, modelled on an iconic 1980s' Apple advert, in which Hillary Clinton appeared as the Big Brother figure speaking in robotic tones to massed ranks of workers, ending in an appeal to vote for Obama. Eventually Philip de Vellis was tracked down as the source of the attack ad. In an interview he described his 'citizens' ad' as marking a new dawn for the ability of ordinary people to upset the traditional balance of power where the media and politicians seek to arbitrate and frame the public agenda.

The battle for agenda control is one that politicians are finding increasingly difficult to manage. Britain's 1997 Labour campaign was considered to be a landmark in party electioneering and it took place in a context where UK broadcasters have a public service obligation to provide impartial electoral coverage. Nevertheless, Norris and colleagues found that 'the party and the news agendas remained worlds apart' (1999: 181).

Are the Media Decisive?

Can the media actually win elections for parties? This was the UK *Sun*'s claim after the Conservatives won the 1992 general election. It claimed in a front-page banner headline that: 'IT WAS THE SUN WOT WON IT.' Research shows that there is a correlation between voting behaviour and newspaper reading habits but it cannot confirm anything about the direction of influence. It is more probable that my reading of a left-leaning newspaper simply reinforces my pre-existing voting preferences rather than actually shaping them in one direction or another. Studies of the 1992 and 1997 British general elections concluded that newspapers had a limited effect on the voting decision of their readers (see Curtice and Semetko, 1994; and Norris et al., 1999). These findings have to be set in the context of Britain's highly partisan press. In countries where the press is considered a more impartial source (some parts of Spain's regional press, for example), the press may be more influential.

The media's role in shaping voters' preferences needs to be considered beyond that of suggesting that they may set the issue agenda. They can be crucial in making some candidates, and certain of their traits, more salient than others. According to Weaver 'this kind of media influence probably has more influence on voters' early perceptions of the campaign, and the final choices available at election time, than does issue agenda setting' (1996: 215). Patterns of voter media exposure, prior knowledge and opinions, discussions with others and motivation to follow the campaign all affect how campaigns impact on citizens. The media's role in providing the resources apparently to make sense of what we see, hear and read, their provision of the seemingly commonsense assumptions upon which to judge candidates and issues may, however, be their most crucial function, as I shall discuss next.

Making Sense of It All

Whatever the agenda of objects might be (issues, candidates), each of these objects has a set of attributes that can be examined for their impact on perceptions and opinions. Referred to by McCombs as the second level of agenda setting effects (see Ghanem, 1997), these attributes can tell us not only what to think about but also what to think. In this way, the media 'frame' stories and 'prime' us to respond in certain ways.

Priming. 'Priming' refers to a process developed in psychological research whereby activating certain associations in our memory, we are led to confer greater importance to some criteria or terms than others. For example, if news constantly emphasizes a leader's responsibility for a problem, we will be more likely to judge him or her on the basis of their handling of that issue. In campaigns the media's capacity to make some features more salient than others in relation to image and, to a lesser extent, issues ensures that their role is highly significant.

Framing. The concept of framing was introduced into mass communication studies by Todd Gitlin in his 1980 study of the student political movement, *The Whole World is Watching*. Developed in the work of Iyengar and Kinder (1987), Iyengar (1991) later examined the impact of episodic and thematic framing. Episodically framed stories concentrate on specific events illustrating general themes while thematically framed stories present more general, fact-based stories. In experimental research he found we were more likely to attribute individual responsibility in stories told in an episodic way. Stories of suicide bombing in Iraq would be understood simply as the work of bloodthirsty fanatics, while stories focusing on trends in the security situation would lead us also to think about structural reasons for the events. Iyengar's work suggested that media influence in political communication is related to how they tell the story and who they make responsible in the stories they tell.

Definitions of framing and frame refer, first, to *the idea of selection*. Framing is a result of inclusion and exclusion of contents. 'To frame – Entman explains – 'is to select some aspects of a perceived reality and make them more salient in communicating a text, in such a way as to promote a particular problem definition, causal interpretation, moral evaluation, and/or treatment recommendation for the item described' (1993: 52). Second, most definitions have to do with *the way things are understood* or, more precisely, mentally organized. A frame is a 'central organizing idea or story line that provides meaning' (Gamson and Modigliani, 1987: 143). Third, the idea of the *context of an issue* has also been related to the notion of frame. As Rachlin puts it, 'fundamental assumptions will be identified that serve to provide the "frames" or contexts within which the events are presented' (1988: 3). Fourth, applied to newsmaking, the frame is seen as the *story line*, angle, or news judgement.

The media help us make sense of the political world. As Lang and Lang (1983) showed in their landmark study of the Watergate affair the context in which news is presented determines to a large extent whether a problem comes to be perceived as important and politically relevant. Issues require constant coverage to cross the threshold of public consciousness and displace other concerns. But for them to matter, the public must be able to locate them on the political landscape and this is what the media do. Media framing is key. Campaigns seek to co-opt the media into defining candidates, parties and issues on their terms. They don't always succeed. In the 2004 US presidential elections, John Kerry's floral surfing shorts framed him as the effete liberal his opponents wanted him to be seen as. The photograph of Sarkozy mounted on a white horse in the Auvergne during the 2007 French presidential campaign, provided the visual correlate of his campaign themes of dynamism and masterful leadership.

These examples point to a further dimension of media framing, one of which campaign strategists have to be aware. Framing occurs within cultural and historical contexts. In Spanish politics, for example, the civil war (1936–39) is an ever-present historical reference. Politicians seeking political advantage often seek to frame issues in its polarizing terms and these can be too easily adopted by the media. As Edelman puts it:

The models, scenarios, narratives, and images into which audiences for political news translate that news are social capital, not individual inventions. They come from works of art in all genres: novels, paintings, stories, films, dramas, television sitcoms, striking rumours, even memorable jokes. For each type of news report there is likely to be a small set of striking images that are influential with large numbers of people. (1988: 1)

We are not passive consumers of framed news. Our own capacities, experience and prejudices – platforms of understanding – come into play in interpreting what the media places before us. However, in Street's words. 'The mass media may not be the cause of votes and attitudes, but they may be responsible for legitimating the operation of particular agendas and ideologies' (2001: 98). The media in all its forms and formats provide the resources from which we fashion our understanding of the political world not least during election campaigns. They are not, however, our only sources. *Influentials* are also a significant route of influence as I shall discuss next.

The Influentials

In 2003, Keller and Berry published *One American in Ten Tells the Other Nine How to Vote, Where to Eat, and What to Buy.* They identified around 10 percent of the American population as *influentials*. The *influentials* are the minority of those who have substantial influence on a significant number of their peers. Based on public opinion polls from the Roper centre, Keller and Berry identified *influentials* who tell us 'what to do, what to buy, who to vote for and they have the answer to any question or they know someone who knows'. Their research applies the hypothesis formulated by Lazarsfeld, Berelson and Gaudet (1944/1948) of the *two-step flow* theory according to which a minority of opinion leaders act as the intermediaries between the media and the majority (see Figure 12.1).

According to Weimann (1994), more than 3900 studies of *influentials*, of opinion leaders and their personal influence, have been carried out since Lazarsfeld, Berelson and Gaudet's pioneering study. These studies have examined issues such as who are the *influentials*, how they influence others and what is the nature of their influence. In its 2003 study of online *influentials*, the Institute for Politics, Democracy and the Internet (2004) found that they actively spread information and influence others: 44 per cent are asked for advice and information about a range of issues including career choices, computers, government and politics, restaurants or web sites. The study's authors concluded that:

> A new community of citizens online is defining the 2004 presidential campaign. These citizens are Internet-oriented and politically energized, and they support their candidates by visiting their Web sites, joining Internet discussion groups, reading political Web logs and making political contributions over the Internet. (2004: 1)

Figure 12.1   The two-step flow model

Evidence from Barack Obama's 2008 nomination campaign suggested that these trends were set to continue.

Campaign Persuasion

One of the most difficult to prove and yet most studied areas of campaign effects is that of the shaping of electoral preferences. Persuading people to vote for you is, of course, the whole point of election campaigns. Yet, as we have seen, mediated campaigns result in strategic communications focusing on media as their chief venue of political communication, leading some commentators to speak of a 'bystander' public (Lang and Lang, 1983). Candidates and parties tailor their communication to capture as much positive free media coverage as possible. Apart from being the main way of reaching the voter, it is also a way of ensuring that campaign communications may be received in a context where they may be considered to have some credibility. The perception of source impartiality is a key factor in inclining voters to accept the truth of a message. However, even though campaigns often cannot control the context in which their message is communicated, it is in their hands to ensure that the message is potentially persuasive in itself.

The analysis of the persuasive characteristics of communication has been interestingly explored from the perspective of social psychology. Robert Cialdini carried out extensive fieldwork examining persuasion and influence in various occupational contexts. In particular, he observed the work of those great persuaders, car salesmen, to learn what it is that persuades us to consent to making a significant purchase from someone we hardly know. Recalling the insights provided from political marketing (see Chapter 4), we can see that there are some interesting analogies to be made with what might decide our vote. Cialdini (1993) identifies the following six 'decision triggers' in the process of persuasion:

The suggestion of scarcity and/or uniqueness. This principle suggests that opportunities seem more valuable to us when they are limited and that our desire for something increases when we think it is difficult or almost impossible to have, than when it is freely available. If, by not accepting something, we can be convinced that we might lose out, we will be more motivated to accept it than if the offer were placed in the context of what we might gain. This has interesting implications for how politicians frame policy proposals.

Liking. If we like someone we are far more likely to be influenced by her. Social psychologists have found that what makes us like others are factors such as physical attractiveness, similarity, contact and cooperation and the receiving of compliments. If we consider someone to be physically attractive, we are far more likely to attribute to him positive traits. Telegenic political candidates are at a significant advantage compared to their plainer rivals. Having similar interests, background, views and dress sense also produces an attraction. Cultivating attractiveness through emphasizing commonalities ('I'm a pretty regular kind of guy'; 'I had a tough childhood'), bestowing compliments and seeking areas of cooperation is a powerful spur to acceptance of a message. Political candidates often play to this, targeting specific sets of supporters by choosing a particular holiday location (Clinton going on a hiking holiday in 1995) or hunting and fishing in Siberia (Putin in 2007). In transactions with what Cialdini (1993: 203–5) calls 'compliance professionals' (salespeople of all kinds), he advises us to separate our liking for them from the transaction itself. This may be more difficult in politics where, as we shall see, the candidate's character is part of what we 'buy'.

Reciprocation. The rule of reciprocation suggests that where we receive a favour or gift we feel under a strong obligation to reciprocate. Charity organizations often use this principle, sending a free pen or cards with their campaign literature. According to Cialdini (1993: 26), it is no coincidence that two Washington outsiders, Carter and Clinton, had difficulty getting legislation through Congress. No one was indebted to them and therefore no one felt obliged to make reciprocal concessions.

Authority. There are many good reasons for obeying those who know more or have more experience than we have. Authority can flow from expertise but it can also be simulated. For example, the symbols and trappings of authority make us more likely to obey the person who possesses them: a title, certain kinds of clothes, physical appearance – height is strongly associated with authority – all conspire to create the impression that their possessor warrants our obedience even though there may be no substantial reason for this to be so. In this sense, political incumbents enjoy a significant advantage.

Social proof. Experiments have shown that when we watch comedy programmes with canned laughter we find them funnier and laugh longer than when we watch them without (Cialdini, 1993: 116–17). The reason is that we look for guidance about what is correct by seeing what others think. The principle of social proof suggests that we are more likely to accept something if evidence is provided that others do too. A political candidate who is widely recognized, has name recognition, and has an established level of support enjoys an automatic advantage that her lesser-known challenger has to surmount, hence the well-known advantages of incumbency.

Commitment and consistency. Social psychology research shows that we have a deep underlying need to be consistent in attitudes and choices or at least to see ourselves in that way. According to Leon Festinger's theory of cognitive dissonance (1957), where we perceive dissonance between two cognitions (an emotion, belief or attitude), we seek to filter out the conflicting cognition or acquire new cognitions to reduce the perceived conflict. In other words, the perception of inconsistency in our beliefs and behaviour causes psychological tension that we dissipate through changing our beliefs to suit behaviour rather than the other way around. Making a commitment provides a strong spur to being consistent. However small the commitment – signing a petition, doing some canvassing for a political party – the pressures for consistency come from outside and from our own wish to align our self-image with our actions.

The set of principles derived from the study of the psychology of compliance that act as useful shortcuts for decision-making in a complicated, information-rich world and understanding routes of influence can help us identify persuasion's power and deflect it where it veers dangerously close to manipulation. Each of these decision triggers can be translated into firm policy and communication tactics and strategies. According to Westen, they need too to be supplemented by attention to the emotional narrative of a campaign:

> If you think the failure to tell a coherent story, or to illustrate your words with evocative images, is just the 'window dressing' of a campaign and makes little difference in the success or failure of a candidacy, you're missing something very important about the political brain. Political persuasion is about networks and narratives. (2007)

Getting the persuasive messages through may be one of the most challenging goals for a campaign team. Political advertising can play only a limited role and campaigns are always vulnerable to the distorting effects of media influence and opposition strategies. However, it may be the case that the latter two can only be significantly influential when there are notable flaws in a candidate's or party's approach. Take the Kerry 2004 presidential campaign. His insistence on playing the military service card, despite the apparent incongruence of his later opposition to the Vietnam war and unclear stance on the Iraq invasion, left him open to the charge of inconsistency and, more seriously, lack of credibility. It was precisely on this last issue that he was attacked in the videos released by the Swift Boat Veterans for Truth who questioned the truth of his war record. Paying attention to the cognitive and emotional tone and coherence of campaign messages and strategy, to all that can contribute to their persuasive quality, is still almost certainly

worth doing even if, in the end, we are less commonly persuaded by campaigns than might be thought.

Conclusion

In conclusion, campaigns have the '*potential* capacity to matter both for civic
engagement and for political persuasion' (Norris, 2000: 9). In his study of
American presidential campaigns, Campbell concludes that campaign
effects 'are neither large or minimal in an absolute sense, but sometimes
large enough to be politically important' (2000: 7). For these reasons, election campaigns will continue to be significant sites for communicating politics and parties and candidates will continue to pour money into them.
Another way of putting it is to say that campaigns may matter less than the
politicians and their campaign consultants suppose for deciding electoral
outcomes, yet their effects for education, mobilization, persuasion, reinforcement and activation are real enough to justify the effort and expense.

13

Political News and Comment

Introduction

News is a nebulous entity: it is not simply what happens in the world; newspapers do not straightforwardly 'mirror' reality. As writers from Walter Lippmann onwards have recognized, news is a product, a construction arising out of a particular set of historical, economic, cultural and institutional circumstances.[1] It involves processes of selection, interpretation, the application of formulae and judgement. It is an eminently human practice, closely bound up in specific understandings of significance and of what can be set before the public as justified belief, often summed up by the notion of 'news values' (see below). However, it is also about 'events', things which happen: a suicide bombing, a natural disaster, pigs on the run. Notwithstanding its constructed, manufactured or framed nature, news, unlike fiction, should have some connection, however spurious, to events that can be pinpointed in time and space. The time-worn expression that 'newspapers are the first draft of history' just about holds true despite the many reservations and caveats that can be entered against it.

The fragility of news' connection to events and of an overly realist account of news is particularly apparent in examining the reporting of politics. Much of political news consists of the relaying of opinion, speculation and rumour dressed up as fact. Politicians vie with journalists to shape public perceptions to their own ends. At times, and in particular journalistic and political cultures, journalists connive in the production of news as politics rather than politics as news (see Hallin and Mancini, 2004). As Edelman put it:

> The spectacle constituted by news reporting continuously constructs and reconstructs social problems, crises, enemies and leaders and so creates a succession of threats and reassurances. These constructed problems and personalities furnish

the content of political journalism and the data for historical and analytic political studies. They also play a central role in winning support and opposition for political causes and policies. (1988:1)

News has long been partly constitutive of politics itself and this is especially apparent when crisis, division and scandal sweep the political stage. The drama of Nixon's resignation in 1974, of Clinton's difficulties about a White House intern in 1998, were narratives in which major political actors took the leading roles in stories told by the media, often considered political actors in their own right (see Cook, 2005).

Understanding political news – the principal aim of this chapter – is a complex task and ever more so in a rapidly changing news environment in which the central role of the 'professional mediators' – the journalists – is being challenged (see Blumler and Gurevitch, 2005: 108-9). This chapter will first examine political news as *a kind of knowledge and practice*, examining in detail *the relationship to sources*; it will then examine *the types of political journalist* inhabiting the news and commentary zoo and, finally, explore some of *the forces driving change*, sometimes in apparently contradictory directions, in our understanding of political news.

'Known Knowns' in Political Journalism

Political journalism is one of the most extensively researched areas of journalism studies. Notwithstanding this, identifying a corpus of accepted findings is no easy matter. This, in part, is due to what have been described as research 'blind spots', including the absence of substantial historical and comparative studies which would allow us to be clear about what is meant by 'political journalism' and political news (Kuhn and Neveu, 2003: 2–3).

I will argue next, however, that there are a number of 'known knowns'[2] about political journalism, some of which are shared to a degree with the rest of journalism (see Figure 13.1). I have divided them into three.

First, when we examine what kind of thing political journalism is – what is its ontological status – we can define it as *a certain kind of practice arising in a particular set of cultural and historical circumstances* which at the same time constantly change and bear upon its form and content. This is true of journalism in general. Political news and journalism, however, could be said to have a particularly delicate relationship to their historical and cultural setting. A little like a rare orchid which requires precise climatic and soil conditions in order to flourish, the conditions necessary for the healthy practice of political journalism are not easily achieved and always in danger of being undermined.

The second known refers to *the knowledge claims* – the epistemological status – upon which political news and journalism are based. In common with

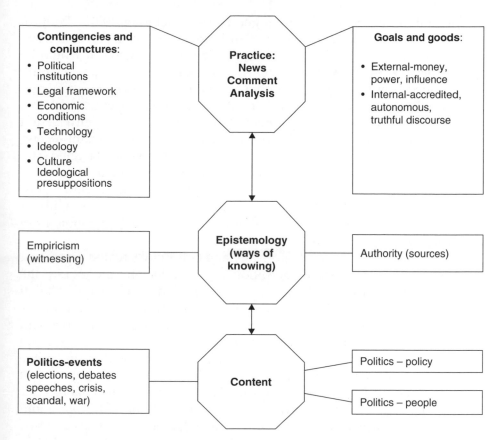

Figure 13.1 Known knowns: characteristics of political journalism

other forms of journalism, these flow both from the standpoint of the witness but primarily from source relationships.

Finally, the distinguishing mark of political journalism and news is its *content*. As we shall see, there are debates about alleged shifts in content, generally along the lines that political news has become more focused on personalities, drama and conflict (Franklin, 2004). Notwithstanding the evidence for this, it continues to be the case that news bulletins, blogs and newspapers are full of talk about politics understood as the events, deeds and words of those engaged in public life. I will next examine in more detail journalism as practice and as epistemology.

Political Journalism as Practice

Political journalism, like all human practices, arose out of a set of activities undertaken by communities with shared rules and aims directed towards

the pursuit of internal and external goods (see MacIntyre, 1997).[3] Political
journalism might often pursue power and influence – what can be termed
external goods – but without a distinguishing internal good, it would be
impossible to know what political journalism is. Broadly speaking, it could
be described as organized, autonomous and accredited discourse about politics including news, comment and opinion. It can be independent, biased,
partisan, policy or personality oriented. However, for it to be journalism it
must have some connection – however tenuous – first with truth, second
with someone or thing who assumes responsibility for what is claimed, and
third, with a perspective which is distinct from the prevailing political powers, even though it might coincide with specific political viewpoints.
Without connection to truth, it is at best fiction and at worst lies; without
accountability it may be no more than rumour and without autonomy from
political power, it is no more than propaganda.

Reporting politics is also a historically and culturally situated practice. It
arises where the conditions are propitious; it is moulded by and moulds the
social and political circumstances in which it finds itself. Authoritarian
regimes, such as Robert Mugabe's post-2000 Zimbabwe and Kim Jong Il's
North Korea, attempt at least to control if not extinguish independent
reporting of politics. Indeed, the history of the development of political
journalism is the history of the struggle to cast off government control of the
free flow of information about politics. It is also about the development of
an understanding and practice of political journalism as an area distinct, for
instance, from political publicity. Neveu remarks that 'the shift from publi-
cist to political journalism is a clear, international trend from the second half
of the nineteenth century onwards' (2003: 28) while recognizing that in
countries such as France and Italy, for example, the close political paral-
lelism between journalists and politicians and the tardy development of
journalism as an autonomous area of practice meant that journalists continued to be, in effect, political publicists for much longer.

The story of the reporting of parliament in Britain illustrates these themes
well. In the same way that government executive discussions are even
today considered out of media bounds, eighteenth-century politicians did
not permit the reporting of parliamentary debates, in part to control the
flow of information to the monarch. Politicians' growing recognition of
public opinion as a force in the land prompted practical developments as
elementary, for example, as ensuring that newspaper reporters would have
a space in parliament – the Press Gallery – reserved for them (in 1803) and
that they would be allowed to take notes (from 1828), something previously
forbidden.

Reporting of parliament became a mainstay of British political news,
opening up the political space to greater public scrutiny and giving rise to
Thomas Babington Macaulay's (1800–1859) famous statement that: 'The

gallery in which the reporters sit has become a fourth estate of the realm.'[4] Gallery reporters, of which Charles Dickens was perhaps the most famous representative, set great pride on the accuracy and speed with which they reported parliamentary debates and for these purposes, the practice of shorthand came to be seen as an essential skill for the journalist's craft. In 1881 the Parliamentary Press Gallery was formed, opening its doors to provincial reporters, followed three years later by the establishment of the Parliamentary Lobby. This gave journalists access to the parliamentarians' Lobby of the House of Commons where they hung around hoping to be approached by members of parliament (MPs) since they were not permitted to speak to them unless spoken to first.

The twin developments of Lobby and Gallery journalism gave much of twentieth-century British political journalism its distinctly deferential flavour. Writing about British political journalism in the 1950s, a distinguished *Daily Mirror* reporter recorded how: 'journalists operated their own code of behaviour – a kind of unwritten statute of limitations. An unwritten understanding of when and how to break the rules of convention' (Goodman, 2003: 271). These conventions included never mentioning the existence of the Lobby and, as a Lobby journalist, never identifying an informant without specific permission (the so-called reporting on Lobby terms).

The practice of much twentieth-century political reporting in Britain took place in a cultural context of male dominance of journalism, limited news outlets and pronounced social deference and difference: Winston Churchill would never have deigned to address a newspaper editor let alone a mere reporter. It was also a time of the decline of Empire and of adjustment to post-world war realities. These and other factors marked the character of British political news and reporting in the past. Different factors, as we shall see, mark it now and yet, as a practice, it bears the marks of the continuities of its defining goals and goods and the contingencies of its past. This is true for all political news. Two examples from the Arab Gulf show this: as we saw in Chapter 9, Arab broadcast news is a very different creature since the birth of Al Jazeera in 1996; on the other hand, at the beginning of the twenty-first century much of the Arab Gulf press continued to reflect the political and cultural conventions of authoritarian states, compromising to some extent its status as political news.

Political Journalism as Epistemology

The greater part of journalism is based on appeals to authority, the authority of sources. Journalists also derive their knowledge of events from being witnesses to them, but this is rarer than is often thought. Stories are structured around claims to facts and truth provided by sources sometimes

named and sometimes not. The fact that 'minister x' or 'aide y' said something becomes the basis for news. Authority, in other words, is considered a
good enough reason in journalism for us to believe that something is the
case or not. Journalists ground this belief in the perceived reliability of the
information source, either because it contains (in the case of a document) or
is a witness to what is stated or, more commonly, because their information
source lays claim to having a reliable source of information. In the latter
case, the underlying assumption is that there is ultimately someone who
knows. If there were not, all journalism would be only gossip and rumour
(which, of course, it sometimes is).

Most of what we know – language, tests for evaluating knowledge claims –
is based, quite reasonably, on what we have learnt from others. This is a
very respectable yet often unacknowledged intellectual approach to gaining
knowledge. Presenting news and comment on the basis of authority constitutes a tacit tradition partly constitutive of what journalism is. It is, very
especially, the life-blood of political reporting which is one of the most
source-bound areas of news which, together with the subject matter it deals
with, makes political news one of the most contentious fields of reporting.

Political journalism maps power: most fundamentally, who has it, who
hasn't and why; more sophisticatedly, it charts the tides in the affairs of men
and women, the shifts in thought, the movement of ideas in a critical and
scrutinizing fashion. It provides ways of knowing and interpreting the
political world and therefore it is a battle place among those who seek to
shape the meaning and understanding of politics.

Political News and Sources

Various metaphors have been employed to describe the source–political
journalist relationship: images of 'the Beltway' and 'village' emphasize the
cosy, insider world inhabited by journalists and politicians; images of 'incest'
and a dog's relation to a lamp-post underline opposite extremes of their
interaction; certainly it is a field of journalism in which source–reporter relationships are often particularly: (a) regular, (b) personal, (c) competitive, and
(d) confidential. As one journalist put it, 'many – perhaps even most – political stories owe far more to a quiet "secret" chat or tip-off than to open, vol-
unteered quotes' (Goodman, 2003: 31). Politicians and particularly their
aides and communication advisors are in regular, close contact with journalists; they often socialize with them, travel with them. Each needs the other
and this mutual need powerfully structures political reporting. At the same
time, mutual need is shot through with underlying tension.

As we saw in Chapter 3, politicians seek control; journalists, novelty and
revelation. Conflict, then, is frequently the order of the day and, as scholars

like Patterson have shown (1994), conflict itself is sought by journalists as the *leitmotif* of politics. So, for example, in the view of some scholars, 'the index- ing hypothesis – selecting content patterns that are cued by the positions of decisive actors in a political conflict – still explains most routine political reporting' (Bennett, 2004: 292). Other scholars have looked to the model of 'primary definition' to explain the dynamics of source–reporter relationship (Gitlin, 1980; Hall, 1982; Herman and Chomsky, 1988). In this view, sources are the forces who hold the balance of power, using their institutional muscle as well as logistical and ideological resources to ensure that certain stories are told and others not. For many commentators, Tony Blair's election in 1997 marked a sea-change in UK government-media relations, shifting power into the hands of the professionalized government and party sources who used their strategic understanding of the media to ensure their message prevailed (see Barnett and Gaber, 2001; Jones, 1995, 1997, 2001). Source power is explored in agenda setting and agenda building studies of the media.[5]

However, when suspicion dominates the relation between journalists and official sources, when sources lose credibility during times of crisis and scan- dal or because of the excesses of media management, it becomes ever clearer that structural constraints do not tell the whole story of journalists' relation- ships to sources (see, for example, Canel and Sanders, 2006; Negrine, 1996; Schlesinger and Tumber, 1994). The balance of power shifts and the media appear to have the upper hand, driving the political news agenda despite politicians' best efforts to regain control. Something of this happened to the Clinton presidency where the alleged and/or real scandals of Whitewater and Lewinsky dominated headlines despite the White House's attempts to move the agenda onto the President's policies.

It is also the case that politicians are not the only sources attempting to dominate the political news agenda. As we saw in earlier chapters, NGOs, pressure groups and lobbyists have become increasingly adept media strate- gists and use multimedia approaches to move their issues onto journalists' radar screens. The source-journalist relationship is probably too multilay- ered to be captured by one single hypothesis or theory. It depends on a num- ber of factors including the media's resources; the kind of issue being covered; and the integrity and energy of the journalist. So, for example, a poorly resourced newspaper is far more likely to be source dominated; jour- nalists reporting scandal and crisis will rely heavily on non-official sources; a lazy journalist will be less likely to check out the alleged 'facts' of a news release. Scant resources, poor journalistic integrity and, what one might term, low issue excitement factor will tend to favour source dominance while the contrary will shift the balance of power towards journalists (see Figure 13.2).

So far we have examined the source-journalist relationship within a broadly sociological framework. Cottle (2003) sets out two other approaches

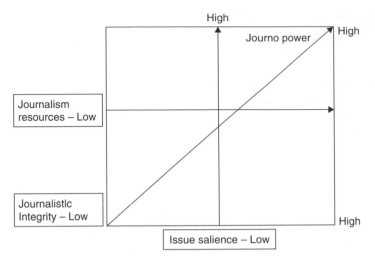

Figure 13.2   Journalist–source relationship

to this relationship, the first of which he terms the 'culturalist' perspective and the second the 'communicative' approach (see Table 13.1).

The culturalist approach examines how the source-journalist relationship is structured by the story-telling resources of particular communities. So, for example, political scandal stories (see Canel and Sanders, 2006) have predictable casts of villains, media events tell stories about contests (the Watergate hearings, for example), conquests (Pope John Paul II's visit to Poland in 1979) and coronations (election victory) (see Dayan and Katz, 1994). Drawing on insights from a number of scholars (see, for example, Bird and Dardenne, 1988; Schudson, 2000), news is shown to be partly a function of the cultural repertoires available at any given time and place. Finally, Cottle points to an approach where emphasis is placed on the contingencies of the communication acts themselves and the institutional settings in which they take place. Communication encounters in interviews, for example, have changed over time and a close study of their characteristics can reveal a great deal about the dynamic and open nature of some source/media exchanges

As Cottle is himself at pains to point out (2003: 17), these approaches to thinking about source/media relations are not mutually exclusive. Together they highlight their complex, multi-layered character.

The Political News Zoo

The twenty-first-century political news zoo, like the rest of journalism, is characterized by intense commercial pressures, news hyper-inflation and

Table 13.1 Sources, power and the media (after Cottle, 2003)

	Sociological perspective	Culturalist perspective	Communicative perspective
Type of power in play	Strategic	Symbolic	Communicative
Research approach	■ Ethnography ■ Content analysis	■ Textual analysis: discourse/content analysis	■ Textual analysis: discourse/content analysis ■ Conversational analysis ■ Historical analysis
Theoretical models	■ Primary definition ■ Agenda setting/building ■ Framing ■ Indexing	■ Narrativity ■ Media events	■ Ritual and social drama ■ Institutional frameworks and settings
Nature of source/journalist relationship	■ Complicity ■ Competition	■ Story-telling: production of compelling story lines, plots and characters	■ Dynamic ■ Undetermined ■ Driven by institutional conventions and possibilities
Type of agency	■ Play of social interests serving personal, economic and/or ideological goals.	■ Cultural resources provide scripts and references giving primacy to form over content.	■ Contingent on performative and institutional factors and resistant to ideological or textual closure.

the opening up of spaces and opportunities for redefining political news. This last development is particularly notable in relation to the increasing blurring of the private and the public in political journalism, extending the range of 'acceptable' subjects.

Political journalism straddles, then, a variety of modes, formats and styles. The development of the blogosphere and the advent of user-generated content (UGC) have expanded these. A journalist can be chronicler, newshound, interrogator, pundit, performer or critic. As I shall explore next, roles are not mutually exclusive: the pundit is often critic and very often performer.

Political Journalist as Chronicler

The nineteenth-century Gallery reporter of the British parliament comes as close as anything to the model of the journalist as straightforward chronicler of events, recorder of the words and deeds of the politicians. The faithful reproduction of parliamentary debates remained a feature of British newspaper journalism until the late 1980s, but the agreement by MPs to permit the televising of Parliament in 1989 led to the development of parliamentary coverage on broadcast channels and the decline of press parliamentary reporting (Straw, 1993). Since 1998 the BBC has broadcast live and recorded coverage of British parliamentary proceedings on the BBC Parliament channel. C-Span in the United States, the Knesset channel in Israel, the Australian ABC NewsRadio and from 2005, the Venezuelan ANTV are among some of the channels performing a similar function across the world. As with all mediated representations, though, the broadcasting of parliamentary proceedings introduces its own distorting effects into the events it is showing. First, the logic of audiovisual representation encourages an emphasis on those elements – clothes, gestures, noise, placing and so on – which play to the media's narrative mode. Second, the institutions themselves take great care to regulate the kinds of images and sounds which can be made available to the watching public. The British parliament, for example, prohibits certain kinds of camera angle and, despite the attempts of broadcasters, refuses to permit a 'public gallery' view of events in parliament.

The development of the internet provided new opportunities for opening up parliament to the public gaze. The modern Scottish parliament, established in 1999, first webcast parliamentary proceedings live in May 2000. Its London counterpart launched a pilot project in January 2002; in September 2004 Parliamentlive.tv was established to webcast all public UK parliamentary proceedings. Similar developments can be found at local government level. Webcasting would seem to suggest the ultimate disintermediation of the reporting of political events. The traditional political news intermediaries – political journalists – can simply be bypassed. This is partly true. As we saw, it would be wrong to think of broadcast and web parliamentary coverage as being straightforwardly unedited. If anything, the politicians' editorial control becomes more dominant as broadcasters seek to negotiate the terms of entry. However, politicians have a vested interest in engaging publics and, as can be seen in the EU's proposed communication policy (2007), are keen to use the technological means at their disposal to overcome public disengagement from political institutions. The chronicler journalist has, to an extent, been displaced by technological developments in many parts of the world. However, far from diminishing the range and scope of political journalism, there are strong arguments and considerable evidence to suggest that it has flourished in a number of different guises.

Political Journalist as News Reporter

Political news, as we saw earlier, shares some of the imperatives of general news reporting in the Western tradition. The Lobby journalists, the White House press corps, the Brussels pack are assigned to structured news beats, applying the routine news values (see Galtung and Ruge, 1965), covering the events of their particular patches: briefings, press conferences, news releases and so on. In part, the logic of newspaper sections and broadcast specialisms ensure that there will be a steady stream of material to fill the 'news holes'. 'Politics' continues to be a key section of most generalist newspapers and news programmes

Journalists do not, of course, simply gather the news. There are some who also pursue stories, who investigate and actively scrutinize the activities of the political classes. The results of their work can be found in current affairs programmes such as *60 Minutes*, the BBC's *Panorama* or Spain's *El Mundo* newspaper. Some newspapers opt for an 'investigative' approach to the news. The UK's *Guardian* seeks to have roving reporters with 'a very sharp eye for a story', specialists in their chosen areas. David Hencke, Westminster correspondent, for example, was expected, in the words of his former editor, to 'hang loose and speak to all those people you don't have time to speak to if you're following a lobby agenda' (personal interview, Preston, 2000). Investigative journalists seek to move away from the official source agenda and ruffle a few feathers.

Political Journalist as Critic

As Neveu puts it: 'The political journalist is both an insider, who knows the codes and secrets of the tribe, and a critic, whose point of honour is to decipher for the audience the secrets of their political competitor-colleagues'

(2003: 31). The journalist critic can be considered along a kind of continuum, which ranges from the political sketch writers – and their cousins in political humour shows – to the bitingly acerbic shock jocks who have no pity for their political victims.

Political sketch writers are a kind of subspecies of critic. They write or provide amusing yet tellingly acerbic vignettes of political performance and character. One of the most talented, Mathew Parris, who worked as *The Times'* sketch writer, described his task as being similar to that of a theatre critic. It is a type of political journalism which requires a particular kind of political humus. The British parliament's Prime Minister's Question Time provides a particularly rich soil for political sketch writers.

Political Journalist as Pundit and Commentator

Strictly speaking a pundit is an expert in an area of specialism. However, it has also come to mean a commentator and opinion leader who makes up for lack of expert knowledge with the pungency of his or her opinions. One of the earliest British exponents of this second type of punditry was the *Daily Mirror*'s William Connor (1909–1967), known as Cassandra. However, he was very much a lone voice. Up until the 1960s political columnists were relatively rare beasts on British newspapers (Young, 2003: xv) even though their presence – as successors to seventeenth-century essayists – can be traced to the nineteenth century (see Silvester, 1997). Political commentary abounded in leader columns, but most comment appeared without a writer's byline. In other parts of Europe, political commentary tended to be the pursuit of party politics by other means (Neveu, 2003). In the United States, political columnists have long enjoyed a position of esteem, advising politicians from a position of Olympian detachment. From the 1930s onwards, Walter Lippmann wrote his nationally syndicated column, 'Today and Tomorrow', the precursor to writers such as William Safire of the *New York Times* and Maureen Dowd of the *Washington Post*. In the United States, as McNair noted, columnists became 'significant social and political actors in their own right – journalists of particular influence, whose opinions mattered as much as their reporting skills' (2000: 63). They are journalists who have achieved an authoritative voice through long experience of politics and proven analytical acuity, often supplemented by claims to some kind of insider knowledge.

Since the 1960s Britain, too, saw a significant expansion of the punditocracy. By the 1990s Tunstall (1996) estimated that the high-priests of British political punditry between them published 300,000 words per week, the equivalent of three full-length books. Their subjects were policy and the great debates and questions of the time. These must-read commentators included the *Guardian*'s Hugo Young (1938–2003), whose criticism of Blair and the Iraq war prompted a four-page letter from the then prime minister defending his policy (Rusbridger in Young, 2004: xii). Young himself noted the huge expansion of the commentariat from the days of Cassandra to the over 200 newspaper columnists identified by a Blair staffer at the beginning of the twenty-first century (Young, 2004: xv). Their ranks have been swelled by commentators working on radio, television and, increasingly, the internet. Political journalists employed by the major television channels and radio stations often become an 'expert' resource for the anchorman/woman, asked to provide instant analysis of a political interview or campaign event moments after it has happened. 'What did you make of that?' the presenter will ask the journalist, who is expected to make sense of and contextualize what the public has just heard or seen.

This sense-making punditry is increasingly seen on the internet. Many mainstream news organizations have an internet presence in which their pundits harvest what they consider key comment on the web while maintaining an ongoing commentary themselves. *The Times'* 'Comment Central' is a good example, run by its Comment editor as 'Daniel Finkelstein's rolling guide to opinion on the web', it began on 4 September 2006. His 'Daily Fix' features commentators who have transcended their traditional media careers to become star internet pundits.

Journalistic punditry ranges from the fine-honed, informed judgments of journalists such as Peter Riddell of *The Times* to the savage style of commentators in the populist press. Punditry as polemic and partisan comment have become common in a number of countries where the radio has become the medium of choice for a journalism of outrage and controversy. In Spain, for example, where measured independent punditry is relatively rare, during the Socialist president, José Luis Rodríguez Zapatero's first term of office (2004–08), radio commentators became the principal warriors in the country's political and cultural wars. The conservative radio station Cadena COPE became embroiled in controversy because of its attacks, led by star presenter, Federico Jiménez Losantos, on Catalonian nationalism, leading to the threat in 2005 that its licence to broadcast in Catalonia would be revoked. Intemperate language, exaggeration and partisanship characterize this kind of punditry. It is contrived to pursue a specific political agenda, confirm its audience's political opinions and win market share, serving both an ideological and market logic. The audience leader in US cable television news, Fox News, has found this to be a winning formula, although it protests otherwise. Accused of conservative bias (see Frankel, 2003; Noah, 2005), it is nevertheless careful to claim in its logo that it is 'Fair and Balanced' and that it 'Puts the News in Context'. However, the Project for Excellence in Journalism found that: 'Cable audiences are more likely than those for other media to hear reporters' opinions about the news' and that Fox News 'has abandoned the more disinterested neutral voice of traditional broadcasting.

It is a clearly American channel, with the US government frequently referred to in the first person plural — "we" and "us."' (2006).

The expansion of polemical punditry has been particularly notable in the United States. The contentious years of the Bush presidencies (2000–04 and 2004–08) saw a polarization and sharpening of political commentary as exemplified by Ann Coulter, Ms Right as *Time* magazine described her in its 2005 profile which stated:

> Coulter epitomizes the way politics is now discussed on the airwaves, where opinions must come violently fast and cause as much friction as possible [...] It is almost impossible to watch her and not be sluiced into rage or elation, depending on your views. As a congressional staff member 10 years ago, Coulter used to help write the nation's laws. Now she is far more powerful: she helps set the nation's tone.

High-decibel punditry may be in part a consequence of the number of voices struggling to make themselves heard in the contemporary media cacophony. The concern must be that it makes it increasingly difficult to have an intelligent conversation about the pressing issues of the time. Hugo Young, the antithesis of the Coulter style, explained that he saw his principal task as being that of 'enlightening readers who may want to understand what is going on. I don't see myself as a player, more as a watcher, a finder-out, a discloser, an alerter, a reporter' (2004: xviii).

Political Journalist as Interrogator

The political interview is one of the main tools in the journalist's kit-bag in his or her role as 'finder-out'. It was not always so. One of the British inventors of the probing political interview, Robin Day, described how until the 1950s, in the United Kingdom interviews were conducted on the politician's rather than the journalist's terms. For broadcast interviews, questions had to be submitted in advance and they were conducted in the deferential tones that are more usually adopted by journalists living under authoritarian regimes. By the later 1950s, however, the principle was established that 'broadcasters had a right and a duty to put awkward questions on behalf of the public' and in doing so, the interview became 'an important source of news and a part of the political process' (Day, 1989: 105).

This journalistic self-image as tough tribune of the people or, in more traditional terms, the public's watch-dog, reflects a view of journalism's purpose in line with survey findings both of UK and US journalists' views of news media roles (see Weaver, 1998; and Table 13.2). 'Investigating claims and statements made by the government' is the role accorded the highest percentage of

Table 13.2 Journalists' views on news roles

Question: 'The list below describes some of the things that the news media do or try to do. How important do you think each of these things is?'
Percentage saying 'Extremely important'.

	US journalists		British journalists
	1992 **n = 1,156**	**2002** **n = 1,149**	**1994-1995** **n = 726**
A: Get information to the public quickly	69	59	88
B: Provide analysis and interpretation of complex problems	48	51	83
C: Provide entertainment and relaxation	14	11	47
D: Investigate claims and statements made by the government	67	71	88
E: Stay away from stories where factual content cannot be verified	49	52	30
F: Concentrate on news which is of interest to the widest possible audience	20	15	45
G: Discuss national policy while it is being developed	39	40	64
H: Develop intellectual and cultural interests of the public	18	17	30
I: Be an adversary to public officials by being constantly sceptical of their actions	21	20	51
J: Be an adversary of businesses by being constantly sceptical of their actions	14	18	45
K: To set the political agenda	5	3	13
L: Influence public opinion (see note below)	–	–	–
M: Give ordinary people a chance to express their views on public affairs	48	39	56

Note: A question on this news role [L] was not included in the surveys of journalists.
Sources: Delano and Henningham (1995), Weaver and Wilhoit (1996), Weaver et al. (2007).

those saying it is an extremely important, a role exemplified by programmes such as CNN's *Crossfire*. It is a kind of political journalism which embodies the premise that journalists speak for the people, bestowing a vicarious legitimacy on their task of scrutinizing the activities of public officials.

However, this seemingly straightforward account of what certain kinds of political journalists do – while representing an accurate self-image – tells only a small part of the increasingly complex story of twenty-first-century political news. In this final section, I will examine some of the interacting trends and forces which are moulding the contemporary political news environment.

Changing News Environment

Media researchers, educationalists and journalists all agree that the practice of journalism is facing qualitatively new challenges even if they don't quite agree about their precise nature (see, for example, Butterworth, 2006; Dahlgren and Gurevitch, 2005: 380-83; Lemann, 2006). Broadly speaking, these challenges flow from developments which are changing the context of political news. The proliferation of media outlets and the introduction of user-friendly technology are two drivers of change. Political news is no longer confined to items on the nightly bulletins or reports in the politics sections of the world's major newspapers. Political correspondents are no longer the only mediators of politics and politics itself appears to have widened its range of reference.

Industrialized democracies face their own particular challenges. Media organizations compete to shore up an increasingly fragmented audience share, whose younger members are uninterested in traditionally presented political news (see BBC, 2002). Nevertheless, intense competitive pressures and a crowded news market on a global scale are contributing to the creation of an environment where media executives seek formats to shore up market share. Entertainment values – personalization, controversy and celebritization – frequently trump informational ones. As traditional venues for political news lose audience, talk shows, radio phone-ins, comedy programmes, such as Jon Stewart's *the News Show*, become the sites from which people pick up their news about politics. In this concluding section, I will examine two features of the changing news environment: first, the development of what I shall call 'performance journalism' and, in second place, debates about the status of journalism in a world of blogs and user-generated content (UGC).

Performance Journalism

Across media systems, even those which espouse public service values, politics 'must fight for its place in reporting and scheduling more often on the basis of its news value or likely audience appeal' than because of the intrinsic value once accorded to its coverage by 'sacerdotal' understandings of the journalist's role (Blumler and Gurevitch, 2005: 109). Reflecting on contemporary US political reporting, one American academic W. Bennett concluded: 'even though reporters may continue to rely on officials to identify what matters, they are decidedly less deferential in representing official views, often introducing more negativity and journalist-driven commentary into the news mix, while playing up scandal and celebrity angles over political analysis of power and policy' (Bennett, 2004: 285).

As well as resulting in performance politics, these tendencies have also led to what could be called performance journalism, defined by three key characteristics. First, it privileges the protagonism of the professional mediator, who may no longer proceed from the world of political traditional journalism, but is just as likely to be a comedian or talk show host. *The Tonight Show* host, Jay Leno, and the queen of talk shows, Ophrah Winfrey, are unequivocal media stars and significant mediators of political news. Their position lies at the antipodal opposite to the journalists without bylines of *The Economist* and formerly of newspapers such as *The Times*. Entertainment values weigh more heavily so that, for example, the personality and appearance of the journalist matter: even staid political correspondents are coached on body language and news anchors are hired for their looks as well as their expertise.[6] A Catalan academic wrote of the emergence of the 'star-journalist' being a specifically Spanish phenomenon (Gubern, 2007). It is, however, a development transcending national barriers, owing much to broader structural imperatives.

Second, performance journalism courts and seeks out controversy. The negativity and scandal-driven narratives of political news became particularly striking in the 1990s (see Canel and Sanders, 2006; Thompson, 2000; Tumber and Waisbord, 2004). This feature remains characteristic of mainstream political reporting and has, if anything, intensified. Although cultural distinctions apply (see Sanders, 2004), political news is increasingly irreverent and covers any and all aspects of a politician's life including his/her eating and sexual habits, holiday choices and clothes and hair-style, all considered fair game for comment and exposure (see Schudson, 2005: 191; Stanyer and Wring, 2004).

Opinion-driven political news is a third characteristic of performance journalism. Reporting of substantive political issues still exists, but is very often laced with comment and interpretation. When the BBC's radio journalist John Humphries interviewed the future leader of the UK's Labour Party, Gordon Brown, he repeatedly asked him whether he thought the British people liked him. The interview was duly dissected by political editor Nick Robinson, in a display of psychoanalysis as political news (22 March 2007, BBC).

Performance journalism is a far cry from the authoritative, sober reporting of a *New York Times* or of the major international news agencies. Cultural, social and political factors still matter (see Schudson, 2005; Zelizer, 2005). However, as noted earlier, the proliferation of media outlets, the development of access friendly technology together with the permeation of politics into every nook and cranny of personal life, have changed the context of political news. They have also provided the conditions for developments I will consider in the final section of this chapter.

Political News Without Journalists?

After the 7 July 2005 London bombings, the BBC was flooded with photographs submitted by its audience. The experience led to the permanent establishment of a three-person pilot unit established earlier that year to make use of what has become known as user-generated content (USG), media content largely produced by those who primarily consume it. The social networking sites YouTube and Facebook took off after 2005 and 2004 respectively. These and other developments led *Time* magazine to designate 'You' as the 2007 person of the year. The USG world has developed apace with that of the blogosphere, the realm of bloggers who took advantage of the introduction of software in 1999 to produce their amalgam of internet diary and comment board. USG and blogging blur the boundaries of journalism's traditional interpretative authority; views about their implications for its future can be summarized in simple terms into three camps: blog triumphalism; media mainstreamism and professional-amateur (pro-am) realism.

Blog triumphalism heralds the advent of the army of bloggers as the beginning of the end for the mainstream media. According to the blog monitoring site technorati.com, there were over 27 million blogs by the summer of 2006, from 15,000 blogs in 2002, and their number was doubling every five months. This growth contrasts with declining audiences for newspapers and network news in the Anglo-American audiences. In 2004, five of eight US media markets experienced audience losses; online, ethnic and alternative media were the only ones to pick up audience (see Project for Excellence in Journalism, 2006). For radio show host and conservative blogger, Hugh Hewitt:

> There is too much expertise, all of it almost instantly available now, for the traditional idea of journalism to last much longer. In the past, almost every bit of information was difficult and expensive to acquire and was therefore mediated by journalists whom readers and viewers were usually in no position to second-guess. Authority has drained from journalism for a reason. Too many of its practitioners have been easily exposed as poseurs. (2006)

Hewitt's critique is an ideological one, directed at journalists' self-definition of themselves as an occupational group seeking to be objective in their pursuit of the news in the interest of the common good. According to Hewitt, this was always a chimera, especially given what he considers to be the liberal bias of the American press. For blog triumphalists, the blogging explosion simply contributes to the decline of the mainstream's press authority, ever less trusted by the public (see Project for Excellence in Journalism, 2007) and shaken by ethical scandals such as plagiarism at *The New York Times* in 2003 and CBS's lack of rigour in reporting a negative story about President George W. Bush's military service in 2004.[7] The fact that the debunking of CBS's reporting came from the work of bloggers and that year for the first time ever they joined the ranks of the professional mediators by receiving official press accreditation for the US Democratic convention, prompted *The New York Times* to declare 2004 the year of the blog.

Media mainstreamism. Journalist and Dean of the Columbia Journalism School, Nicholas Lemann, represents what could be termed media mainstreamism. He takes a more sceptical view of blogging's potential and what, more generally, is described as citizen journalism, arguing for the continued relevance of mainstream journalism. In an article entitled 'Amateur Hour: Journalism without journalists', Lemann suggests that far from representing a radical change, blogging is a throwback to the late seventeenth-century tradition of opinion-driven Stuart England pamphleteers such as Daniel Defoe and Joseph Addison. In his words: 'The more ambitious blogs, taken together, function as a form of fast-moving, densely cross-referential pamphleteering – an open forum for every conceivable opinion that can't make its way into the big media' (7 August 2006). In Lemann's view, this activity in no way substitutes that of the reporter, 'a distinct occupational category'. Its distinction – a set of practices and principles oriented to reporting affairs and events without fear or favour – represents the real break with tradition and, states Lemann, cannot simply be replaced by the work of amateurs on the internet, where 'everyone is a millenarian'.

A more nuanced version of this view, was expressed by the *Time* magazine editor in their special issue on Web 2.0, the second generation of the internet where USG and social networking sites have taken off:

> Journalists once had the exclusive province of taking people to places they'd never been. But now a mother in Baghdad with a videophone can let you see a roadside bombing or a patron in a nightclub can show you a racist rant by a famous comedian. These blogs and videos bring events to the rest of us in ways that are often more immediate and authentic than traditional media. These new techniques, I believe, will only enhance what we do as journalists and challenge us to do it in even more innovative ways'. (Stengel, 25 December 2006 – January 2007).

Pro-am realism. Stengel argues that the new techniques should be harnessed by the professional mediators to buttress mainstream media's traditional interpretative power. This, however, perhaps underestimates some of the real power shifts which are taking place in the world of journalism, where amateurs are learning to do the work of professionals, and professionals are having their work judged and improved by amateurs. Pro-am (professional-amateur) realism recognizes the changing context of political news in the twenty-first century, where newsmaking, production and distribution can be open to anyone, at any time and any place. Participatory or citizen journalism represents this trend. It is journalism carried out by citizens, by non-professional mediators. The media for this journalism can be classified into two types (see Lasica, 2003).

First, media which invite, use or consist of audience participation. This would include material such as user comments attached to news stories, personal blogs, photos or video footage captured from personal mobile cameras, or local news written by residents of a community. Sontag noted its development in the 2003 Iraq War: 'where once photographing war was the province of photojournalists, now the soldiers themselves are all photographers' (2004: 27). News stories can be initiated and driven by such material. In March 2007, the English cricketer, Andrew Flintoff, lost his captaincy when shots of a drunken late-night escapade were captured on mobile phones.

The participatory format has always been common for radio, but it has become increasingly used for political television programmes. The BBC's *Question Time* depends on the participation of a selected audience of ordinary people who put questions to politicians. It was used for the first time in Spain for political leaders in March 2007, in imitation of a French programme. 'Tengo una pregunta para usted, Señor Presidente-I have a question for you Mr President' was billed as being the first time on television that the public carried out the interview (27 March 2007, TVE advertisement, *El Mundo*, 69).[8]

Second, citizen journalism can be found on the independent news and information websites which collect together and rely on participatory input. This would include, for example, the *Chicago Tribune*'s consumer reviews and the *Drudge Report*. Media such as South Korea's OhmyNews.com represent a structural and philosophical commitment to participatory journalism. Founded in 2000 with the slogan 'Every Citizen is a Reporter', it relies principally on the work of citizen journalists who must sign up to an ethics code and submit their copy for editorial clearance and review.

Citizen journalism is audience driven. Like blogging, it largely retains its amateur ethos but there are signs that some of the disciplines of professional mediators are beginning to be adopted.

Clearly, the principal providers of political news – the established media organizations – are not about to disappear. They remain the main sources for most of us for our news about politics. However, as *The State of the News*

Media 2007 overview spells out, major challenges lie ahead including the question of what journalists should be doing in a changed news environment where the economic model for news seems ever shakier as advertising increasingly migrates to the internet; how media organizations should be using the internet and, most fundamentally of all, whether news – and in our case political news – will continue to constitute the public square and be delivered principally by media organizations.

14

Creating the Conditions for Conversation: Ethics and Political Communication

Introduction

Political communication necessarily involves thinking about normative issues in relation to practices, conduct and institutions. Considering the work of lobbyists, political reporters, election campaigners and politicians, or of media and political institutions immediately raises questions about power and justice, methods and ends, truth and deception, the kinds of issues explored by ethics and political philosophy. Normative concerns run through the work of a great number of political communication scholars. Critiques of political journalism (Barnett and Gaber, 2001), packaged politics (Franklin, 2004), irresponsible media (Lloyd, 2004), political economy (Herman and Chomsky, 1988; McChesney, 2008) all implicitly suggest that matters are not as they should be. Once we debate the question of how things should be, we enter the realm of ethics.

However, ethics itself has come under attack in the twentieth century. 'Ethics' and its cognate forms are frequently used terms of praise or denigration: we speak of an 'ethical foreign policy', 'unethical legal practices'; ethics is used in conjunction with areas of human activity as in 'medical ethics' or 'business ethics' or to describe the content of declarations of lists of guiding principles as in 'code of ethics'. Often it is held up as an ideal, almost impossible to obtain in the circumstances of the 'real' world. Certain contrapositions of 'ethics' provoke wry laughter: 'ethics' and 'journalism', 'ethics' and 'lawyers'. Or, as encapsulated in the title (although not the contents) of the only modern study of political communication and ethics, *Political Communication Ethics: An Oxymoron?* (Denton, 2000). Somehow the notion of 'ethics' is simultaneously held to be significant and valuable while at the same time only strictly relevant to those naïve or idealistic enough to believe humans capable of principled conduct. There is an underlying assumption that self-interest and ethical behaviour are fundamentally opposed and where they come into conflict the former will win the day. So why do we continue to talk about ethics when it appears to be an unrealizable goal or a muddle of conflicting unverifiable opinions? The answer may lie in a more precise understanding of what ethics means. This chapter will first *examine perspectives that seek to banish ethics from the world of politics* followed by *an exploration of how ethics might be reclaimed*. It will then examine how *the wells of political communication have been poisoned* by the fundamental doubt that rhetoric itself is unethical, making the argument that *political communication can be ethical* but only where certain kinds of strategies are pursued in the particular circumstances of our world a the beginning of the twenty-first century.

Banishing Ethics

Machiavelli and Ends as Criteria of the Good

Niccolò Machiavelli (1469–1527) is often taken to be the defender of amorality in politics. His thought is regarded as the acme of expediency and *realpolitik*, the political thinker whose most famous book, *The Prince*, is allegedly on the desk of every major politician. This reputation is not entirely undeserved, as the following advice to leaders who wish to maintain their position shows:

> He must be prepared to vary his conduct as the winds of fortune and changing circumstances constrain him and [...] not deviate from right conduct if possible, but be capable of entering upon the path of wrongdoing when this becomes necessary. (ch. XVIII, 62)

This apparently amoral approach to politics does, nevertheless, employ conceptions of the good. Even *The Prince*, his most extreme expression of 'power politics', recognizes the notion of 'good' ends. For Machiavelli, the highest good is maintenance of power and every action should serve this goal. Obedience to the moral laws should, for example, be sacrificed at the altar of power as it is this that is the higher good. In Machiavelli's view the appearance of moral goodness matters more than the reality:

> A ruler, then, need not actually possess all the above-mentioned qualities [those classified as good], but he must certainly seem to. Indeed, I shall be so bold as to say that having and always cultivating them is harmful, whereas seeming to have them is useful. (ch. XVIII, 62)

This, he believes, is an effective way to retain power because 'men are so naïve, and so much dominated by immediate needs, that a skilful deceiver always finds plenty of people who will let themselves be deceived'. His ethical thinking appears to be summed up by the principle of 'the end justifies the means'.

But what does this well-known expression mean? In one sense, it simply says that any action which is exclusively a means leading to a good end is justified: taking up jogging in order to become healthier would be one example. This suggests that how we define 'means' is crucial to our evaluation of the phrase. There may, for instance, be circumstances where the 'means' are in fact 'ends'. Take, for example, the dropping of the atomic bombs on Hiroshima and Nagasaki in 1945. The ends sought – the surrender of Japan and the end of the Second World War without further massive loss of American lives – were good. However, can we consider the 'means' purely as means in the way that something like jogging might be? The indiscriminate annihilation of hundreds of thousands of human lives constitutes by any measure an action bounded by an end. As an intentional voluntary human action it cannot but evince an ethical quality: in other words, it registers the presence of motives, actions and consequences that matter both for the agent and for those affected.

Returning to Machiavelli, rather than being an advocate of amorality – a position claiming that there are no human goods or value – Machiavelli's position is closer to utilitarianism, which champions a view of morality where only outcomes determine what is good. Means in themselves have no moral identity; they can be considered neither good nor bad because, for utilitarians, only the ends or consequences can be strictly defined as having value. Thus, 'the end justifies the means' cannot mean 'a good end justifies a bad means' for, whenever the end is good, according to utilitarian logic, so is the means. If I can preserve power through corruption and murder, then these means are good. As can be seen from the earlier example, however, this position ultimately corrupts the possibility of morality. It does not accept that means themselves can also be human actions and thus have a moral identity. So, for example, torturing a prisoner to death in order to obtain information to forestall a terrorist attack may be portrayed as a means of obtaining a good end; however, it is also an action of which one can ask whether it is good or not.

The Death of Humanity

The very notion of moral life refers to that area of conduct to which there is an alternative and in which behaviour could have been otherwise. Therefore, the ethical perspective implies a commitment to the view that human beings can be held responsible for their actions and are, thus, in some measure free. One prevalent understanding of the human being in contemporary Western society is particularly lethal to this. This view, popular in much post-modern thought, construes humans as society's constructs encapsulated in the philosopher, Richard Rorty's pronouncement that: 'Socialisation goes all the way down' (1989: 185). If it is true that what I am is a cultural artefact with a biological residue at its core, then human agency is squeezed out. It would no longer make sense to blame or praise human beings for actions that are the result of preordained scripts. Key, then, to the ethical perspective (and to our entire legal system) is the notion of the human being as a subject who acts and is not merely acted upon. This was something the philosopher, Hannah Arendt, concluded after observing the trials of Nazi war criminals:

> The trouble with the Nazi criminals was precisely that they renounced voluntarily all personal qualities, as if nobody were left to be either punished or forgiven. They protested time and time again that they had never done anything out of their own initiative, that they had no intentions whatsoever, good or bad, and that they only obeyed orders. (2003: 114)

Here all sense of the human person is extinguished and with it the possibility of being responsible for our actions.

Reclaiming Ethics

Arguing against the notion of human goods or values and even against the idea that we can have a stable view of what it is to be human, are effective ways to undermine the possibility of ethics. Before setting out arguments against this view, it is probably as well to clarify what I mean by 'ethics'. Its Greek roots – *ethikos* – link it to the study of character, and moral philosophers from Aristotle onwards have taken it to be the study of the grounds and principles for right and wrong human behaviour. Values, such as courage, self-control, generosity, are considered as notions of the good that function as criteria in making choices and judgements. Discussion and controversy arise in the clash of different values or principles. *Moralis* is the Latin translation of the Greek word and the term from which we derive the more restricted notions of morals and morality centred on the notion of obligation.[1] Borrowing from Rhonheimer's account of the 'moral perspective' (2000), I propose next to explore what I continue to call the ethical perspective by examining it briefly in relationship to human conduct, knowledge, freedom and responsibility, and context.

Ethics and Human Conduct

What does ethics bring to the discussion when we say that someone 'ought to' do something, or that certain behaviour is good or bad, correct or incorrect? If I want to pass my driving test, I *ought* to study the Highway Code. But this is different from what we might consider to be a *moral* obligation to study the Code if I wish to drive legally on the roads. In the latter case, *moral* refers to a specific quality of our voluntary actions which affects us and those around us. I can be a good or bad driver but when we mean this in an ethical sense, we refer to the *kinds* of actions we carry out, not to my level of driving skills. When we speak of unethical behaviour, we impute responsibility to someone for a certain kind of conduct. Taking to the roads without knowing how to drive correctly and killing a child in the process is more than incompetence. I have not only driven incorrectly, been a bad driver in that sense, but also been a bad driver in the sense that the decision and action of driving – to the extent that they were mine – were defective in those circumstances for me. In other words, the ethical quality of action refers both to the interrelationship and to the kinds of wants, intentions and choices of a human subject, and whether, in a certain sense, they get these 'right' in any given circumstances. In the case of the reckless driver, he thought it was good to drive – he wanted to show off to his friends – and made a practical decision to do so. The desire to win approval overrode concerns for others' safety; the action was out of kilter with the requirements of reality.

This example indicates that the primary, albeit by no means exclusive, focus of ethics is human conduct from a first person perspective (see Rhonheimer, 2000). Ethics is concerned with what I do and therefore to know what ethics means it helps, as Aristotle stated, to have experience of human life. Being ethical does not depend on knowledge of codes and moral treatises but involves the application of reason to the practical realities of life. Indeed, reading about ethics is as likely to make one ethical as reading a book about football will make someone a good footballer.

Regarding conduct as the chief focus of ethics does not imply an atomized, individualistic vision, as we shall see later. Nor does it suggest that questions about principles, codes, rights, evaluative terms and regulations are not part of the subject matter of ethics. All these areas are, of course, open to, and have been subject to, ethical inquiry. Ethics necessarily implies judgement and reasoning and hence is a theoretical but, most importantly, a practical enterprise.

Ethics and Knowledge

Questions of ethics arise in the course of human action and our reflection upon it. They presuppose that conduct – ours, of governments, parents or policemen – can be queried concerning its rightness or goodness for ourselves or our communities.

The fact that we can reflect upon human conduct and have intelligible discussions about its rightness or wrongness suggests a further characteristic of ethics, namely that it constitutes a certain kind of knowledge about the world. The claim that ethics is a domain where we can obtain knowledge, where what can be called truth and error exists (see Lovibond, 2002: 16) is fundamental to establishing whether it is possible to have a conversation about ethics at all. Ethical relativists[2] and nihilists would reply that it is not (see Sanders 2003). In their view, appeals to principles and establishment of common standards founder on the idea that all assumptions about value are either equally valid, meaningless or concerned with upholding vested interests.

There are, however, good reasons to suggest that there is more to ethics than these views would allow. When, for example we examine ethical language and discussion we find they have a curious feature: they appear to be about certain kinds of facts that have a singular force in our lives. The motivational aspect of ethical thought has been interpreted from various perspectives but one of particular interest to us here is the view that a certain act was performed because of the value the agent saw in it (see Lovibond, 2002: 5–7). It appears to be the case that if we consider something valuable, we are ready to consider that it is of constant and permanent value. In the ethical outlook, there is a commitment to the notion that it is possible to identify common and permanent values which arise out of our shared humanity (see Warnock, 2001:163). For these kinds of explanations to have purchase at all, the reasons put forward for the value of an act must be in some way accessible. What count as reasons for being compassionate, not using torture, keeping a promise are recognizable to others. The sociologist, Margaret Archer, puts this idea in a slightly different way:

> Humanity, as a natural kind, defies transmutation into another and different kind. It is this which sustains the thread of intelligibility between people of different times and place…It is this too which underpins our moral and political responsibilities to humankind despite the socio-cultural differences of groups. (2000: 17)

It is true that different people have different sensitivities and that values emerge through our involvement in specific communities. In this sense, then, we can say with Lovibond that: 'The ethical […] pertains to what people learn to value through immersion in a community acquainted with ideas of right, duty, justice, solidarity, and common social or cultural interests extending beyond the lifetime of the present generation' (2001: 33). Thus, if we think of knowledge as being about how things are in the world, then we can argue that ethics is about a certain kind of knowledge and therefore has an identifiable rational structure. We will sometimes disagree because, as thinkers like Raz have pointed out, the question of the universality of value is complex and one to which we may both answer affirmatively and negatively (2001: 2): values change over time, our ethical notions may be rationalizations of culturally inculcated views. This is all true. Yet it is possible to construct a space where reflective scrutiny of prevailing ethical values takes place and where revision can occur even from within one's own ethical outlook. Beliefs about values, no less than about facts, are true if there are good reasons to hold them to be true. Take the belief that democracy is a good thing. Many people hold this view because they have sound reasons for doing so. Just as we have mathematical knowledge, we also have axiological knowledge that in part arises from the facts of experience

Freedom and Responsibility

One of the paradoxes of the modern era is the great store set by the notion of individual freedom and the simultaneous denial by much contemporary thought that we are in fact free.[3] And yet, our common practical, daily experience is that of our ability to make choices about what we want and what we do. Our wanting and doing are made possible by our capacity to make judgements about reality, in which our reason and emotions come into play, and make decisions. Where our actions are the fruit of this dominion over will and reason, we can say they are free and therefore have a moral quality. The very young or those with certain types of psychological disorder, for example, who do not have this dominion over will or reason, cannot be said to be free in a way that allows their actions to be ethically significant. One of the horrors of torture is that it seeks to crush this most intimate freedom, the freedom that allows us to have a sense of self, the possession of our desires, thoughts and feelings.

If we understand the notion of 'freedom' correctly, it must imply the ability to *explain* one's conduct. Being free means taking charge of behaviour and giving reasons for actions. Therefore, the notion of freedom raises the issue of responsibility, attending to the consequences of our actions. If choices cannot be explained, if we cannot give reasons for what we do, we might be considered at the least intellectually deficient. In reality, we are always responsible for what we freely do and thus, strictly speaking, the idea that freedom exists without responsibility is false.

However, we have to accept that in a very real sense freedom does exist without responsibility. Politicians lie and journalists distort the truth. For practical purposes, they have freedom without responsibility. The complexity of social institutions and the ways they can powerfully structure agents' options, interests and desires mean that ethics cannot be considered solely from the personal or transactional perspective. I shall consider this issue next.

Ethics and Context

We cannot always act on the terms of our own choosing and the study of ethics recognizes the truth of the Greeks' view that 'to live the good life one must live in a great city' (cited by Solomon, 2003: 215). There are certain contexts in which the possibility of being or doing good is at the very least heavily circumscribed. Legal, institutional and economic contexts are key to the goals of fostering justice and human dignity. Having the means to ensure the right institutional conditions is as, if not more, important than agreeing about the right goals. Achieving an environment in which political bribery and corruption, for example, are eliminated is related not only to personal rectitude but also to the institutional means and design that are put in place. As Aristotle recognized, the reign of justice and peace among human beings is not natural. But this is not to say with Thomas Hobbes that *homo homini lupus* – man is a wolf for man – that justice and peace are unnatural and can only be imposed by despotic means. The human inclination to life in society can be explained by reasons of utility but it can also be argued that at the root of community and society is a primordial desire to unite with others in love and friendship.

In the classical, Aristotelian view, ethics is a sub-division of political philosophy. Ethics is about the good life for the citizen ,which is the *raison d' être* of the polis. For this reason, Aristotle greatly admired Sparta, since he considered that its institutional arrangements schooled its citizens in virtue. A rather different view, grounded in Machiavelli, suggests that: 'Ethics must take very seriously the idea [...] according to which many of the usual norms of individual ethics are valid only when those to whom they are addressed live in the framework of an order guaranteed by state power' (Hösle, 2004: 87). This, in my view, goes too far. State power certainly acts as a guarantor of ethical action and the latter's possibility is enhanced where the conditions of civic life and virtue are assured.

It may also be the case that institutional arrangements are a necessary but not sufficient condition for the possibility of certain kinds of ethical practice. However, it is hard to understand the assertion that the content of ethical norms is grounded in the conditions provided by state power.

Poisoning the Wells

'To poison the wells' was an expression coined by the great British Catholic theologian, John Henry Newman (1801–1890), to denote ways in which audiences can be pre-disposed against one side in an argument by hearing a damaging or negative accusation about them. Many politicians find themselves in this position today. One reasonably consistent and universal finding is that people across the world have a fairly low opinion of their political leaders and those who serve them. Working for the persuasion industries is not high on anyone's list of greatly esteemed jobs. Writing about Britain, journalist George Pitcher wrote: 'spin-culture has undermined the credibility of communications professionals. The truth is that they are not believed' (2002: 63). Doctors, chefs, footballers, all enjoy greater social prestige than politicians, lobbyists and government press officers. Distrust of politicians is linked to a fundamental suspicion about the very possibility of ethical political communication.[4]

Ethical political communication faces three kinds of challenges: the first refers to the basic issue of designing organizations and institutions so that they are able to provide adequate political communication for the purposes of citizenship; the second challenge involves that of ensuring that the pressures of media logic do not become the principal drivers of political communication; the third and most fundamental challenge is to justify the very basis of the rhetorical enterprise so seriously called into question by its misuse.

Attending to Justice

In his *Commentary on the Book of the Powerful*, the thirteenth-century philosopher and theologian, Thomas Aquinas states that: 'The corruption of justice has two causes: the false prudence of the wise man and the violence of the powerful.' Where governments do not act to protect the weak and media organizations do not recognize their social responsibilities, they do indeed corrupt justice.

Some media organizations, particularly those funded by the public purse, refer to their duties of 'social responsibility' or to 'public service' or the 'public interest'. Underlying this language is the notion of justice. Justice can be thought of as the virtue that seeks to establish the right ordering of our relationships to others. If we are just, we learn to relativize our own interests and desires so that where my actions affect others, we recognize that it is not enough to justify them on the basis that they satisfy my interests. It is unjust to kill my neighbour simply because he annoys me; denying people the essential goods for their well-being, let alone their existence, is unjust because they are deprived of the possibility of living full human lives.

The administration of justice is necessary in a world of scarce or unevenly distributed goods, of which news and information are one example, and most would accept that the state should have some role in ensuring that the weakest members of society can obtain both social and material goods. Regulation should be about promoting environments in which common or public goods are not the preserve of the few.

In this regard, the field of political communication presents a mixed picture. Institutional, cultural and regulatory environments vary considerably in relation to the various dimensions of political communication. For example, the regulatory environment in the United States ensures that, to a great extent, campaign success remains in thrall to big money whereas its lobbying industry is, compared to that in the European Union, rather more accountable. The analytical complexity of understanding the dynamics of political communication and the practical difficulties involved in getting institutional arrangements right can act as brakes to action. However, there are examples of legislative initiatives that attempt to 'attend to justice'. Mexico offers an interesting case in point. Concerned by the US-style costs and negativity of the country's 2006 election campaign, its congress decided to ban paid for broadcast political advertising in November 2007.[5] It will be interesting to see whether this development has an impact on the character and quality of campaign communication.

Understanding the impact of regulatory, institutional and cultural contexts, developing those that attend to justice is one of the major challenges facing researchers, politicians and citizens in the twenty-first century.

The Dramatization of Politics

The mediatization of political communication, the need to feed the monster of 24-hour news and comment and its appetite for spectacle where stories of conflict and personal and public failure dominate, has been one of the most widely discussed and criticized developments in contemporary democracies (see Lloyd, 2004). It is true that ordinary acts of kindness, straightforward goodness and the daily plod of policy work do not translate well into dramatic spectacle. This has always been the case. As we have seen in previous chapters, however, there appears to be an accelerated dynamic at work, pushing some media to ratchet up the thrill quotient and some political communicators to focus principally on convincing story lines. As a *Washington Post* journalist put it about the Clinton second-term presidency:

> The mundane reality of White House life was that the top players spent perhaps half their time either talking to the press, plotting press strategy, or reviewing how their latest efforts had played in the press. They did not let Clinton have the briefest exposure to journalists without rehearsing what he would say to this or that question, lest he serve up an unscripted sound bite that would mar the day's story line. The modern presidency was, above all, a media presidency. (Kurtz, 1998: xxiv)

Providing an attractive script becomes a major aim of political communicators, something that professional mediators simultaneously indulge and seek to unmask. Political reporters and commentators engage in a game of knowingness – they reveal the scaffolding behind the stage – and complicity – their theatricality feeds the dramatic production. In the meantime, the public searches in vain for honest brokers. Again, commentating on the Clinton presidency, Kurtz described his fellow journalists as being almost exclusively interested in 'conflict, in drama, in behind-the-scenes maneuvering, in pulling back the curtain and exposing the Oz-like manipulation of the Clinton crowd' (1998: xix).

Mazzolini and Schulz suggest that: '"Media politics" does not mean "politics by the media"' (1999: 259–60). This may be so. In the end, political leaders still make the decisions to go to war, to raise taxes, to decide spending priorities in ways and for reasons not wholly determined by the media. Politics is indeed always mediated but – and this is the charge about late twentieth- and early twenty-first-century politics – its mediatization is a compelling reality in certain kinds of constitutional democracies. This development requires agreement on fundamentals, as argued by Lloyd (2004), if political communication is not to dissolve wholly into soap opera, scandal-ridden, control freakery politics. Again, it requires close examination of institutional and agent level solutions.

In Defence of Rhetoric

A *Guardian* editorial, referring to Blair's reaction to an opposition statement on immigration, declared 'how typically New Labour – opportunistic, strong on rhetoric and totally lacking in substance' (7 February, 2005). The comment echoes a centuries' old view regarding the essentially disreputable nature of persuasive communication. As we saw in Chapter 2, the practices of the Sophists made Plato suspicious of the whole rhetorical enterprise in much the same way as journalists and citizens became suspicious of 'spin' at the end of the twentieth century.

The Oxford English Dictionary definition of a spin-doctor, as 'a spokesperson for a political party or politician employed to give a favourable interpretation of events to the media', suggests the existence of an inherently tendentious relationship to the truth as claimed by critics. By the beginning of the twenty-first century, 'spin' had become a totemic word, symbolizing what was wrong with contemporary politics. As one journalist put it: 'spin means a lack of substance, interpretation parading as fact, image creation at the expense of tangible evidence. The unfortunate implication is that there is little of value or substance in our institutions' (Pitcher, 2002:7).

The charges against rhetoric understood as spin can be summarized as follows:

- It is essentially manipulative in its methods, using emotion and specious arguments to gain the assent of its audience.
- It has replaced dialectic in political discourse; appearance is presented as reality and sound bites replace substance in politics.

- It is used to disguise the real purposes of the person who employs it, generally to pursue their interests not those of their audience.

It is certainly true that persuasive communication always runs the risk of falling into manipulation. However, the art and science of rhetoric employed in leading someone to accept a statement or fact as true or convincing can hardly be considered in itself unethical. It is what teachers and parents do every day.

As we saw in Chapter 2, communication has a semantic dimension, understood as the meaning of signs and their relationship to reality; it has a syntactical dimension where language is considered as a structured system of signs. It also has a pragmatic dimension that is related to understanding how to communicate effectively. This is the domain of rhetoric or persuasive communication.

Rhetoric is necessary because communication is not easy. We inhabit a complex and richly textured world that we do not always find easy to understand. Our communicational repertoire and style are shaped by a multiplicity of factors and, in our attempts to understand and be understood, we learn to use and develop them. Successful communication, then, entails not only knowing what to say but also how to say it. Manipulative methods, unworthy goals and intentions can always be found in persuasive communication, but this does not transform it into an intrinsically unethical practice.

Talk matters in politics. Politics seeks constitutional and institutional arrangements that can ensure the peaceful co-dwelling of a plurality of free people with a multiplicity of interests and distinct goods. Words are politicians' ordinary currency. Like money they can be devalued or achieve an inflated value. But words are what we have as agents in the public realm. This was noted by an English academic writing in the *Guardian* about politicians' use of rhetoric in the run up to the Iraq invasion:

> When, in recent years, has speaking in public mattered so much? Rhetoric – the art of using language so as to persuade or influence others – is a kind of action. How do you prepare a country for war? With words. It is difficult to think of a geopolitical 'crisis' where the crisis has depended more on talk. There has been no recent invasion or outrage to make military action seem unavoidable. Nothing has 'happened'. Words alone must create the necessity for 'doing something'. (Mullan, 11 September 2002)

Rhetoric's power and the potential for its abuse suggests that we should think carefully about ways to promote conditions, practices and institutions that aspire to the creation of a conversational culture; a culture that accepts rhetoric but one too where we understand and differentiate rhetoric's rightful place in politics. This will be the subject of my final reflections on communicating politics in the twenty-first century.

Creating the Conditions for Conversation

The classical Greek view of politics places communication at its core:

> This is how we know that man is a political animal [...] man alone possesses the power of speech [...] the power of speech is intended to point out the useful and the harmful, or the just and unjust. For it is a property of man that he alone, among all the animals, has a sense of good and evil, the just and unjust. Having these things in common [community, *koinonia*] is what constitutes the family and the state. (I Politics, 1253, a7–q8)

Communication is in part how community is established and, for communication to occur, there must, in general terms, be a presumption of the trustworthiness of those with whom we communicate. Trust-engendering communication and the establishment of community have an intrinsic connection. The analysis and practice of political communication cannot but involve ethical questions about the relationship between personal agency and institutions in achieving communication about politics directed towards social and personal goods such as justice and truthfulness.

This fact can help us think about the values we might want to foster in our communicational relationships and institutions in certain types of politically organized society. There is an undoubted tension between the universal applicability of these values and the particular historical and cultural trajectory of each political community.

The democratic constitutional state found in the western tradition has a long complex history and expresses a rich ethos (see Bobbitt, 2003). Its general early twenty-first century form is that of a democracy limited in relation to rights under the rule of law that upholds shared understandings of the common good. This is not a culturally neutral product and, I would argue, its maintenance and nurture require a strong commitment to certain principles. However, it is also true that the nature of politics is about finding, in conditions of conflict and disagreement, the basis for a degree of consensus.[6] What holds in the political realm, apart from the coercive force dischargeable by state power, is attention to the conditions of what could be called *do-ability*. Politics is about this: recognizing that in all likelihood there is not full agreement on what constitute the highest values to be pursued. In these circumstances, the kind of approach advanced by philosopher John Rawls (1921–2002) may be one to be recommended. The Rawlsian commitment to the idea of 'public reason' that has at its kernel an *agreement* about what might be shared political common goods, implying too an agreement to disagree about other goods that are not politically relevant, that are not, in other words, goods that we believe the coercive power of the state should impose.

Working out comprehensive answers to these questions for political communication is beyond the scope of this book. However, in conclusion, I offer some thoughts on communicating politics in the new millennium in ways that allow political communication to flourish. They relate to what might be involved in creating conditions for a conversation about politics.

Contemporary Political Communication and the Conversational Mode

It might seem surprising to consider political communication in the context of conversation. Clearly political communication in all its varieties is of wider range. It involves argument, debate, speech-making, news, comment, infotainment even; it appeals to logic and emotion. However, I would like to suggest that the conversational mode is the one that most closely approximates to what twenty-first-century conditions permit and require if political communication is to flourish.

Conversation is characterized among other things by:

- **The principle of cooperation**. Good conversation is about engaging listeners not simply addressing them or directing messages to them in megaphone fashion. A good conversationalist does not use language in a purely instrumental way to achieve her immediate goals. She introduces her counterparts into her world of meaning.
- **The distribution of speakers' rights**. No one is excluded from the conversation nor does any one speaker dominate. All are given their chance to contribute even if they do not wish to take it.
- **Mutual respect among speakers**. Respect, courtesy even, is the climate of those who converse. Neither cynics nor fanatics engage in conversational intercourse: the first because they believe there is no truth, and the second because they believe they have a monopoly of truth.
- **Spontaneity and informality**. Conversations have rules, but they are governed by a lightness of touch and have an open and even playful character.

These characteristics are precisely those that many of the new modes of communication permit and require: an examination of internet blogs, discussion groups, call-in programmes show that we are becoming increasingly accustomed to truly interactional communication. Even if old-style fine rhetoric still has its place – witness some of Barack Obama's inspirational speech-making in the 2008 US presidential primaries – the switch to a more conversational mode has major implications for political communication of all kinds.

Credibility, Trustworthiness and Truthfulness

Trustworthy communication is key for achieving conditions in which conversation about politics is possible. Communication that inspires trust does so on various grounds including a presumption that it is not engaged in deception, but in trying to know what is the case, in trying to be truthful.

Take truthfulness. The condition *sine qua non* for all communication is a commitment to truthfulness. If lying – communicational deception – were generalized, social life would become all but impossible. Truthfulness has been defined as 'that type of justice which constitutes the communicational basis of human co-dwelling' (Rhonheimer, 2000: 361). A lie is a deliberately false statement which, where a communicational context exists, undermines community and withdraws recognition of the person deceived as our equal. The notion of 'communicational context' is important for assessing whether the conditions for lying exist. In a game of bluff, for example, the rules permit deception, and to deceive in those circumstances would not constitute an injustice and, thus, the deceptions would not be lies. Or, again, in a situation where someone threatens to murder us to obtain certain information, we can hardly be said to be unjust in deceiving the potential murderer. War too is an exceptional situation where there has been a breakdown of the communicational context of the human community. But even here there are certain acts directed to re-establish that community in which truthfulness should be observed. The First World War Christmas truce celebrated by German, French, British and Belgian soldiers is an example of one of these.

A commitment to truthfulness should not be confused, however, with legitimate practices in certain circumstances that involve reserving aspects of the truth. For example, providing details of military operations would be truthful, but utterly irresponsible. Presenting an argument or ourselves – as we do when we apply for a job – in the best light is also perfectly licit.

In communicating politics, however, the truthfulness of the communicator or the communication may not be sufficient to engender trust. Trust, the reliance that we deposit in another person's or institution's capacity and/or disposition for carrying out or evincing certain actions and aptitudes, can be engendered by specific kinds of knowledge and experience of the source. They include practices that exhibit:

- **Transparency**. Inviting scrutiny about one's past or being open about one's present and future actions and goals builds institutional and personal credibility and authority.

- **Accessibility**. We live in information-rich times. Controlling access to information is still possible, as a number of governments have shown, but ultimately it little serves the purposes of establishing authoritative and high quality communication. In the words of a British journalist: 'The goal should be to invest systematically in creating a context for informed and intelligent debate by making relevant information as accessible as possible, rather than using the control of access to information as the basis of authority' (Pitcher, 2002: 67).

- **Accountability**. In the First Report of the Committee on Standards in Public Life established by John Major's government to remove sleaze, seven principles were set down for those who serve the public. They included the principle of accountability according to which those in public life are accountable for their decisions and actions to the public, to whom they should submit themselves for appropriate scrutiny. Mechanisms to ensure that all those engaged in communication must respond, account for, what they communicate are a powerful means to build trust.

Broadly speaking, these three principles can provide the necessary framework in an information-rich world for not only credible but also trustworthy and truthful communication.

The Conversationalists

The terms of the conversation must be set by the institutional and organizational arrangements in place. But whether a conversation can occur at all depends on the presence of conversationalists. These include the politicians and journalists, but, most importantly, you and me. Without our presence and without our commitment to the fundamental conditions of the conversation – mutual respect, speakers' rights, trust-building practices – it will not happen. This, I believe, is the greatest challenge facing political communication practitioners and scholars: to foster and to understand the existence of discriminating conversation in all its modalities. Not everyone has to be a campaigner, a political activist, a blogger or even, in most democracies, a voter. However, to acquire and to exercise powers of discrimination and judgement is the very least we can aspire to as citizens.

In her analysis of the failure of political society in 1930s Germany, Arendt stated: 'without taking into account the almost universal breakdown, not of personal responsibility, but of personal *judgement* in the early stages of the Nazi regime, it is almost impossible to understand what actually happened' (2003: 24). Unreason, fear and ignorance become levers for hatred and violence when manipulated by the unscrupulous and the powerful. Kenya and

Pakistan in 2007 provided tragic examples of the failure of words: the words of Benazir Bhutto were not enough to quell the rising tide of fanaticism; together with other factors, the words of Kenyan leaders Mwai Kibaki and Raila Odila were sufficient to awaken the fear of the tribal other.

Educating us all as to the power of rhetoric in all its forms, to the form and content of rigorous argument, to the necessity and workings of political communication and to the qualities of good conversation are urgent tasks for this century.

Notes

Part One

Chapter 2

1   Each of these perspectives is not a watertight compartment: theories and models from one approach can elide into another and significant thinkers have been influential in more than one approach. This is particularly the case for the critical and hermeneutical perspectives. In both the analysis of culture is key. I should add too that my analysis is clearly not exhaustive and anyone interested in exploring theoretical perspectives in more detail should look at some of the excellent guides around such as D. McQuail's (2005) *McQuail's Mass Communication Theory*. London: Sage.
2   A third person perspective aspires to scientific objectivity so that any findings I might make would be entirely replicable by another observer. The first person perspective, however, starts from the premise that the reality we can know can only start from the meditating subject.
3   I use the 'conversation' metaphor in the final chapter, but this does not imply that I underestimate the force of structural factors as I explain there.

Chapter 3

1   It should be noted that Plato himself adopted a more favourable view of rhetoric in his later dialogue, *Phaedrus*, where he sketches out the possibility of an ideal philosophical rhetoric. The speaker is virtuous, knows the subject and his/her audience and moves them to know and experience the truth.
2   In 2003 there was a serious outbreak of the SARS influenza virus in South-East Asia. The Chinese Propaganda Department's attempts to control reporting of the outbreak because of the potential for widespread social and economic panic became a catalyst for more general concerns about information control in China. The Propaganda Department's efforts extended beyond censorship. Journalists at the progressive Chinese daily, *Southern Metropolis News*, published stories without clearance from their local propaganda department. Several of its editors were subsequently convicted on charges ranging from corruption to embezzlement.
3   The Irish-American journalist, Finley Peter Dunne (1867–1936), coined this phrase but in the context of criticism of press power.

Chapter 4

1   The quotation in full is: 'All the world's a stage, and all the men and women merely players' (William Shakespeare, *As You Like It*, Act II, scene 7).
2   Burke's most significant works include *A Grammar of Motives* (1969) and *The Philosophy of Literary Form* (1973).

3   See, for example, Spanish President Zapatero's statement that his party represented 'progress, future and peaceful coexistence' against the 'apocalyptics who are always mistaken announcing misfortunes', *ABC*, 3 January 2008; and *El País*, 31 January 2008. It should also be said that certain statements and actions of the Spanish bishops lent themselves to unsympathetic interpretation.
4   Rumours about Barack Obama's supposed Muslim faith began appearing on the internet in 2007. The reality is that his middle name is Hussein and his Kenyan father was from a Muslim background as was his Indonesian stepfather. Obama himself is a practising Christian.
5   René Girard's most influential work is found in *La Violence et le Sacré* (1972) [*Violence and the Sacred*]; *Des choses cachées depuis la fondation du monde* (1978) [*Things Hidden since the Foundation of the World*]; *Je vois Satan tomber comme l'éclair* (1999) [*I See Satan Fall Like Lightning*].
6   Clinton polled 39.1 per cent against Obama's 36.4 per cent in contradiction to polling predictions. See Mark Blumenthal's article (9 January 2008) 'New Hampshire: So What Happened?' for an analysis as to why the pollsters got the results so wrong: http://www.pollster.com/blogs/new_hampshire_so_what_happened.php (accessed 10 January 2008).

Chapter 5

1   These quotations and others from Bernays are taken from interviews with him towards the end of his life, shown in the BBC series *The Century of the Self*, aired on British television in 2002. The quotation from Dick Morris later in the chapter is from the same programme.
2   The *Journal of Political Marketing* was established in 2002 and the *Journal of Public Affairs* in 2001.
3   This intelligence was gathered for Clinton by the firm of Mark Penn and Doug Schoen. Known in 2007 as Penn, Schoen and Berland Associates, the company describes itself on its website as having 'nearly 30 years of experience in leveraging consumer opinion to provide clients with a competitive advantage'. It has worked on campaigns across the world, including Tony Blair's 2005 campaign and the Serbian opposition campaign in 2000. The firm also worked for Republican Michael Bloomberg in his mayoral campaign for New York City. Mark Penn was engaged in 2007 by the Hillary Clinton 2008 campaign team as its chief strategist.

Part Two

Chapter 6

1   The remark was made by Labour MP, Gerald Kaufman, and cited by his colleague, Denis Healy, in his memoirs *The Time of My Life* (1989).
2   As well as the academic discussions of the subject, a number of journalists and communication specialists have written articles, books (MacIntyre, 2000; Rawnsley, 2001; Oborne, 2005); diaries (Campbell and Stott, 2007); and even a novel (Price, 2005) about the communication controversies and personalities of the Blair years.
3   See http://www.the-hutton-inquiry.org.uk/content/transcripts/hearing-trans15.htm where an account of a typical day in the life of the Prime Minister's Spokesman can also be found.
4   'The Mountfield Report' noted that 'insufficient emphasis is placed by civil servants involved in policy development on the communication strategy that every important initiative or decision will require. Some observers have noted something approaching disdain for media and communications matters' (1997: 25).

5   This is not to say that communication was never considered important by pre-Blair governments. Harold Wilson understood its importance as did Margaret Thatcher. However, within the mechanisms of government itself – as the Phillis Review found – communicators were isolated and without the kind of status enjoyed by civil servants involved in policy work (see Phillis, 2004).

6   The Mountfield review was undertaken by a team chaired by Robin Mountfield, the Permanent Secretary of the Office of Public Service, and included Alastair Campbell and Mike Granatt, the head of the GICS, after concern was expressed by the new Labour government about the quality of government communication. Its conclusions were published in November 1997. See Lord Mountfield (November 1997) *Report of the Working Group on the Government Information Service*, Cabinet Office, HMSO.

7   Neither event was directly attributable to Kelly's suicide. Campbell had been thinking about resignation for some time (see Campbell, 2007: 518, 725). The review arose out of a recommendation of the Public Administration Select Committee's (PASC) inquiry into the Jo Moore/Martin Sixsmith affair in its *Eighth Report, These Unfortunate Events: Lessons of the Recent Events at the Former DTLR* (HC 303).

8   This is as distinct from e-democracy, a term used to describe online interaction facilitating direct democracy, civic and third-sector action.

Chapter 7

1   A YouGov poll broadcast on Channel 4 News on 17 June 2007 reported that Cameron was regarded as 'lightweight' by a net rating of + 50 while Brown, Blair's successor, was seen as 'heavyweight' by + 44: http://www.channel4.com/news/articles/politics/domestic_politics/exclusive+tories+virtually+unchanged/564702 (18 June 2007).

2   The analogy with dog whistles arises from the fact that, like the high-pitched sound that can only be heard by dogs, communicators can insert trigger words or themes which will call in the core constituency, but will be unnoticed by the wider public. The term originated in Australian politics in the late 1990s and was used by John Howard's party to win the 2001 elections. The term entered British politics when Howard's campaign organizer, Lynton Crosby, joined Michael Howard's campaign to win the 2005 UK elections for the Conservative Party.

3   While the internet is difficult to control this does not stop a large number of governments from trying and succeeding. North Korea controls all computers and Chinese attempts to erect a Great Firewall of China are well documented (see Goldsmith and Wu, 2006). In May 2007 the *opennetwork* initiative research group reported that internet filtering by governments was increasing and the following month Amnesty International issued a warning about the erosion of freedom of speech online (see Tran, 6 June 2007).

4   It is also known as the EDSA Revolution. EDSA stands for *Epifanio de los Santos Avenue*, a main highway in Metro Manila and the main site of the demonstrations.

5   An advert published anonymously in an evening newspaper on the anniversary of the massacre in 2007 stated 'Paying tribute to the strong-(willed) mothers of June 4 victims'. The newspaper's editors were sacked.

6   Iraqi citizens have endured similar kinds of attacks since the invasion of their country in 2003 and many of them would seem to be most accurately described as acts of terrorism.

7   This phrase is associated with Margaret Thatcher, who said in a speech to the American Bar Association in July 1985: 'Democratic nations must try to find ways to starve the terrorist and the hijacker of the oxygen of publicity on which they depend.' It was the argument she used to justify the 1988 Broadcasting Ban prohibiting the direct broadcasting of the representatives of certain Northern Ireland organizations or those seeking support for them after a number of controversial interviews and programmes made by UK broadcasters with representatives of banned Irish republican organizations. The ban made broadcasters more cautious but they quickly found ways round it – recording interviews with actors speaking the words – and it is questionable whether it was of any help in tackling the roots of the problems in Northern Ireland.

8 Some of this discussion is based on research conducted with Maria Jose Canel in papers presented in Lincoln (UK), Paris, New York and Pittsburgh.
9 However, those who formed part of the 2004 PSOE electoral team consider that the election was already moving their way even before the bombings. Conversation with Luis Arroyo, 9 February 2008.
10 The discovery of an ETA plot to bomb Madrid's other main railway station the previous Christmas Eve, as well as the arrest of two ETA members on 28 February 2004 transporting 500 kilogram's of explosives in a city south of Madrid, led most mainstream politicians to declare ETA responsible on the morning of the attacks.

Chapter 8

1 The campaign was explained by the then head of Westminster Strategy, Michael Burrell, in a seminar run by the author for MA political communication students at the University of Sheffield in November 2000.
2 In the late 1980s, the author was in charge of 'press and parliamentary' relations for a trade association. Administrative tasks such as media monitoring were contracted out as were specific campaigns on an ad hoc basis.
3 The lower figure is provided by a EU lobby network organization. See: http://www.eulobby.net/eng/Modul/Abstract/ReadAbstract.aspx?Mid=1457&ItemID=528. The second figure is given by Corporate Europe Observatory (www.corporateeurope.org) (see Barbara Gunnell (7 February 2005) 'In Brussels, the Lobbyocracy Rules'. *The New Statesman*.
4 Many PR and lobbying companies undertake unpaid – *de bono* – work for good causes.
5 The British equivalent, the Association of Professional Political Consultants set up in 1994, has 38 members which, according to its website, 'represent more than four-fifths of the political consultancy sector (measured by turnover)'. See: http://www.appc.org.uk/index.cfm/pcms/site.aboutus.home/ (accessed 12 July 2007).

Chapter 9

1 The sub-national – the local or regional context of political communication – is perhaps the most neglected area of study of all (see Franklin and Murphy (1991) in the British context).
2 These figures are all for 2007 and taken from company websites and the CIA World Factbook. The computer figure is taken from a *Times* report on 13 November 2007 (see: http://business.timesonline.co.uk/tol/business/industry_sectors/technology/article2863079.ece).
3 'Technological determinism', the view that social and economic developments are determined by technology, belongs to a nineteenth-century view of the world where 'progress' is considered the natural dynamic for human kind. Twenty-first-century developments such as global warming make this a difficult creed to uphold.
4 Statutory regulation is the chief form by which the structure and terms of the global conversation are controlled and this is still primarily nationally controlled. Some states devolve this power to quasi-independent regulators. A good example is OFCOM. Established in Britain in 2003, it describes itself as the 'independent regulator and competition authority' for the UK communications industry. Self-regulation, where practice is governed by voluntary codes and guidance, is typically carried out by market-based institutions such as Britain's Press Complaints Commission.
5 All figures are taken from company websites accessed in October 2007.
6 There is a voluminous literature in this area. See, for example, Thussu, D. (2000) *International Communication: Continuity and change*. London: Arnold. A UNESCO commission chaired by Sean MacBride produced a report entitled *Many Voices, One World* (1980) championing a new and more equitable world information order.

7 The European Peace of Westphalia in 1648 is generally regarded as the moment when sovereignty was accepted as the defining governing principle of statehood. The export of this system around the world helped form the basis for the development of diplomacy and of the international state system (see Bobbitt, 2003: ch. 7).

8 Herman and Chomsky's classic book offers a 'propaganda model' of the relationship between the media and political power, arguing that the facts of political economy, that corporate media are money-making enterprises dependent on political power for a favourable economic and regulatory environment, mean that the media tend to favour and serve the interests and world-view of dominant elites. Their views have proved influential turning up either implicitly in the work of Michael Moore or explicitly in a video released in 2007 by Osama bin Laden on the anniversary of the 9/11 attacks.

9 Pacifists argue that no war is just. There is, however, a just war tradition that establishes certain conditions for judging whether war is justified or not.

10 See Chapter 4 in Taylor, 1997, for a very helpful account of the notion and application of 'PSYOPS' in the latter part of the twentieth century. Usually associated with military operations, Taylor cites the following 1990 US army definition of psychological operations: 'Planned operations to convey selected information and indicators to foreign audiences to influence their emotions, motives, objective reasoning, and ultimately the behavior of foreign governments, organizations, groups and individuals. The purpose of psychological operations is to induce or reinforce foreign attitudes and behavior favourable to the originator's objectives' (1997: 150).

11 Slobodan Milosevic (1941–2006), the Serbian leader, may have deserved this epithet and some Serbs too. However, Croats and Bosnian Muslims also committed atrocities, as did Albanian Kosovars against Serbians, and these were marginalized in the Western telling of the story. See P. Goff (2000) (ed.), *The Kosovo News and Propaganda War*. IPI: Vienna.

12 There are no agreed figures on civilian casualties. NATO air-strikes killed between 1500 (NATO figures) and 5000 (Yugoslav government figures). Civilians killed by Kosovar and mainly Serbian ground-forces are estimated at between around 4000 (humans rights groups) and 10,000 (US State Department).

Part Three

Chapter 10

1 The phrase was cited in an interview with Douglas Keay, published in *Woman's Own*, 31 October 1987. A transcript, however, of Mrs Thatcher's actual words found on her Foundation's website shows that the phrase comes later than quoted in the interview and that her precise words were: 'There is no such thing as society. There is a living tapestry of men and women and people and the beauty of that tapestry and the quality of our lives will depend upon how much each of us is prepared to take responsibility for ourselves and each of us prepared to turn round and help by our own efforts those who are unfortunate.' Extract from transcript: http://www.margaretthatcher.org/speeches/displaydocument.asp?docid=106689 (accessed 3 April 2007).

2 Habermas himself acknowledged the influence of Arendt's thought on his work, especially her account of the character of action as being fundamentally uncoerced, public and communicational in nature. See his (1983) 'Hannah Arendt: On the Concept of Power, in *Philosophical-Political Profiles*. London: Heineman.

3 The anti-Iraq war rallies of 15 February 2003 drew millions of protestors across the world. The Rome rally of three million is listed in the 2004 Guinness Book of Records as the largest anti-war rally in history.

4 There is now a vast literature on this subject covering, for example, the potential of e-democracy, e-government and blogging to unharness the democratic energies of the people. See, for example, P. Ferdinand (2000) *The Internet, Democracy and Democratization*. London: Routledge; B. Axford and R.Huggins (2001) (eds) *New Media and*

Politics. London: Sage; D. Saco (2002) *Cybering Democracy*. Minnesota: University of Minnesota Press; A. Chadwick (2006) *Internet Politics: States, Citizens and New Communication Technologies*. Oxford: Oxford University Press.

Chapter 11

1 Some scholars (see, for example, Brady, Johnston and Sides, 2006: 1–4) take a parsimonious approach to the definition of 'political campaign', restricting it to refer to campaigns directed at winning elections. This has the virtue of simplifying the field of analysis.
2 The long-term effects were examined for the 12 months preceding the campaign which, the authors acknowledge, is a shorter period than is desirable to determine whether any differences found are the result of news use or of more persistent predispositions in those surveyed (see Norris et al., 1999: 13).
3 Campaigning is forbidden as is the publication of polls. In fact, candidates bypass the first by orchestrating campaign friendly photo ops showing them with family or relaxing. Controlling poll information has become almost impossible at a time when voters can access the information through overseas internet sites.
4 Hilary Clinton's campaign for the presidential nomination provoked great interest in the issue of voters' views on the possibility of a female president. While opinions polls consistently showed there would be no broad objection from the American public to a female president, further research by Streb and colleagues (2007) found a 'social desirability' effect. In other words, people responded favourably to the question of a female president because they wished to be 'politically correct' and observe prevailing social norms regarding gender equality. In fact, Streb and colleagues' research found that around 26 per cent of the public 'is angry and upset' at the idea of a female president, with no difference observed across demographic groups.
5 The internet was used mostly for information and persuasion purposes in the 1992 election. It began to be used for direct advertising by presidential candidates in the 1996 race (see Kaid, 2004b: 180–1).
6 TV PEBs should be 2'40'', 3'40'' or 4'40'' in length. The current rules and guidance governing UK party election broadcasts can be found on OFCOM's website at: http://www.ofcom.org.uk/tv/ifi/codes/legacy/programme_code/pc_section_four and http://www.ofcom.org.uk/tv/ifi/guidance/ppbrules/Minutes of the meetings of the Broadcasters' Liaison Group are also available online.
7 This is the view of Mark Blumenthal, responsible for Mystery Pollster, a US polling website. He argues that bloggers will play an influential role in the 2008 Presidential election on sites such as those run by Matt Drudge or Mickey Kaus.

Chapter 12

1 All figures are from the US Federal Election Commission. See: http://www.fec.gov/press/press2005/20050203pressum/20050203pressum.html (accessed 20 July 2007).
2 Survey panel research selects is a form of longitudinal study that observes the same units (these could be, for example, individuals, households or companies) and items at regular intervals over long periods of time. Panel data compares variables between individuals and how they change over time.
3 This is the case for many voters, especially those living in single winner voting systems in countries such as India, the United States and the United Kingdom. A large proportion of votes are simply 'wasted' in systems where the winner takes all. In the 2005 UK general elections, for example, 52 per cent of the votes were cast for losing candidates.
4 The Marcos presidency in the 1970s and early 1980s was characterized by a showbiz, vaudeville style where the Marcos couple would often break into song. This tradition has

continued in Filipino politics: campaigning politicians are as likely to sing at a rally as to give a speech. However, it appears that movie star politics might be on the wane. In the 2007 elections, two stars ran for the Senate and lost (private communication with Montemayor, 31 January 2008).

5   Randomized experiments are a reliable way to infer causation. For human beings, they would require a large group to be randomly divided with one or more variables being applied in one group and not the other (the obligation to read newspapers, for example). Measurements of differences in, say, levels of political knowledge might then be inferred to newspaper readership because of the equivalence between the two groups in everything other than the manipulated variable.

Chapter 13

1   There is a vast literature spanning over 50 years, examining the nature and construction of news. Landmark studies include those by: Gans (1979), Lippmann (1922), Schudson (1995), and Tuchman (1978).

2   At a US Department of Defense briefing on 12 February 2002, the then Secretary of Defense, Donald Rumsfeld, declared that 'there are known knowns, there are things we know that we know. There are known unknowns, that is to say there are things that we now know, we don't know, but there are also unknown unknowns, there are things we do not know, we don't know, and each year we discover a few more, of those unknown unknowns.'

3   I use the term 'good' or 'goods' here and elsewhere in the book in the sense of something that is valuable.

4   This phrase was contained in an essay on 'Hallam's "Constitutional History"' published in September 1828 in the *Edinburgh Review*. The origins of the term 'fourth estate' are not entirely clear. In *Heroes and Hero Worship* (1839), Thomas Carlyle attributed it to the political thinker and essayist, Edmund Burke. However, the phrase cannot be found in his published works. Essayist William Hazlitt (1778–1830) used it to refer to William Cobbett (1763–1835) in his sixth essay in *Table Talk* on the character of Cobbett (1821). The Oxford English Dictionary ascribes the first use of the phrase with reference to the press to Lord Henry Brougham (1778–1868) in a parliamentary debate in 1823.

5   Agenda-setting research comprises a significant swathe of political communication studies. McCombs and Shaw's 1972 article examining correlations between the agenda of issues in newspaper content (in amount and prominence of coverage) and public ranking of the importance of these issues was the groundbreaking study which launched a thousand more. Theirs focused on what has since been called 'public' agenda setting. It has been followed by studies in media and policy agenda setting, i.e., the influences that bear on the media and policy agenda or what has also been called 'agenda building'.

6   Interview with Ric Bailey, 20 October 2006, BBC's Chief Advisor-Politics. See Poindexter and colleagues (2007) for debates about women journalists and their 'unsuitability' for TV after a certain age as compared to their male counterparts. The first female solo anchor of a major television network in the United States, Katie Couric, was appointed in 2006 by CBS News. There was some criticism of her journalistic credentials for one of the main jobs in American news journalism (Winzenburg, 2006).

7   American researchers found that in the United States, 'since the early 1980s, the public has come to view the news media as less professional, less accurate, less caring, less moral and more inclined to cover up rather than correct mistakes' (*The State of the News Media, Public Attitudes*, 2007).

8   The programme achieved 30.3 per cent of audience share, making it the second most seen show in peak-time viewing. That figure was surpassed by the opposition leader, Mariano Rajoy, when he appeared on 19 April, three weeks later. The format was imported from France's TF1's 'J'ai une question à vous poser'.

Chapter 14

1   Of course, ethics as a field of moral philosophy is vast. Interested readers can consult my thumbnail sketch of ethics in journalism in *Ethics and Journalism* (2003). More comprehensive treatments can be found in Scruton's *Modern Philosophy: A Survey*. London: Arrow Books (1997), or Rhonheimer's excellent study of moral philosophy (2000). Best of all, they could look at the work of the philosophers themselves.

2   Relativism is often confused with a commitment to an ethic of toleration. Toleration involves a specific moral commitment, not relativist at all, to tolerate other ethical viewpoints without necessarily endorsing them.

3   Evolutionary psychologists suggest that we are gene machines whose actions are determined by the innate biological imperative to perpetuate our genes. Apparently altruistic acts are genetically driven; 'love', 'generosity' are biological strategies. These explanations have a specious plausibility. They 'explain' everything and yet understand nothing.

4   The picture is more mixed for journalists. In Britain and the United States, the news reporter is not generally trusted, although television presenters – and in the United Kingdom, the BBC – enjoy significantly better trust ratings. In other parts of the world, Nigeria and Indonesia, for example, journalists are trusted more than their governments (see Globescan, 2006).

5   The measure was opposed by two main groups on the grounds that banning paid spots is against freedom of expression. The groups were, on the one hand, the business sector through the Mexican Chamber of Commerce and, on the other, a group of leading Mexican intellectuals and journalists. The legislation limits presidential campaigning to three months before election day and forbids political parties from insulting political institutions and candidates

6   In his *Politics and Passion: Towards a More Egalitarian Liberalism*. New Haven and London: Yale University Press (2005), Michael Walzer states 'opposition and conflict, disagreement and struggle where the stakes are high – that's what politics is' (p. 117). He points to a number of activities in democratic politics, including campaigning, that are directed at success rather than understanding and it is, of course, the case that much deliberative politics involves non-deliberative actions.

Bibliography

Ableson, D. (2002) *Do Think Tanks Matter? Assessing the Impact of Public Policy Institutes.* Montreal: McGill-Queen's University Press.

Ableson, D. (2004) 'The business of ideas: The think tank industry in the USA', in D. Stone and A.Denham (eds) *Think Tank Traditions: Policy Research and the Politics of Ideas.* Manchester: Manchester University Press, 215–31.

Abramowitz, A. (1996) 'Bill and Al's excellent adventure: Forecasting the 1996 presidential elections'. *American Political Quarterly* 24: 434–43.

Aizpeolea (23 June 2007) 'La Moncloa mira a la Casa Blanca y a Downing Street', *El País*, 28.

Alexander, J., B. Giesen and J. Mast (2006) *Social Performance: Symbolic Action, Cultural Pragmatics, and Ritual.* Cambridge: Cambridge University Press.

Altheide, D. L. (1976) *Creating Reality: How TV News Distorts News Events.* Beverly Hills, CA: Sage.

Amis, M. (18 September 2001) 'Fear and Loathing'. *The Guardian*, G2, 2–3.

Anderson, B. (1991) *Imagined Communities.* London: Verso.

Ansolabehere, S. and S. Iyengar (1995) *Going Negative: How Political Advertisements Shrink and Polarize the Electorate.* New York: The Free Press.

Archer, M. (2000) *Being Human: The Problem of Agency.* Cambridge: Cambridge University Press.

Arendt, H. (1958) *The Human Condition.* Chicago: The University of Chicago Press.

Arendt, H. (2003) *Responsibility and Judgment.* Edited with an introduction by J. Kohn. New York: Schocken Books.

Aristotle (1978) *Politics.* London: Penguin.

Aristotle (1991) *On Rhetoric: A Theory of Civic Discourse.* New York/Oxford: Oxford University Press.

Ashley, J. (8 January 2007) 'Control freaks beware, the big clunking fist is after you', *The Guardian*: http://www.guardian.co.uk/commentisfree/story/0,,1984890,00.html (accessed 4 April 2007).

Aviles, J. (21 April 2004) 'The Madrid massacre: The Iraq connection'. Real Instituto Elcano de Estudios Internacionales y Estratégicos: http://www.realinstitutoelcano.org/analisis/imprimir/485imp.asp (accessed 1 June 2004).

Bale, T. and K. Sanders (2001). 'Playing by the book: Success and failure in John Major's approach to prime ministerial media management'. *Contemporary British History*, 15(4): 93–110.

Barnett, S. and I. Gaber (2001) *Westminster Tales: The Twenty-First Century Crisis in British Political Journalism.* London/New York: Continuum.

Baudrillard, J. (1988) *America.* London: Verso.

BBC (2002) *'Beyond the Soundbite': BBC Research into Public Disillusion with Politics.* BBC: London.

BBC (9 March 2005) 'Mobile growth fastest in Africa': http://news.bbc.co.uk/1/hi/business/4331863.stm (accessed 3 May 2007).

BBC (18 March 2005) 'Voters don't trust politicians': http://news.bbc.co.uk/1/hi/uk_politics/4360597.stm (accessed 20 June 2007).

BBC (20 January 2006) '"Evo Fashion" arrives in Bolivia': http://news.bbc.co.uk/1/hi/world/americas/4630370.stm (accessed 13 January 2007).

BBC (10 July 2006) 'Cameron defends "hoodie" speech': http://news.bbc.co.uk/ 1/hi/uk_politics/5163798.stm (accessed 5 March 2007).

BBC (22 March 2007) *The Today Programme*. BBC.
BBC Editorial Guidelines: http://www.bbc.co.uk/guidelines/editorialguidelines/advice/terrorismlanguage/ (accessed 26 June 2007).
Bennett, W. (2004) 'Gatekeeping and press–government relations: A multigated model of news construction', in L. L. Kaid (ed.) *Handbook of Political Communication Research*. Mahwah, NJ: LEA, 283–314.
Bernays, E. (1923/2004) *Crystallizing Public Opinion*. Montana: Kessinger Publishing.
Berrocal, S. (2003) (ed.) *Comunicación política en televisión y nuevos medios*. Madrid: Ariel.
Bird, E. and R. Dardenne (1988) 'Myth, chronicle and story: Exploring the narrative qualities of news', in J. W. Carey (ed.) *Media, Myths and Narratives*. Newbury Park: Sage, 67–87.
Birnbaum, J. (22 June 2005) 'The Road to Riches Is Called K Street', *The Washington Post*, A01.
Bishop, G. (2005) *The Illusion of Public Opinion: Fact and Artefact in American Public Opinion Polls*. Lanham, MD: Rowman & Littlewood.
Blair, T. (12 June 2007) 'Lecture by the Prime Minister the Right Honourable Tony Blair MP on public life', London: Reuters.
Blumenthal, S. (1980) *The Permanent Campaign*. New York: Simon & Schuster.
Blumler, J. G. and M. Gurevitch (1995) *The Crisis of Public Communication*. London: Routledge.
Blumler, J. G. and M. Gurevitch (2005) 'Rethinking the Study of Political Communication', in J. Curran and M. Gurevitch (eds) *Mass Media and Society*, London : Arnold, 104–21.
Blumler, J. G. and D. Kavanagh (1999) 'The Third Age of Political Communication: Influences and Features'. *Political Communication*. 16(3): 209–30.
Bobbitt, P. (2003) *The Shield of Achilles: War, Peace, and the Course of History*. London: Penguin.
Brady, H. E., R. Johnston and J. Sides (2006) 'The study of political campaigns', in H. E. Brady and R. Johnston (eds) *Capturing Campaign Effects*. Ann Arbour: The University of Michigan, 1–26.
Brookes, R., J. Lewis and K. Wahl-Jorgensen (2004) 'The media representation of public opinion: British television news coverage of the 2001 general election'. *Media, Culture and Society*, 26: 63–80.
Burke, K. (1969) *A Grammar of Motives*. Berkeley: University of California Press.
Burke, K. (1973) *The Philosophy of Literary Form: Studies in Symbolic Action*. Berkeley: University of California Press.
Butler, P. and N. Collins (1996) 'Strategic analysis in political markets'. *European Journal of Marketing*, 30(10/11): 32–44.
Butler, P. and N. Collins (1999) 'A conceptual framework for political marketing', in B. Newman (ed.) *Handbook of Political Marketing*. Thousand Oaks, CA: Sage, 55–72.
Butler, D. and D. Kavanagh (1997) *The 1997 British General Election*. Basingstoke: Macmillan.
Butterworth, T. (17 February 2006) 'Time for the last post'. *The Financial Times*.
Calhoun, C. (1992) *Habermas and the Public Sphere*. Cambridge, MA: MIT.
Campbell, A. and R. Stott (eds) (2007) *The Blair Years: Extracts from the Alastair Campbell Diaries*. London: Hutchinson
Campbell, A., P. Converse, W. Miller and D. E. Stokes (1960) *The American Voter*. New York: John Wiley.
Campbell, J. (2000) *The American Campaign: US Presidential Campaigns and the National Vote*. College Station: Texas A&M Press.
Canel, M. J. and K. Sanders (2004) 'The Madrid Bombings and the 2004 Spanish General Elections: Framing an effective communication response'. Paper presented at *Internationalization of Political Marketing: Americanization or Plain Globalization?* Paris. Seminar organized by IAMCR Political Communication Research Section & IPSA Research Committee in Political Communication.
Canel, M. J. and K. Sanders (2006) *Morality Tales: Political Scandals and Journalism in Britain and Spain in the 1990s*. New Jersey: Hampton Press.
Carruthers, S. (2000) *The Media at War: Communication and Conflict in the 20th Century*. Basingstoke: Palgrave MacMillan.
Castells, M. (1996) *The Rise of the Network Society*. Oxford: Blackwell Publishers.
Chadwick, A. (2006) *Internet Politics: States, Citizens, and New Communication Technologies*. New York and Oxford: Oxford University Press.

Chaffee, S. (1975) *Political Communications: Issues and Strategies for research*. London: Sage.

Cialdini, R. (1993) *Influence: The Psychology of Persuasion*. New York: Quill William Morrow.

Claybrook, J. (27 July 2005) http://www.citizen.org/pressroom/release.cfm?ID1999 (accessed 28 November 2007).

Cleaver, H. (no date) *The Zapatistas and the Electronic Fabric of Struggle*: http://debreu.eco. utexas.edu/Homepages/faculty/Cleaver/zaps.html (accessed 12 September 2007).

Clinton, B. (2005) *My Life*. London: Arrow books.

Clinton, H. (2004) *Living History*. London: Headline Book Publishing.

Coates, S. (31 March 2007) 'MPs call for lobbyists to end secrecy over clients'. *The Times*: http://www.timesonline.co.uk/tol/news/politics/article1593647.ece (accessed 20 April 2007).

Coates, T. (2004) *The Hutton Inquiry 2003*. London: Uncovered Editions.

Cohen, B. (1963) *The Press and Foreign Policy*. Princeton, NY: Princeton University Press.

Cohen, J. and A. Arato ([1992]1997) *Civil Society and Political Theory*, Cambridge, MA: MIT Press.

Collins, N. and P. Butler (1996) 'Positioning political parties: A market analysis'. *Harvard Journal of Press and Politics*, 1: 63–77.

Cook, T. (2005) *Governing with the News: The News Media as a Political Institution*. Chicago: University of Chicago Press.

Corner, J. and D. Pels (eds) (2003) *Media and the Restyling of Politics*. London: Sage.

Cornwell, E. (1965) *Presidential Leadership of Public Opinion*. Bloomington: Indiana University Press.

Cottle, S. (2003) 'News, public relations and power: mapping the field', in S. Cottle (ed.) *News, Public Relations and Power*. London: Sage, 3–26.

Coxall, B. (2001) *Pressure Groups in British Politics*. Harlow: Pearson Education.

Crick, B. (1982) *In Defence of Politics*. London: Penguin.

Curtice, J. and H. Semetko (1994) 'Does it matter what the papers say?' in A. Heath, R. Jowell and J. Curtice (eds) *Labour's Last Chance?* Aldershot: Dartmouth.

Cutlip, S., A. Center and G. Broom (1994) *Effective Public Relations* (7th edn). Upper Saddle River, NJ: Prentice Hall.

Dahlgren, P. (2005) 'The internet, public spheres, and political communication: dispersion and deliberation'. *Political Communication*, 22: 147–62.

Dahlgren, P. and M. Gurevitch (2005) 'Political communication in a changing world', in J. Curran and M. Gurevitch (eds) *Mass Media and Society*, London: Arnold, 375–93.

Davis, A. (2002) *Public Relations Democracy: Public Relations, Politics and the Mass Media in Britain*. Manchester: Manchester University Press.

Davis, R. (1999) *The Web of Politics: The Internet's Impact on the American Political System*. New York: Oxford University Press.

Day, R. (1989) *Sir Robin Day, Grand Inquisitor: Memoirs*. London: George Weidenfeld & Nicolson.

Dayan, D. and E. Katz (1994) *Media Events: The Live Broadcasting of History*. Cambridge, MA: Harvard University Press.

De Tocqueville, A. (1848/1994) *Democracy in America*. New York: Everyman Library.

De Zengotita, T. (2005) *Mediated: How the Media Shape Your World*. London: Bloomsbury.

Delano, A. and J. Henningham (1995) *The News Breed: British Journalists in the 1990s*. London: The London College of Printing and Distributive Trades.

Denham, A. and M. Garnett (1998) *British Think Tanks and the Climate of Opinion*. London: UCL Press.

Denham, A. and M. Garnett (2004) 'A "hollowed-out" tradition? British think tanks in the twenty-first century', in D. Stone and A. Denham (eds) *Think Tank Traditions: Policy Research and the Politics of Ideas*. Manchester: Manchester University Press, 232–46.

Denton, R. (2000) (ed.) *Political Communication Ethics: An Oxymoron?* Westport, CT: Praeger.

Denton, R. and G. Woodward (1998) *Political Communication in America*. New York: Praeger.

Dewey, J. (1927) *The Public and Its Problems*. New York: Henry Holt.

Downs, A. (1957) *An Economic Theory of Democracy*. New York: Harper & Row.

Drezner, D. and H. Farrell (2004) 'The power and politics of blogs'. Paper presented at the *American Political Science Association Annual Conference*, Chicago, 2–5 September.

Durham Peters, J. and P. Simonson (2004) (eds) *Mass Communication and American Social Thought. Key Texts 1919–1968*. Lanham, MD: Rowman & Littlefield.

Edelman, M. (1967/1985) *The Symbolic Uses of Politics*. Urbana and Chicago: University of Illinois Press.

Edelman, M. (1988) *Constructing the Political Spectacle*. Chicago: University of Chicago Press.

Electoral Commission (2003) *Party Political Broadcasting: Report and Recommendations*. London: The Electoral Commission.

Electoral Commission (2006) *Election 2005: Campaign Spending. The UK Parliamentary General Election*. London: The Electoral Commission.

El-Nawawy, M. and A. Iskandar (2002) *Al-Jazeera: How the Free Arab News Network Scooped the World and Changed the Middle East*. Cambridge, MA: Westview Press.

Eliasoph, N. (2004) 'Can we theorize the press without theorizing the public?' *Political Communication*, 21: 297–303.

Entman, R. (1993) 'Framing: toward clarification of a fractured paradigm'. *Journal of Communication*, 43(4): 51–8.

Entman, R. (2003) 'Cascading activation: Contesting the White House's frame after 9/11'. *Political Communication*, 20: 415–32.

Eulau, H., S. Eldersveld and M. Janovitz (eds.) (1956) *Political Behavior: A Reader in Theory and Research*. New York: Free Press.

Ericson, R., P. Baranek and J. Chan (1989) *Negotiating Control: A Study of News Sources*. Milton Keynes: Open University Press.

Evans, R. and D. Leigh (16 March 2004) 'Downing St forced to reveal secret meetings'. *The Guardian*: http://www.guardian.co.uk/guardianpolitics/story/0,,1170149,00.htm (accessed 26 March 2007).

Fallows, J. M. (1997) *Breaking the News: How the Media Undermine American Democracy*. New York: Vintage Books.

Festinger, L. (1957/1962) *A Theory of Cognitive Dissonance*. Palo Alto, CA: Stanford University Press.

Finkelstein, D. (29 March 2006) 'Let me flog you a used car'. *The Times*.

Finkelstein, D. (31 May 2006) 'Buffoons? No it gets worse'. *The Times*.

Finkelstein, D. (4 April 2007) 'Welcome to a new era: the politics of "but"'. *The Times*.

Fishkin, J. (1995) *The Voice of the People*. New Haven: Yale University Press.

Fisk, R. (11 October 2001) 'A bold and original TV station that America wants to censor'. The *Independent*.

Frankel, A. (2003) *Lies and the Lying Liars Who Tell Them: A Fair and Balanced Look at the Right*. New York: Dutton Books.

Franklin, B. (2004) *Packaging Politics: Political Communications in Britain's Media Democracy*. London: Edward Arnold.

Franklin, B. and D. Murphy (1991) *What News? The Market, Politics and the Local Press*. London: Routledge.

Franklin, B. and J. Richardson (2002) 'Priming the parish pump: Political marketing and news management in local political communications networks'. *Journal of Political Marketing*, 1(1): 117–47.

Gaber, I. (19 June 1998) 'A world of dogs and lamp-posts'. *New Statesman*, 14.

Galtung, J. and M. Ruge (1965) 'The structure of foreign news'. *Journal of Peace Research*, 2: 64–91.

Gamson, W. and A. Modigliani (1989) 'Media discourses and public opinion on nuclear power: A constructionist approach'. *American Journal of Sociology*, 95(1): 1–37.

Gans, H. (1979) *Deciding What's News*. New York: Pantheon Books.

Gardels, N. (Winter 2005) 'The rise and fall of America's soft power'. *New Perspectives Quarterly*, 22(1): http://www.digitalnpq.org/archive/2005_winter/02_gardels.html (accessed 5 July 2007).

Garnham, N. (2000) *Emancipation, the Media and Modernity*. Oxford: Oxford University Press.

Ghanem, S. (1997) 'Filling in the tapestry: The second level of agenda setting', in M. McCombs, D. Shaw and D. Weaver (eds) *Communication and Democracy: Exploring the Intellectual Frontiers in Agenda-Setting Theory*. Mahwah, NJ, and London: LEA, 3–14.

Giddens, A. and D. Willetts (May 2007) 'Have the Conservatives really changed?' *Prospect*: http://www.prospect-magazine.co.uk/printarticle.php?id9303 (accessed 12 June 2007).

Gimson, A. (12 January 2008) 'Obama's soaring rhetoric captures the mood of nation'. *The Daily Telegraph*, 20–1.

Girard, R. (1989) *The Scapegoat*. Baltimore, MD: Johns Hopkins University Press.

Girard, R. (6 November 2001) Interview with Henri Tincq: http://www.uibk.ac.at/theol/cover/girard_le_monde_interview.html (accessed 7 January 2007).

Gitlin, T. (1980) *The Whole World is Watching: Mass Media and the Making and Unmaking of the New Left*. Berkeley: University of California Press.

Globescan (2006) *BBC/Reuters/Media Center Poll: Trust in the Media*: www.globescan.com/news_archives/bbcreut.html (accessed 20 December 2007).

Goffman, E. (1959) *The Presentation of Self in Everyday Life*. New York: Doubleday.

Goffman, E. (1986) *Frame Analysis: An Essay on the Organization of Experience*. Boston, MA: Northeastern University Press.

Goldsmith, J. and T. Wu (2006) *Who Controls the Internet? Illusions of a Borderless World*. Oxford: Oxford University Press.

Goodman, G. (2003) *From Bevan to Blair: Fifty Years' Reporting from the Political Front Line*. London: Pluto Press.

Gould, P. (1998) *The Unfinished Revolution: How the Modernisers Saved the Labour Party*. London: Little Brown.

Graber, D. (1985) 'Magical words and plain campaigns'. *Society*, May/June, 38–44.

Graber, D. (2003) 'Terrorism, censorship and the 1st Amendment: In search of policy guidelines', in Pippa Norris, M. Kern, and M. Just (eds) *Framing Terrorism: The News Media, the Government and the Public*. New York and London: Routledge, 27–42.

Graham, R. (2005) *Anarchism: A Documentary History of Libertarian Ideas*. Vol. 1. Montreal: Black Rose.

Grant, W. (1995) *Pressure Groups, Politics and Democracy in Britain*. Basingstoke: Macmillan (2nd edn).

Gubern, R. (5 February 2007) 'La hiperinflación mediática'. *El País*.

Habermas, J. (1962/1989) *The Structural Transformation of the Public Sphere*. Cambridge: Polity Press.

Hacker, K. (2004) (ed.) *Presidential Candidate Images*. Lanham and Boulder, CO: Rowman & Littlefield.

Hafez, K. (2007) *The Myth of Media Globalization*. Cambridge: Polity Press.

Hague, R. and M. Harrop (2001) *Comparative Government and Politics: An Introduction*. Basingstoke: Palgrave Macmillan (5th edn).

Hall, S. (1973) 'Encoding/decoding in television discourse: Stencilled paper'. Birmingham Centre for Contemporary Cultural Studies: University of Birmingham.

Hall, S. (1982) 'The rediscovery of ideology: Return of the repressed in media studies', in M. Gurevitch, T. Bennett, J. Curran and J. Woollacott (eds) *Culture, Society, Media*. London: Methuen, 56–90.

Hallin, D. (1986) *The Uncensored War*. Oxford: Oxford University Press.

Hallin, D. and P. Mancini (2004) *Comparing Media Systems: Three Models of Media and Politics*. Cambridge: Cambridge University Press.

Hames, T. and R. Feasey (1994) 'Anglo-American think tanks under Reagan and Thatcher', in A. Adonis and T. Hames (eds) *A Conservative Revolution?: The Thatcher-Reagan Decade in Perspective*. Manchester: Manchester University Press.

Harris, R. (2 June 2007) 'Why does David Cameron despise the Tories?' *Mail on Sunday*: http://www.mailonsunday.co.uk/pages/live/articles/news/newscomment.html?in_article_id459352&in_page_id1787 (accessed on 3 June 2007).

Harrop, M. (1990) 'Political marketing'. *Parliamentary Affairs*, 43: 277–91.

Hellweg, S. (2004) 'Campaigns and candidate images in American presidential elections', in K. Hacker (ed.) *Presidential Candidate Images*. Lanham and Boulder, CO: Rowman & Littlefield, 21–47.

Hellweg, S., M. Pfau and S. Brydon (1992) *Televised Presidential Debates: Advocacy in Contemporary America*. Westport, CT: Greenwood.

Henneberg, S. (2004) 'Political Marketing Theory: Hendiadyoin or Oxymoron'. School of Management Working Paper Series. Bath: University of Bath.

Henneberg, S. (2006) 'Leading or following? A theoretical analysis of politicial marketing postures'. *Journal of Political Marketing*, 5.

Henneberg, S. and N. O'Shaugnessy (2004) 'The growth of symbolic government?' Paper presented at *Internationalization of Political Marketing: Americanization or Plain Globalization?* Paris, 1–2 July 2004. Seminar organiZed by IAMCR Political Communication Research Section & IPSA Research Committee in Political Communication.

Henneberg, S. and N. O'Shaugnessy (2007) 'Theory and concept development in political marketing: Issues and an agenda'. *Journal of Political Marketing*, Special Issues on Theory and Concept Development in Political Marketing, 6(2/3).

Hennessy, P. (17 June 2007) 'Cameron u-turn: No more 'heir to Blair'. *The Sunday Telegraph*, 1.

Herbst, S. (1993) 'The meaning of public opinion'. *Media, Culture and Society*, 15: 437–54.

Herbst, S. (2001) 'Public opinion infrastructures: Meanings, measures, media'. *Political Communication*, 18: 451–64.

Herman, E. and N. Chomsky (1988) *Manufacturing Consent*. New York: Pantheon Books.

Hess, S. and M. Kalb (2003) *The Media and the War on Terrorism*. Washington DC: The Brookings Institute Press.

Hewitt, H. (2005) *Blog: Understanding the Information Revolution That's Changing Your World*. Nashville, TN: Thomas Nelson.

Hewitt, H. (30 January 2006) 'The media's ancien régime: Columbia journalism school tries to save the old order.' *The Weekly Standard*: http://www.weeklystandard.com/Content/Public/Articles/000/000/006/619njpsr. asp?pg2 (accessed 19 March 2007).

Hiebert, E. R. (2003) 'Public relations and propaganda in framing the Iraq war: A preliminary review'. *Public Relations Review*, 29: 243–55.

Hogan, K. (2005) *The Science of Influence*. New Jersey: John Wiley & Sons.

Hogg, S. and J. Hill (1995) *Too Close to Call: Power and Politics – John Major in No. 10*. London: Little, Brown.

Horrock, N. (12 October 1975) 'The Warren Commission didn't know everything', *New York Times*.

Hösle, V. (2004) *Morals and Politics*. Notre Dame, IN: University of Notre Dame Press.

Hovland, C.I., I. J. Kelly and H. Kelley (1953) *Communication and Persuasion*. New Haven: Yale University.

Ingham, B. (1991) *Kill the Messenger*. London: HarperCollins.

Ingham, B. (2003) *The Wages of Spin: A Clear Case of Communications Gone Wrong*. London: John Murray.

Institute for Politics, Democracy and the Internet (2004) *Political Influentials Online in the 2004 Presidential Campaign*. Washington DC: The George Washington University.

Iyengar, S. (1991) *Is Anyone Responsible? How Television Frames Political Issues*. Chicago: University of Chicago Press.

Iyengar, S. (2005) 'Speaking of values: The framing of American politics'. *The Forum*, Stanford University, 3: 3.

Iyengar S, and D. Kinder (1987) *News That Matters: Television and American Opinion*. Chicago: University of Chicago Press.

Iyengar, S. and R. Simon (2000) 'New perspectives and evidence on political communication and campaign effects'. *Annual Review of Psychology*, 51: 149–69.

James, H. (20 January 2005) Speech at the CPPS Seminar 'What future for government communications?' http://www.cabinetoffice.gov.uk/about the cabinet office/speeches/james/html (accessed 4 September 2006).

Johnson, P. (1991) *The Birth of the Modern: World Society 1815–1830*. London: HarperCollins.

Johnson-Cartee, K. and G. Copeland (2004) *Strategic Political Communication: Rethinking Social Influence, Persuasion, and Propaganda.* Lanham: Rowman & Littlefield Publishers.

Johnston, A. (1990) 'Trends in political communication: A selective review of research in the 1980s', in D. Swanson and D. Nimmo (eds) *New Directions in Political Communication: A Resource Book.* Newbury Park, CA: Sage, 329–62.

Jones, N. (1995) *Soundbites and Spindoctors.* London: Cassell.

Jones, N. (1997) *Campaign 97.* London: Indigo.

Jones, N. (2001) *The Control Freaks: How New Labour Gets Its Own Way.* London: Politico's.

Jordan, G. (1998) 'Politics without parties'. *Parliamentary Affairs*, 51(3): 314–28.

Kaid, L.L. (2004a) (ed) *Handbook of Political Communication Research.* Mahwah, NJ: LEA.

Kaid, L.L. (2004b) 'Political advertising', in L.L. Kaid (ed.) *Handbook of Political Communication Research.* Mahwah, NJ: LEA, 155–202.

Kaid, L. L. and C. Holtz-Bacha (2006a) 'Political advertising in international comparison', in *The SAGE Handbook of Political Advertising.* Thousand Oaks, CA, London and New Delhi: Sage, 1–14.

Kaid, L. L. and C. Holtz-Bacha (eds) (2006b) *The SAGE Handbook of Political Advertising.* Thousand Oaks, CA, London, New Delhi: Sage.

Kaid, L. L. and C. Holtz-Bacha (eds) (1995) *Political Advertising in Western Democracies: Parties and Candidates on Television.* London: Sage.

Kallas, S. (18 June 2007) 'Speech on European transparency initiative to the federation of European and international associations established in Belgium (FAIB)', Brussels: http://europa.eu/rapid/pressReleasesAction.do?referenceSPEECH/07/405&formatHT ML&aged0&languageEN&guiLanguagefr

Katchadourian, R. (15 May 2006) 'Behind enemy lines'. *The Nation*: http://www.thenation.com/doc/20060515/khatchadourian (accessed 12 January 2008).

Kavanagh, D. (1995) *Election Campaigning: The New Marketing of Politics*, Oxford: Blackwell.

Keller, E. and J. Berry (2003) *The Influentials: One American in Ten Tells the Other Nine How to Vote, Where to Eat, and What to Buy.* New York: Simon & Schuster.

Kellner, D. (2003) *Media Spectacle.* London and New York: Routledge.

Kernell, S. (1986/1993) *Going Public: New Strategies of Presidential Leadership.* Washington DC: Congressional Quarterly.

Kline, D. And D. Burstein (2005) *Blog! How the Newest Media Revolution is Changing Politics, Business, and Culture.* New York: CDS Books.

Knightley, P. (2004) *The First Casualty: The War Correspondent as Hero and Myth-Maker from the Crimea to Kosovo.* Baltimore, MD: Johns Hopkins University Press.

Kotler, P. and N. Kotler (1999) 'Political marketing: Generating effective candidates, campaigns, and causes', in B. I. Newman (ed.) *Handbook of Political Marketing*, Thousand Oaks, CA: Sage, 3–18.

Kotler, P. and S. J. Levy (1969) 'Broadening the concept of marketing'. *Journal of Marketing*, 33: 10–15.

Kuhn, R. and E. Neveu (2003) (eds) *Political Journalism: New Challenges, New Practices*, Routledge: London.

Kunczik, M. (1996) *Images of Nations and International Public Relations.* New York: Lawrence Erlbaum Associates.

Kurtz, H. (1998) *Inside the Clinton Propaganda Machine: Spin Cycle.* London: Pan.

Lakoff, G. (2002) *Moral Politics: How Liberals and Conservatives Think.* Chicago: University of Chicago Press.

Lakoff, G. (2004) *Don't Think of an Elephant: Know Your Values and Frame the Debate.* Vermont: Chelsea Green.

Lang, G. and K. Lang (1983) *The Battle for Public Opinion: The President, the Press and the Polls during Watergate.* New York: Columbia University Press.

Lasica, J. D. (7 August 2003) 'What is participatory journalism'. *Online Journalism Review.* USC Annenberg: http://www.ojr.org/ojr/workplace/1060217106.php

Lazarsfeld, P.F., B. Berelson and H. Gaudet (1948) *The People's Choice: How the Voter Makes up His Mind in a Presidential Campaign.* New York: Columbia University Press.

Lees-Marshment, J. (2001) *Political Marketing and British Political Parties*. Manchester: Manchester University Press.

Lemann, T. (7 August 2006) 'Amateur hour: Journalism without journalists'. *The New Yorker*.

Leonard, M., A. Small with M. Rose (February 2005) *British Public Diplomacy in the 'Age of Schisms'*. London: The Foreign Policy Centre.

Lieven, A. and D. Chambers (13 February 2006) 'The limits of propaganda'. *The Los Angeles Times*.

Lilleker, D. and J. Lees-Marshment (2005) (eds) *Political Marketing: A Comparative Perspective*. Manchester: Manchester University Press.

Lippmann, W. (1922; reprint 1965) *Public Opinion*. New York: Free Press.

Lloyd, J. (2004) *What the Media Are Doing to Our Politics*. London: Constable.

Lock, A. and P. Harris (1996) 'Political marketing – *Vive la Différence*'. *European Journal of Marketing*, 30(10): 14–24.

Louw, E. (2003) 'The "war against terrorism": A public relations challenge for the Pentagon'. *Gazette: The International Journal for Communication Studies*, 211–30.

Lovibond, S. (2002) *Ethical Formation*. Cambridge, MA: Harvard University Press.

Maarek, P. (1995) *Political Marketing and Communication*. London: John Libbey.

Maarek, P. (2003) 'Government communication to the public and political communication', in P. Maarek and G. Wolfsfeld (eds) *Political Communication in a New Era: A Cross-National Perspective*. London: Routledge, 157–70.

Maarek, P. and G. Wolfsfeld (eds) (2003) *Political Communication in a New Era: A Cross-National Perspective*. London: Routledge.

MacIntyre, A. (1997) *After Virtue. A Study in Moral Theory*. 2nd edn. London: Duckworth.

MacIntyre, D. (2000) *Mandelson: And the Making of New Labour*. London: Simon & Schuster.

McCarthy, R. (30 May 2003) 'Salam's story'. The *Guardian*.

McChesney, R. (2008) *The Political Economy of Media: Enduring Issues, Emerging Dilemma*s. New York: Monthly Review Press.

McCombs, M. and D. Shaw (1972/1996) 'The agenda-setting function of mass media', in O. Boyd-Barrett and C. Newbold (eds) *Approaches to Media: A Reader*. London: Arnold.

McGinnis, J. (1969/1988) *The Selling of the President*. London: Penguin.

McKinney, M. and D. Carlin (2004) 'Political campaign debates', in L. L. Kaid (ed.) *Handbook of Political Communication Research*. Mahwah, NJ: LEA, 203–36.

McNair, B. (2000) *Journalism and Democracy*. London: Routledge.

McNair, B. (2007) *An Introduction to Political Communication*. 4th edn. London: Routledge.

Machiavelli (2004) *The Prince*. Cambridge: Cambridge University Press.

Mair P. and I. van Biezen (2001) 'Party membership in twenty European democracies 1980–2000'. *Party Politics*, 7(1): 5–21.

Martin, B. and W. Varney (2003) 'Nonviolence and communication'. *Journal of Peace Research*, 40(2): 213–32.

Mazzoleni, G. and W. Schulz (1999) 'Mediatization of politics: A challenge for democracy?' *Political Communication*, 16: 247–61.

Meadow, R. (1980) *Politics as Communication*. Norwood, NJ: Ablex Publishing.

Michie, D. (1998) *The Invisible Persuaders: How Britain's Spin Doctors Manipulate the Media*. London: Bantam.

Miles, H. (2005) *Al-Jazeera: The Inside Story of the Arab News Channel that is Challenging the West*. New York: Grove Press.

Miller, C. (2000) *Politico's Guide to Political Lobbying*. London: Politico's.

Ming-Chen S. with D. Stone (2004) 'The Chinese tradition of policy research institutes', in Diana Stone and Andrew Denham (eds) *Think Tank Traditions: Policy Research and the Politics of Ideas*. Manchester: Manchester University Press, 141–62.

Monzón, C. (1996) *Opinión Pública, comunicación y política. La formación del espacio público*. Madrid: Tecnos.

Mountfield, Lord (November, 1997) *Report of the Working Group on the Government Information Service*. London: Cabinet Office.

Mountfield, R. (2002) 'A Note on Politicisation and the Civil Service': http://www.civilservant.org.uk/politicisation.pdf (accessed on 8 April 2007).

Mullan, J. (11 September 2002) 'Fighting Talk'. The *Guardian*.

Mullins, B. (14 February 2006) 'US lobbying tab hits a record'. *The Wall Street Journal*: http://online.wsj.com/article/SB113988289379073090.html?modtodays_us_page_one (accessed 17 May 2007).

Nacos, B. (2002) *Mass-Mediated Terrorism: The Central Role of the Media in Terrorism and CounterTerrorism*. Lanham, MD: Rowman & Littlefield.

Negrine, R. (1996) *The Communication of Politics*. London: Sage.

Negrine, R. and S. Papathanassopoulos (1996) 'The Americanization of political communication. A critique'. *Harvard International Journal of Press/Politics*, 1(2): 45–62.

Negrine, R. and J. Stanyer (2006) *The Political Communication Reader*. London: Routledge.

Neveu, E. (2003) 'Four generations of political journalism', in R. Kuhn and E. Neveu (eds) *Political Journalism: New Challenges, New Practices*. London: Routledge, 22–44.

Newman, B. (1994) *The Marketing of the President*. Thousand Oaks, CA, London and New Delhi: Sage.

Newman, B. (1999) *The Mass Marketing of Politics: Democracy in an Age of Manufactured Images*. Thousand Oaks, CA, London and New Delhi: Sage.

Newman, B. and R. Perloff (2004) 'Political marketing: Theory, research, and applications', in D. Nimmo and K. Sanders, *Handbook of Political Communication*, 17–44.

Nimmo, D. (1999) 'The permanent campaign: Marketing as a governing tool', in B. Newman (ed.) *The Handbook of Political Marketing*. Thousand Oaks, CA, London and New Delhi: Sage, 73–86.

Nimmo, D. and K. Sanders (1990) (eds) *Handbook of Political Communication*. Thousand Oaks, CA, London and New Delhi: Sage.

Nimmo, D. and D. Swanson (1990) 'The field of political communication: Beyond the voter persuasion paradigm', in D. Swanson and D. Nimmo (eds) *New Directions in Political Communication*. Beverly Hills, CA: Sage, 7–47.

Noah, T. (31 May 2005) 'Fox News admits bias!' *Slate*: http://www.slate.com/id/2119864/ (accessed 5 September 2007).

Noelle-Neumann, E. (1984) *The Spiral of Silence: Public Opinion – Our Social Skin*. Chicago: University of Chicago Press.

Noelle-Neumann, E. and T. Petersen (2004) 'The spiral of silence and the social nature of man', in L. L. Kaid (ed.) *Handbook of Political Communication Research*. Mahwah, NJ: LEA, 339–56.

Norris, P. (2000) *A Virtuous Circle: Political Communications in Postindustrial Societies*. Cambridge: Cambridge University Press.

Norris, P., J. Curtice, D. Sanders, M. Scammell and H. Semetko (1999) *On Message: Communicating the Campaign*. London: Sage.

Norris, P., M. Kern and M. Just (eds) (2003) *Framing Terrorism: The News Media, the Government and the Public*. New York and London: Routledge.

Nunberg, G. (11 April 2006) 'The frame game'. *The New Republic*: http://blogs.tnr.com/tnr/blogs/open_university/archive/2006/11/04/60751.aspx (accessed 12 December 2007).

Nye, J. S. (8 February 2004) 'The benefits of soft power': http://hbswk.hbs.edu/archive/4290.html (accessed 9 July 2007).

O'Shaughnessy, N. (1990) *The Phenomenon of Political Marketing*, Basingstoke: Macmillan.

Oates, S. (2008) *Introduction to Media and Politics*. London: Sage.

Oborne, P. (2005) *The Rise of Political Lying*. London: Free Press.

OFCOM (2005) *Viewers and Voters: Attitudes to Television Coverage of the 2005 General Election*. London: OFCOM.

Ormrod, R. (2006) 'A critique of the Lees-Marshment market-oriented party model'. *Politics*, 2(26): 110–18.

Parris, M. (18 March 2006) 'No more excuses: Just hand in your homework and go, Prime Minister'. *The Times*, 21.

Patterson, T. (1994) *Out of Order*. New York: Vintage Books.

Patterson, T. (2003) *The Vanishing Voter: Public Involvement in an Age of Uncertainty*. London: Vintage Books.

Penn, M. with E. Kinney Zalesne (2007) *Microtrends: The Small Forces Behind Tomorrow's Big Changes*. London: Allen Lane.

Pfau, M. (2002) 'The subtle nature of presidential debate influence'. *Argumentation and Debate*, 38: 251–61.

Phillis, B. (19 January 2004) *An Independent Review of Government Communications*. London: Cabinet Office.

Pickerel , W., H. Jorgensen and L. Bennett (2002) 'Culture jams and meme warfare: Kalle Lasn, Adbusters, and media activism. Tactics in global activism for the 21st century': http:// www.depts.washington.edu/gcp/pdf/culturejamsandmemewarfare.pdf (accessed 20 May 2007).

Pitcher, G. (2002) *The Death of Spin? Communication in the 21st Century*. London: Demos.

Pitkin, A. (1998) *The Attack of the Blob: Hannah Arendt's Conception of the Social*. Chicago and London: The University of Chicago Press.

Plasser, F. and G. Plasser (2002) *Global Political Campaigning: A Worldwide Analysis of Campaign Professionals and Their Practices*. Westport, CT: Praeger.

Plato (1987) *Gorgias*. Indianapolis: Hackett Publishing.

Poindexter, P., S. Meraz and A. Schmitz Weiss (2007) *Women, Men and News: Divided and Disconnected in the News Media Landscape*. London: Routledge, Taylor & Francis.

Power Inquiry, The (2006) *Power to the People: The Report of Power: An Independent Inquiry into Britain's Democracy*. York: York Publishing.

Price, L. (2005) *The Spin Doctor's Diary: Inside Number 10 with New Labour*. London: Hodder & Stoughton.

Project for Excellence in Media (2006) *The State of the News Media 2006: An Annual Report on American Journalism*: http://www.stateofthenewsmedia.org/2006/narrative_cabletv_ contentanalysis.asp?cat2&media6 (accessed 6 February 2007). http://archive.cabinetof- fice.gov.uk/gcreview/News/index.htm (accessed on 20 September 2005).

Project for Excellence in Media (2007) *The State of the News Media: Public Attitudes 2007. An Annual Report on American Journalism*: http://www.stateofthenewsmedia.org/2007/nar- rative_overview_publicattitudes.asp?cat8&media1

Putnam, R. (2000) *Bowling Alone: The Collapse and Revival of American Community*. New York: Simon & Schuster.

Rachlin, A. (1988) *News as Hegemonic Reality: American Political Culture and the Framing of News Accounts*. New York: Praeger.

Rajoy, M. (21 March 2007): http://www.libertaddigital.com:83/php3/noticia.php3?fecha_edi_ on2007-03-17&num_edi_on1465&cpn1276301383&seccionESP_D (accessed 20 May 2007).

Rawnsley, A. (2001) *Servants of the People: The Inside Story of New Labour*. London: Penguin.

Rawnsley, G. (2005) *Political Communication and Democracy*. Basingstoke: Palgrave Macmillan.

Raz, J. (2001) *Value, Respect and Attachment*. Cambridge: Cambridge University Press.

Reynolds, G. (2007) *An Army of Davids*. Nashville, TN: Nelson Current.

Rhonheimer, M. (2000) *La perspectiva del moral. Fundamentos de la ética filosófica*. Madrid: Rialp.

Robinson, P. (2002) *The CNN Effect: The Myth of News, Foreign Policy and Intervention*. London: Routledge.

Rorty, R. (1989) *Contingency, Irony, and Solidarity*. Cambridge: Cambridge University Press.

Rose, R. (2001) *The Prime Minister in a Shrinking World*. Cambridge: Polity Press.

Rosenbaum, M. (1997) *From Soapbox to Soundbite. Party Political Campaigning in Britain since 1945*. Basingstoke: Macmillan.

Rosenblum, M. (1993) *Who Stole the News? Why We Can't Keep Up With What Happens in the World and What We Can Do about It*. New York: John Wiley.

Russell, A. (2005) 'Myth and the Zapatista movement: Exploring a network identity'. *New Media and Society*, 7(4): 559–77.

Sampredo, V. (2005) *12-M Multitudes on Line*. Madrid: Los Libros de la Catarata.

Sanders, K. (2003) *Ethics and Journalism*. London: Sage.

Sanders, K. (2004) 'Spanish politicians and the media: Controlled visibility and soap opera politics', with M. J. Canel, in J. Stanyer and D. Wring (2004) *Public Images, Private Lives: The Mediation of Politicians Around the Globe. Parliamentary Affairs*, 57(1): 196–208.

Schechter, D. (2003) *Media Wars: News at a Time of Terror*. Lanham, MD: Rowman & Littlefield.

Scammell, M. (1995) *Designer Politics*. Basingstoke: Macmillan.

Scammell, M. (1999) 'Political marketing: Lessons for political science'. *Political Studies*, 47: 718–39.

Scammell, M. and H. Semetko (1995) 'Political advertising on television: The British experience', in *Political Advertising in Western Democracies: Parties and Candidates on Television*. London: Sage.

Scheufele, D. (2001) 'Agenda-setting, priming, and framing revisited: Another look at cognitive effects of political communication'. *Communication Abstracts*, 24: 1.

Schlesinger, P. and H. Tumber (1994) *Reporting Crime: The Media Politics of Criminal Justice*. Oxford: Oxford University Press.

Schmid, A. and J. de Graaf (1982) *Violence as Communication: Insurgent Terrorism and the Western News Media*. Beverly Hills, CA: Sage.

Scholte, J. (2000) *Globalization: A Critical Introduction*. Basingstoke: Palgrave Macmillan.

Schudson, M. (1995) *The Power of News*. Cambridge, MA, and London: Harvard University Press.

Schudson, M. (2000) 'The sociology of news production revisited (again)', in J. Curran and M. Gurevitch (eds) *Mass Media and Society*. 3rd edn. London: Arnold, 175–200.

Schudson, M. (2001) 'Politics as cultural practice'. *Political Communication*, 18: 421–31.

Schudson, M. (2005) 'Four approaches to the sociology of news', in J. Curran and M. Gurevitch (eds) *Mass Media and Society*. 4th edn. London: Hodder Arnold, 172–97.

Schultz, D. (1982) *Psychology and Industry Today: An introduction to Industrial and Organizational Psychology*. London: Macmillan.

Schultz, J. (1998) *Reviving the Fourth Estate: Democracy, Accountability and the Media*. Cambridge: Cambridge University Press.

Scruton, R. (August 2007) 'The sacred and the human'. *Prospect* magazine, issue 137.

Seldon, A. (1997) *Major: A Political Life*. London: Weidenfeld & Nicolson.

Seligman, A. (1995) *The Idea of Civil Society*. Princeton, NJ: Princeton University Press.

Seymour-Ure, C. (2003) *Prime Ministers and the Media: Issues of Power and Control*. Oxford: Blackwell.

Shea, D. and M. J. Burton (2006) *Campaign Craft: The Strategies, Tactics and Art of Political Campaign Management*. 3rd edn. Westport, CT: Praeger.

Shoemaker, P. and S. Reese (1996) *Mediating the Message: Theories of Influences on Mass Media Content*. New York: Longman.

Silverstone, R. (2007) *Media and Morality: On the Rise of the Mediapolis*. Cambridge: Polity.

Silvester, C. (1997) (ed.) *The Penguin Book of Interviews*. London: Viking.

Simpson, J. (1999) *Strange Places, Questionable People*. London: Pan Books.

Smith, C. A. and K. Smith (1994) *The White House Speaks: Presidential Leadership as Persuasion*. Westport, CT: Praeger.

Solomon, R. (2003) 'Corporate roles, personal virtues: An Aristotelian approach to business ethics', in D. Statman (ed.) *Virtue Ethics: A Critical Reader*. Edinburgh: Edinburgh University Press, 205–26

Sontag, S. (23 May 2004) 'Regarding the torture of others'. *New York Magazine*, 24–9.

Spiegel (20 June 2005) 'Campaigning without a platform: What Would Angela Merkel Do as Chancellor?': http://www.spiegel.de/international/spiegel/0,1518,361589,00.html (accessed 25 June 2007).

Stanyer, J. (2001) *The Creation of Political News: Television and British Party Political Conferences*. Brighton: Sussex Academic Press.

Stanyer, J. (2004) 'Politics and the media: A crisis of trust'. *Parliamentary Affairs*, 57(2): 420–34.

Stanyer, J. (2007) *Modern Political Communication: Mediated Politics in Uncertain Times*. Cambridge: Polity.

Stanyer, J. and D. Wring (2004) 'Public images, private lives: The mediation of politicians around the globe'. *Parliamentary Affairs*, 57(1): 196–208.

Stengel, R. (25 December 2006 – January 2007) 'Now it's your turn'. *Time Magazine*.

Stevenson, N. (1999) *The Transformation of the Media: Globalization, Morality and Ethics*. London: Longman.

Stone, D. and A. Denham (2004) (eds) *Think Tank Traditions: Policy Research and the Politics of Ideas*. Manchester: Manchester University Press.

Straw, J. (1993) 'Parliament on the spike'. *British Journalism Review*, 4(4): 45–54.

Streb, M., B. Burrell, B. Frederick and M. Genovese (2007) 'Social desirability effects and support for a female American president'. *Public Opinion Quarterly*. Public Opinion Quarterly Advance Access published online on 21 September: 2007,http://americandemocracy.nd.edu/speaker_series/documents/StrebPaper.pdf (accessed 3 January 2008).

Street, J. (2001) *Mass Media, Politics and Democracy*. Basingstoke: Palgrave Macmillan.

Street, J. (2005) 'Politics lost, politics transformed, politics colonised? Theories of the impact of mass media'. *Political Studies Review*, 3: 17–33.

Swanson, D. and P. Mancini (eds) (1996) *Politics, Media and Modern Democracy*. Westport, CT: Praeger.

Swanson, D. and D. Nimmo (1990) *New Directions in Political Communication Research*. Newbury Park: Sage.

Talbot, M. (6 April 2006) 'The Agitator'. *New Yorker*.

Taylor, P. (1997) *Global Communications, International Affairs and the Media since 1945*. London: Routledge.

Tedesco, J. C. (2004) 'Changing the channel: Use of the internet for communicating about politics', L. L. Kaid (ed.) *Handbook of Political Communication Research*. Mahwah: LEA, 507–32.

Thompson, J. (1997) 'Scandal and social theory', in James Lull and Stephen Hinerman (eds) *Media Scandals. Morality and Desire in the Popular Culture Marketplace*. Cambridge: Polity Press, 34–64.

Thompson, J. (2000) *Political Scandal: Power and Visibility in the Media Age*. Cambridge: Polity.

Thunert, M. (2004) 'Think tanks in Germany', in D. Stone and A. Denham (eds) *Think Tank Traditions: Policy Research and the Politics of Ideas*. Manchester: Manchester University Press, 71–8.

Toolis, K. (4 April 1998) 'The enforcer'. *The Guardian*.

Toynbee, P. (22 November 2005) 'It is New Labour, as much as the public, that lacks trust'. *The Guardian*.

Tran, M. (6 June 2007) 'Online freedoms under threat, says Amnesty'. *The Guardian*.

Trent, J. and R. Friedenberg (2004) *Political Campaign Communication: Principles and Practices*. 5th edn. Lanham, MD: Rowman & Littlefield.

Tuchman, G. (1978) *Making News: A Study in the Construction of Reality*. New York: Free Press.

Tuman, J. (2003) *Communicating Terror: The Rhetorical Dimensions of Terrorism*. Thousand Oaks, CA, London and New Delhi: Sage.

Tumber, H. and J. Palmer (2004) *The Media at War: The Iraq Crisis*. London: Sage.

Tumber, H. and S. Waisbord (2004) 'Introduction: Political scandals and media across democracies'. Vol. I, *American Behavioral Scientist*, 47(8): 1031–9.

Tunstall, J. (1996) *Newspaper Power: The New National Press in Britain*. Oxford: Clarendon Press.

UNDR (2006) http://hdr.undp.org/hdr2006/statistics/indicators/124.html (accessed 20 May 2007).

Van Ham, P. (2003) 'War, lies, and videotape: Public diplomacy and the USA's war on terrorism'. *Security Dialogue* 34(4): 427–44.

Waisbord, S. (2000) *Watchdog Journalism in South America: News, Accountability and Democracy*. New York: Columbia University Press.

Warnock, M. (2001) *An Intelligent Person's Guide to Ethics*. London: Duckbacks.

Weaver, D. (1996) 'Media agenda setting and elections', in D. Paletz (ed.) *Political Communication: Approaches, Studies, Assessments*. Vol. II, Norwood, NJ: Ablex Publishing, 211–24.

Weaver, David H. (1998) (ed.) *The Global Journalist: News People Around the World*, Cresskill, NJ: Hampton Press.

Weaver, D. and G. Wilhoit (1996) *The American Journalist in the 1990s: US News people at the End of an Era*. Mahwah, NJ: LEA.

Weaver, D., M. McCombs and D. Shaw (2004) 'Agenda-setting research issues, attributes, and influences', in L. L. Kaid (ed.) *Handbook of Political Communication Research*. Mahwah, NJ, and London: LEA, 257–82.

Weaver, D., R. Beam, B. Brownlee, P. Voakes and G. Wilhoit (2007) *The American Journalist in the 21st Century: U.S. News People at the Dawn of a New Millennium*. Mahwah NJ: LEA.

Wegg Prosser, B. (9 October 2001) 'A spin too far'. *The Guardian*.

Weimann, G. (1994) *The Influentials: People Who Influence People*. New York: State University of New York Press.

Weir, S. (2002) *Evidence to the Select Committee*.

Westen, D. (2007) *The Political Brain: The Role of Emotion in Deciding the Fate of the Nation*. New York: Public Affairs.

White J. (1991). *How to Understand and Manage Public Relations*. London: Business Books.

Whittle, S. (2005) 'Journalists as citizens'. *British Journalism Review*, 16(4): 54–7.

Wilby, P. (13 June 2005) 'Watching brief'. *The New Statesman*, 23.

Wilkinson, P. (2004) 'Terrorism: Implications for world peace': http://www.preparingfor-peace.org/wilkinson.htm (accessed 27 April 2004).

Willnat, L. and A. Aw (2004) 'Political communication in Asia: Challenges and opportunities', in L. L. Kaid (ed.) *Handbook of Political Communication Research*. Mahwah, NJ: LEA, 479–506.

Wilson, Richard (1998), Evidence to the Select Committee on Public Administration, 6th Report: http://www.publications.parliament.uk/pa/cm199798/cmselect/cmpub-adm/ 770/77006.htm (accessed 5 July 2004).

Winter, J. and C. Eyal (1981) 'Agenda setting for the civil rights issue'. *Public Opinion Quarterly* 36: 376–83.

Winzenburg, S. (4 September 2006) 'Is Couric ready for prime-time TV news?' *USA Today*.

Wring, D. (2005) *The Politics of Marketing the Labour Party*. Basingstoke: Palgrave Macmillan.

Yepes Stork, R. (1996) *Fundamentos de Antropologia*. Pamplona: Eunsa.

Young, H. (29 July 2003) 'Every prime minister must have an Alastair Campbell'. *The Guardian*.

Young, H. (2004) *Supping with the Devils*. London: Atlantic Books.

Zaller, J. (1992) *The Nature and Origins of Mass Opinion*. Cambridge: Cambridge University Press.

Zelizer, B. (2004) *Taking Journalism Seriously: News and the Academy*. Thousand Oaks, CA: Sage.

Index

Italic page numbers indicate figures and tables